A Special Issue of
*Neuropsychological Rehabilitation*

# Pathologies of awareness: Bridging the gap between theory and practice

Guest Editors

Linda Clare
*University of Wales, Bangor, UK*

Peter Halligan
*Cardiff University, UK*

Psychology Press
Taylor & Francis Group
HOVE AND NEW YORK

First published 2006 by Psychology Press
27 Church Road, Hove, East Sussex, BN3 2FA

Simultaneously published in the USA and Canada
by Psychology Press
711 Third Avenue, New York, NY 10017

First issued in paperback 2015

*Psychology Press is an imprint of the Taylor & Francis Group, an informa business*



*British Library Cataloguing in Publication Data*
A catalogue record for this book is available from the British Library

ISBN 13: 978-1-138-87767-2 (pbk)
ISBN 13: 978-1-84169-810-6 (hbk)

ISSN 0960-2011

Cover design by Hybert Design
Typeset in the UK by Techset Composition Limited, Salisbury

## Contents*



*This book is also a special issue of the journal *Neuropsychological Rehabilitation* and forms issue 4 of volume 16 (2006). The page numbers are taken from the journal and so begin with p. 353

NEUROPSYCHOLOGICAL REHABILITATION
2006, 16 (4), 353–355

# Editorial

Linda Clare
*School of Psychology, University of Wales Bangor, UK*
Peter Halligan
*School of Psychology, Cardiff University, UK*

## PATHOLOGIES OF AWARENESS: BRIDGING THE GAP BETWEEN THEORY AND PRACTICE

This special issue of *Neuropsychological Rehabilitation* provides an opportunity to characterise some of the key clinical issues concerned with assessing and managing pathologies of subjective or conscious awareness. By conscious awareness, we mean the cognitive processes that provide for our phenomenological experience (reported subjective states) and behavioural responses (objectively perceived actions). In considering subjective awareness, there has been an understandable tendency in the past to focus on clinical disorders given the epistemological and conceptual difficulties of researching and defining the construct of awareness in a "normal" context.

However, we believe it is important to emphasize that normal informational processing and psychosocial systems are the relevant domains over which any perceived clinical disorder of awareness must be meaningfully understood. Elucidating the cognitive processes underlying awareness, and their corresponding phenomenological experiences, provides the necessary theoretical platform to inform assessments and justify interventions aimed at compensating for, and/or reducing the functional consequences of, impaired awareness. This special issue represents an attempt to bring together previously disparate research findings and conceptual issues from relevant fields within medicine and the psychological sciences and, in so doing, provide for a more coherent, comprehensive account which clinicians and

Correspondence should be sent to Linda Clare, School of Psychology, University of Wales Bangor, Bangor, Gwynedd LL57 2AS, UK Tel: 01248 388178, Fax: 01248 382599. E-mail: l.clare@bangor.ac.uk


http://www.psypress.com/neurorehab DOI:10.1080/09602010500465366

theoreticians can use to better understand the apparently obvious but unwieldy construct of awareness.

First, we consider conceptual issues. Contributors to this section critically review the key conceptual frameworks that have been proposed to explain the underlying neuropsychological and psychological processes mediating conscious awareness, and consider the implications for rehabilitation. Papers in this section highlight shortcomings in previous accounts, and allow practising clinicians to identify, compare and contrast current accounts in terms of their underlying assumptions, operational measures and clinical diagnostic potential. Adam Zeman opens this section with a wide-ranging analysis of what we mean by "conscious" and "awareness". He considers the meanings of these terms in the context of a range of contrasts that highlight both the scientific complexity of the issues and the importance of the cultural and social framework within which these constructs are grounded. Awareness, therefore, needs to be approached on a number of levels, all of which may contribute to a comprehensive explanatory account. Peter Halligan continues this theme with a discussion of the nature of consciousness and awareness. He considers some fundamental questions about the nature of conscious experience. Much of our conscious experience arises as a late-stage product following considerable pre-conscious processing, and in clinical cases, it is often the dissociation between explicit accounts on the one hand and behaviour on the other hand that is the most clinically relevant and theoretically striking. Tony Ro and Bob Rafal draw on perspectives from cognitive neuroscience, taking as their starting point the puzzling phenomenon of blindsight, where visual information is processed without apparent conscious awareness. Detailed exploration of the neural processes underlying blindsight suggests possible parallels with the processes available for recovery of visual function, and offers possible directions for developing rehabilitation strategies. Laura Bach and Tony David discuss the relevance of neuropsychological and neuroanatomical models for understanding impairments of social self-awareness following brain injury. They argue that existing cognition-based models do not provide adequate explanations and propose a role for psychological constructs such as "theory of mind". The ecological and phenomenological relevance of cognition-based accounts needs to be further supplemented and contextualised by an appropriate psychosocial framework that considers not just impairments but also relevant issues arising at the personal level, such as volitional choice, phenomenological experience and sociocultural influence. Finally in this section Tamara Ownsworth, Linda Clare, and Robin Morris draw a distinction between focal types of awareness deficit that relate directly to underlying neuropathology and the broader awareness deficits sometimes seen following brain injury or in the early stages of Alzheimer's disease. They argue in the latter case for an integration of cognitive neuropsychological and biopsychosocial explanatory models, emphasising the need to take account of psychological processes and social influences alongside the impact of specific neuropsychological impairments.

In the second section, we consider some of the measures used to assess, and clinical management strategies used in response to, impaired awareness. Not unlike other neurospsychological conditions, many of the symptoms attributed to deficits of conscious awareness are defined ostensibly by the tasks used to reveal them rather than by any fundamental understanding of their nature. Papers in this section, however, aim to demonstrate the extent to which it has been possible operationally to measure components or general features of the construct as delineated either by cognitive theory or more commonly from phenomena seen in clinical practice, and following such assessment, to provide effective rehabilitation interventions. A comparison of the existing approaches to assessment, together with a review of their strengths and limitations, is provided by Ivana Marková and German Berrios. The literature describes a range of approaches for assessing awareness, and these can vary on a number of dimensions. Most importantly, they are based on differing definitions of awareness and are addressed to different objects of awareness, and hence not surprisingly elicit different awareness phenomena. Consequently, there are problems with making comparisons between the results obtained from different measures. This may help to explain some of the contradictory and variable findings reported in awareness studies. Rehabilitation strategies clearly need to be developed specifically for particular impairments of awareness. Finally, Jenny Fleming and Tamara Ownsworth review current treatment-based approaches that have attempted, albeit often on the basis of a very limited theoretical framework, to modify the functional effects of disorders of awareness. The most appropriate intervention for a given individual understandably depends on the nature of, and interactions between, factors contributing to that individual's awareness deficits, whether primarily neurological, psychological or socio-environmental. Key elements of interventions directed at each of these three levels are outlined. Intervention for awareness deficits are not without important ethical implications, and increasing awareness *per se* is not always considered the primary goal of therapy. Instead, treatment directed at awareness deficits is usually conducted in the context of interventions aimed at improving other aspects of cognitive functioning. Since increased awareness might result in increased distress, it is vital that interventions aim to produce functional gains that contribute to enhancing the person's quality of life.

In focusing on disorders of conscious awareness as a crucial and overriding factor when planning specialised rehabilitation, the modest aims of this special issue are to provide a representative snapshot of the current theoretical pitfalls, variety of measures and potential interventions available for clinical practice.

NEUROPSYCHOLOGICAL REHABILITATION
2006, 16 (4), 356–376

# What do we mean by "conscious" and "aware"?

Adam Zeman
*Peninsula Medical School, Exeter, UK*

The concepts of consciousness and awareness are multifaceted, and steeped in cultural and intellectual history. This paper explores their complexities by way of a series of contrasts: (1) states of consciousness, such as wakefulness and sleep are contrasted with awareness, a term that picks out the contents of consciousness: these range across all our psychological capacities; the scientific background of the two concepts is briefly outlined; (2) consciousness is contrasted to self-consciousness, itself a complex term embracing self-detection, self-monitoring, self-recognition, theory of mind and self-knowledge; (3) "narrow" and "broad" senses of consciousness are contrasted, the former requiring mature human awareness capable of guiding action and self-report, the latter involving the much broader capacity to acquire and exploit knowledge; (4) an "inner" conception of consciousness, by which awareness is essentially private and beyond the reach of scientific scrutiny, is contrasted with an "outer" conception which allows that consciousness is intrinsically linked with capacities for intelligent behaviour; (5) finally "easy" and "hard" questions of consciousness are distinguished, the former involving the underlying neurobiology of wakefulness and awareness, the latter the allegedly more mysterious process by which biological processes generate experience: Whether this final distinction is valid is a focus of current debate. Varied interests converge on the study of consciousness from the sciences and the humanities, creating scope for interdisciplinary misunderstandings, but also for a fruitful dialogue. Health professionals treating disorders of consciousness should be aware both of its

---

Correspondence should be addressed to: Adam Zeman, Professor of Cognitive and Behavioural Neurology, Peninsula Medical School, Mardon Neurorehabilitation Unit, Wonford Road, Exeter EX2 4UD, UK. E-mail: adam.zeman@pms.ac.uk

This paper has been adapted, in part, from "What in the world is consciousness?", in press in *Altered States of Consciousness* (*Progress in Brain Research*), edited by Steven Laureys (Elsevier), 2005; "Consciousness", in *Psychogenic Movement Disorders*, edited by Mark Hallett (Lipincott, Williams and Wilkins), 2006, and "Theories of Visual Awareness", in *The Roots of Visual Awareness*, edited by C. A. Heywood, A. D. Milner, and C. Blakemore, *Progress in Brain Research*, Vol. 144 (Elsevier), 2004.

---


http://www.psypress.com/neurorehab DOI:10.1080/09602010500484581

scientific complexities and of its broad cultural background, which influences the public understanding of these conditions.

## INTRODUCTION

Impairment of consciousness is a ubiquitous problem in medicine generally, and especially so in neurology and neurosurgery which focus on the functioning of the chief organ of awareness, the brain. In our everyday practice we routinely categorise states of consciousness, like sleep and coma, and we readily quantify its levels, with tools like the Glasgow Coma Scale (Teasdale & Jennett, 1974) and the Wessex Head Injury Matrix (WHIM) (Shiel et al., 2000); our clinical efforts are often directed toward restoring it, where it has been abolished by injury or disease, and to removing it, for example in anaesthesia and the treatment of insomnia, where it is an impediment to treatment or an unwanted gift. We are, in other words, experts in the assessment and manipulation of consciousness: but what, precisely, is the function we are observing and treating? Is it a straightforward physiological process like digestion, a behavioural output, like dancing a waltz, or an essentially private, scientifically inaccessible, subjective event?

Consciousness is not alone, among psychological concepts, in calling simultaneously for biological, behavioural and first-person styles of exploration. But this requirement seems to be particularly acute in the case of consciousness: this concept, above all others, focuses our attention on the divide between body and mind, the tension between the objective and the subjective realms, analysis by science and synthesis through experience. This is what makes the study of consciousness both so attractive and so difficult. Janus-faced, it looks out on one side towards the sciences of the human body and human behaviour, on the other towards our subjectivity and an ancient set of beliefs about what constitutes personhood. In understanding consciousness we may hope to make sense of a web of interconnected ideas, like the self, the soul and the will. Naturally, many of us have strong background assumptions about the nature of these, which science may be hard-pressed to accommodate fully.

We recently probed these assumptions in a survey of 250 undergraduates at the University of Edinburgh, sampling their views on the relationship of mind to brain (see Figure 1; Liew, Sharpe, Zeman: data submitted for publication). The results are a reminder that consciousness and its associated terms are by no means straightforward terms of science: both consciousness researchers and the wider educated public inherit a vocabulary of terms which are steeped in religious, philosophical and cultural history. This makes it worthwhile to spend a little time at the outset reminding ourselves of the complexities of the concepts of consciousness and awareness. I shall approach these

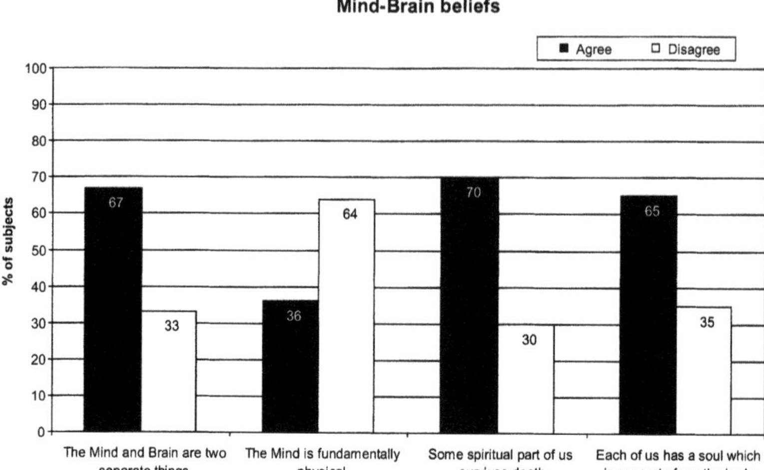


**Figure 1.** The results of a survey of 250 students from several disciplines at the University of Edinburgh on attitudes to mind and brain (Liew, Zeman et al., data submitted for publication).

complexities by way of a series of contrasts designed to highlight the ambiguities which are in play.

I should clarify one potential source of confusion at the outset. "Consciousness" and "awareness" are often used interchangeably in colloquial and medical contexts alike, and by and large I shall do so here. The one exception is outlined in the next section, when "awareness" is used to pick out a particular sense of consciousness.

## WAKEFULNESS VERSUS AWARENESS

Consciousness has two key senses in colloquial English which I shall pick out with the terms *wakefulness* and *awareness* (Zeman, 2001, 2003). Wakefulness is a *state* of consciousness, distinguished from such other states as sleep and coma. These states have degrees: We can be wide awake or half awake, just as we can be lightly or deeply anaesthetised. We are normally confident of our ability to judge an individual's state of consciousness, in this first sense, with the help of objective criteria, like those of the Glasgow Coma Scale: Having one's eyes open is generally an indication of wakefulness, being able to converse pretty much settles the matter.

We usually assume that anyone who is awake will also be *aware*—in other words, not merely conscious but conscious *of* something. Objective criteria are still helpful in ascertaining the presence of consciousness in this second sense—anyone who can obey your instructions and tell you the date is presumably aware—but it has a much stronger connotation of subjectivity than the first sense: As we all know, it is often hard to be sure about what is passing through another's mind on the basis of their behaviour.

The general properties of awareness—the contents of consciousness—have been much discussed. There is a consensus about the following properties: The contents of consciousness are relatively stable for short periods of a few hundred milliseconds, but characteristically changeful over longer ones; they have a narrow focus at a given moment, but over time our awareness can range across the spectrum of our psychological capacities, allowing us to be aware of sensations, percepts, thoughts, memories, emotions, desires and intentions (our current awareness often combines elements from several of these psychological domains); our awareness is personal, allowing us a distinctive, limited perspective on the world; it is fundamental to the value we place on our lives—keeping people alive once their capacity for awareness has been permanently extinguished is widely regarded as a wasted effort (Jennett, 2005).

The relationships between wakefulness, awareness and their behavioural indices are more involved than they appear at first sight (see Figure 2). As a rule, while we are awake we are aware. But the phenomena of wakefulness and awareness do not always run in parallel. The vegetative state, which results from profound damage to the cerebral hemispheres and thalami, with relative preservation of the brainstem, is a state of "wakefulness without awareness". Conversely, when we dream, we are asleep yet aware. Nor can we always rely on behavioural criteria to diagnose consciousness: Patients paralysed for surgery may be fully aware—if the anaesthetic drug has failed to reach them—but completely unable to manifest their awareness; patients "locked in" by a brainstem stroke may appear unconscious until someone recognises their ability to communicate by movements of their eyes or eyelids.

## THE SCIENCE OF WAKEFULNESS AND AWARENESS

Much of contemporary neuroscience, especially cognitive neuroscience, is relevant to these two key senses of consciousness. In this section I shall give a brief, partly historical, sketch of the key findings as a primer for readers who are unfamiliar with this terrain.

Physiological, anatomical and pharmacological advances over the past century have greatly enlarged the scientific understanding of wakefulness, sleep and pathologically altered states of consciousness. In 1929 Hans Berger demonstrated that it was possible to record the brain's electrical activity from the scalp. This provided a tool—the electroencephalogram (EEG)—with which to track the concerted shifts in cerebral activity which accompany changes in conscious state (Berger, 1929). Berger and others

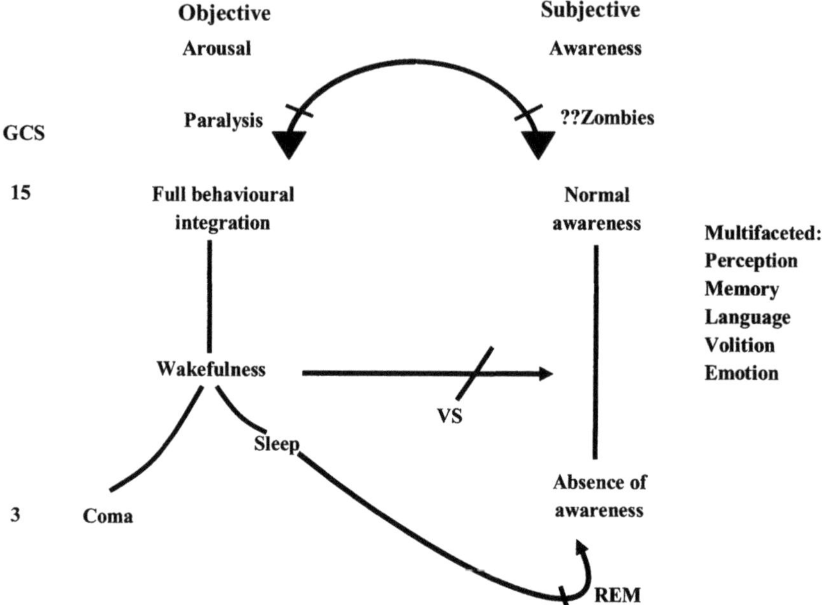


**Figure 2.** Inter-relationships between arousal and awareness. See text for explanation. "Zombies" are theoretical beings discussed by philosophers who display the signs of consciousness, yet lack experience. The plausibility of such beings is controversial.

soon described the fundamental rhythms of the EEG (see Figure 3): beta, at >13 Hz, which accompanies mental effort; alpha, at 8–13 Hz, the signature of relaxed wakefulness; theta (4–7 Hz) and delta (<4 Hz) which predominate in deep sleep.

In the 1950s Kleitman and his co-workers in Chicago discovered that sleep itself has an internal architecture (Aserinsky & Kleitman, 1955; Dement & Kleitman, 1957). Over the first hour of sleep, the sleeper descends through a series of deepening stages into stage III and IV sleep in which slow waves predominate (slow wave sleep, SWS, known as non-REM, NREM, sleep), only to ascend back through these stages into a state resembling wakefulness in its EEG appearance, accompanied by rapid eye movements, profound muscular atonia, autonomic arousal and vivid mentation—dreaming, paradoxical or rapid eye movement sleep (REM) (see Figure 4). This cycle repeats itself four or five times in the course of the night, with decreasing amounts of SWS and increasing amounts of REM as the night proceeds. Recent work on the brain's electrical rhythms has highlighted the potential importance of rapid, widely synchronised, high frequency gamma oscillations (25–100 Hz) in wakefulness and REM (Llinas & Ribary, 1993), although their true significance is not yet clear.

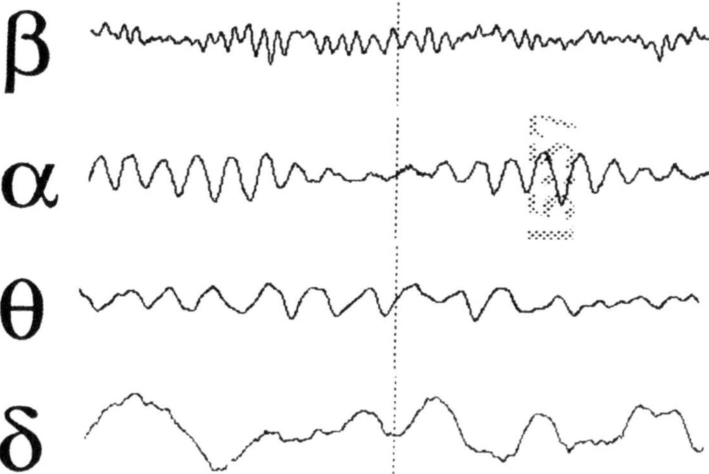


**Figure 3.** The rhythms of the EEG: Records from diagnostic encephalograms performed in four different patients, exemplifying beta rhythm (>14 Hz); alpha rhythm (8–13 Hz); theta rhythm (4–7 Hz); delta rhythm (4 Hz). In each case the dotted line bisects a 2-second sample.

The anatomical and pharmacological mechanisms which control these cycling states have also been clarified over the past hundred years. Moruzzi and Magoun's proposal that the brainstem and thalamus are home to an "activating system" which maintains arousal in the hemispheres has stood the test of time (Moruzzi & Magoun, 1949). However, the notion of a monolithic system has given way to a pharmacologically complex picture of multiple interacting activating systems innervating the cerebral hemispheres widely from the brainstem and diencephalon (Robbins & Everitt, 1995) (see Figure 5). These systems are defined by their neurotransmitters, which

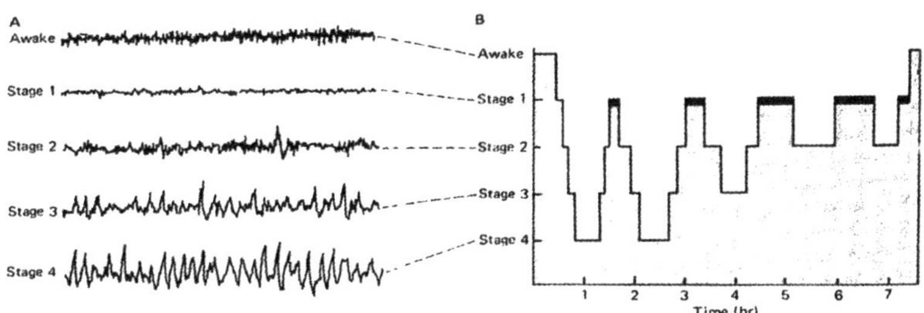


**Figure 4.** The architecture of sleep: An example of sleep staging over the course of a single night. The sleeper passes from wakefulness to deep sleep and then ascends to REM sleep (dark bars). Five similar cycles occur in the course of the night. The EEG tracings to the left show the EEG appearances associated with the stages of sleep; the EEG in REM resembles the "awake" trace.

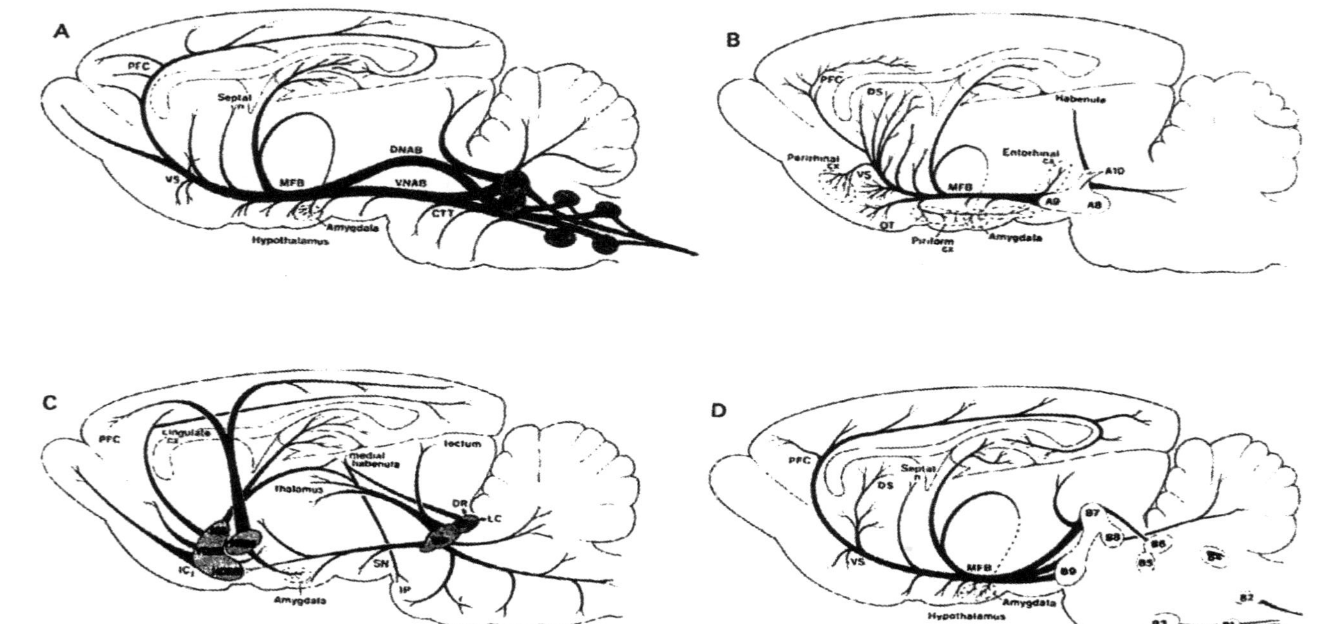


**Figure 5.** The pharmacology of the brainstem activating systems. A: the origin and distribution of the central noradrenergic pathways in the rat brain; B: dopaminergic pathways; C: the cholinergic pathways; D: the serotonergic pathways. CTT = central tegmental tract; dltn = dorsolateral tegmental nucleus; DNAB = dorsal noradrenergic ascending bundle; DR = dorsal raphe; DS = dorsal striatum; HDBB = horizontal limb nucleus of the diagonal band of Broca; Icj = islands of Calleja; IP = interpeduncular nucleus; LC = locus ceruleus; MFB = medial forebrain bundle; MS = medial septum; NBM = nucleus basalis magnocellularis (Meynert in primates); OT = olfactory tubercle; PFC = prefrontal cortex; SN = substantia nigra; tpp = tegmental pedunculopontine nucleus; VDBB = vertical limb nucleus of the diagonal band of Broca; VNAB = ventral noradrenergic ascending bundle; VS = ventral striatum (Robbins & Everitt, 1995).

include acetylcholine, serotonin, noradrenaline, dopamine, histamine, hypocretin and glutamate. The normal succession of conscious states is regulated by these systems: For example, in SWS all these systems become relatively quiescent; in REM periods the ascending cholinergic system becomes disproportionately active; REM periods are eventually brought to an end by rising levels of activity in noradrenergic and serotonergic neuronal groups which had fallen silent at REM onset. Hobson's AIM model attempts to integrate several lines of evidence on the genesis and nature of conscious states (see Figure 6).

The practical upshot of these advances is a useful taxonomy of states of healthy and disordered consciousness. In health, we cycle between wakefulness, SWS, and REM. Pathological states include coma (Glasgow Coma Score <7, eyes closed), the vegetative state mentioned above, brain death and the locked in syndrome (Working party of the Royal College of Physicians, 2003) (Table 1). While wakefulness, SWS and REM are as a rule mutually exclusive, overlaps between these states occasionally occur (Mahowald & Schenck, 1992) (see Figure 7). For example, sleepwalking reflects motor activation of the kind seen during wakefulness occurring at a time when much of the brain is deactivated as during SWS (Bassetti et al., 2000); REM sleep behaviour disorder, in which sufferers enact their

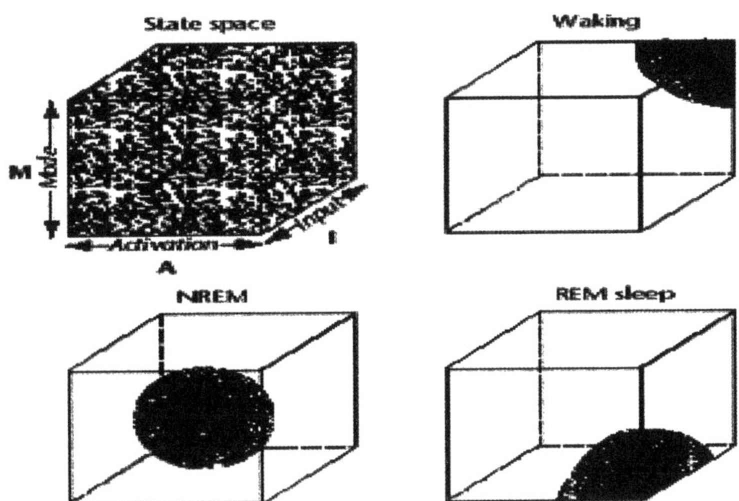


**Figure 6.** The AIM model: Hobson's AIM model locates the three principle states of health consciousness in a "state space" defined by input (I: external in wakefulness, internal during REM), activation (A: high in REM and wakefulness, low in NREM sleep) and mode (M: during REM, prefrontal regions involved in regulation of waking behaviour and encoding of memories are deactivated) (Hobson & Pace-Schott, 2002).

TABLE 1
The differential diagnosis of impaired awareness (Adapted from Working party of the Royal College of Physicians, 2003)

| *Condition* | *Vegetative state* | *Minimally conscious state* | *Locked-in syndrome* | *Coma* | *Death confirmed by brain stem tests* |
|---|---|---|---|---|---|
| Awareness | Absent | Present | Present | Absent | Absent |
| Sleep-wake cycle | Present | Present | Present | Absent | Absent |
| Response to pain | +/ − | Present | Present (in eyes only) | +/ − | Absent |
| Glasgow Coma score | E4, M1-4, V1-2 | E4, M1-5, V1-4 | E4, M1-3, V1 | E1, M1-4, V1-2 | E1, M1-3, V1 |
| Motor function | No purposeful movement | Some consistent or inconsistent verbal or purposeful motor behaviour | Volitional vertical eye movements or eyeblink preserved | No purposeful movement | None or only reflex spinal movement |
| Respiratory function | Typically Preserved | Typically Preserved | Typically Preserved | Variable | Absent |
| EEG activity | Typically slow wave activity | Insufficient data | Typically normal | Typically slow wave activity | Typically absent |
| Cerebral metabolism (positron emission tomography) | Severely reduced | Insufficient data | Mildly reduced | Moderately−severely reduced | Severely reduced or absent |
| Prognosis | Variable: if permanent, continued vegetative state or death | Variable | Depends on cause but full recovery unlikely | Recovery, vegetative state or death within weeks | Already dead |

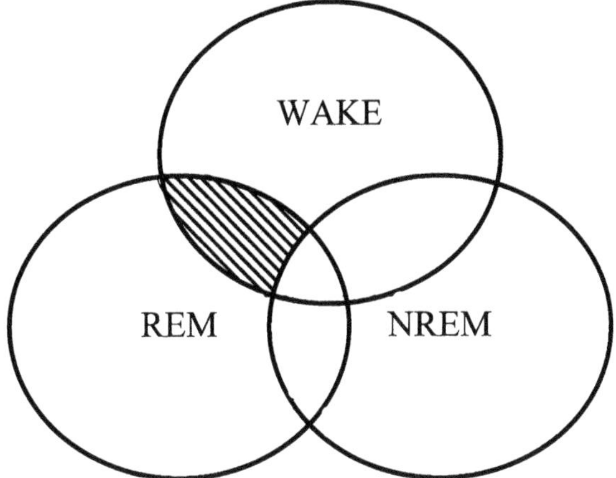


**Figure 7.** State boundary dissociation. The states of wakefulness, REM and NREM sleep are normally distinct. Many parasomnias can be understood as the result of a fusion of two or more states. For example, overlap between the phenomena of REM sleep and wakefulness (shaded) gives rise to REM sleep behaviour disorder; overlap between NREM sleep and wakefulness occurs during sleepwalking and night terrors (Mahowald & Schenck, 1992).

dreams, results from a failure of the normal atonia of REM sleep, allowing dream mentation to give rise to behaviour, like self-defence, of a kind which would normally be confined to wakefulness (Schenck, Bundlie, Ettinger, & Mahowald, 1986).

Knowledge of the neural basis of awareness, of our experience, has also been transformed by the path-breaking work of the past century on the biology of cognition, exploring the neurology of perception, language, memory, emotion, and action. Work on these psychological processes, and their disruption by disease, is demonstrating increasingly fine-grained correlations between features of our experience and details of neural processes. The key role of visual area V4 in the conscious perception of colour, and in its loss in central achromatopsia (Zeki, 1990) (loss of colour vision), and the key role of area V5 in the perception of visual motion, and in its loss in central akinetopsia (Zeki, 1991) are much cited examples. Correlation, of course, does not imply cause. Recent work in this area has tried to tighten the link between brain activity and conscious experience by investigating how cerebral activity changes when our experience changes without any corresponding change in the world: examples include studies of imagery (Ishai, Ungerleider, & Haxby, 2000), hallucinations (Ffytche et al., 1998) and the modulation of awareness by attention or during binocular rivalry (Kanwisher, 2001). A second strategy for defining the neurology of consciousness is to approach awareness by stealth, so to speak, by exploring the neurology of unconscious processing. I shall discuss this line of work and fill out our current picture of the neurological basis of awareness in the section on narrow and broad consciousness below.

## CONSCIOUSNESS VERSUS SELF-CONSCIOUSNESS

The terms "self-consciousness" and "self-awareness" are sometimes used in medical contexts, usually interchangeably, as if their meanings were self-evident. I doubt this: Self-consciousness and self-awareness are peculiarly complex ideas, not too surprisingly, as they combine three others—"self", "conscious" and "aware"—each of which is multifaceted (Berrios & Markova, 2003). I shall try to tease apart the principle strands of self-consciousness/self-awareness.

The distinction between "self" and "other" is biologically crucial. There are many activities which we need to direct towards other objects in the world—like eating them—which it would be disastrous if we directed towards ourselves. We should expect to find strategies for drawing this distinction in the simplest organisms. But "self-consciousness" implies more than an ability to behave differently towards self and other: It requires a representation of self and other. A variety of different kinds of representation fall out of the senses I shall discuss (and number for ease of reference).

The *colloquial* sense of self-consciousness (1)—a proneness to embarrassment in the presence of others—is rather sophisticated, as it implies the person's awareness that the awareness of others is directed on him or her. A second sense (2), *self-consciousness as self-detection*, refers to a family of forms of self-consciousness which are probably present in many animals. This family includes awareness of stimuli which directly impinge on the body (the ant walking up your arm); of proprioceptive information about bodily position which contributes substantially to our body image; of information about actions which we are about to perform or are performing, giving rise to a sense of agency; of information about bodily state (hunger, thirst, etc); and of emotions, like fear or affection, which signal the state of our relationship to objects and to people around us, and without which we are liable to lose the sense of our own reality or that of the world, as in "depersonalisation" and "derealisation".

A third sense, (3)—*self-consciousness as self-monitoring*—extends self-detection in time into past and future, and in range, to encompass more plainly cognitive abilities. It refers to the ability to recall the actions we have recently performed (Beninger, Kendall, & Vanderwolf, 1974), and to our ability to predict our chances of success in tasks which challenge memory (Hampton, 2001) or perception (Smith, Shields, & Washburn, 2003): we undoubtedly possess these abilities, and ingenious experiments in comparative psychology (Beninger et al., 1974; Hampton, 2001; Smith et al., 2003) suggest that many other animals have them too.

Senses (2) and (3) require representation of various activities and capacities of self rather than any unified concept. Senses (4) and (5) draw closer to what we normally have in mind, I suspect, when we speak of self-awareness. The fourth sense, (4)—*self consciousness as self-recognition*—alludes to our ability to recognise our own bodies as our own, for example in mirrors (mirror self-recognition, MSR). Gordon Gallup discovered in the 1970s that if apes are given experience with a mirror they will soon realise that they are looking at themselves, while their monkey cousins apparently fail to grasp this fact despite extensive exposure (Gallop, 1970). Human children develop this ability at around 18 months. Recent evidence suggests that dolphins can also acquire MSR (Reiss & Marino, 2001); there are claims for pigeons and magpies.

Between the ages of 18 months and around 5 years, human children take a further major intellectual stride: they come to appreciate that as well as being objects, which can be inspected in mirrors, they are also subjects, of experience—they possess, in other words, not only bodies, but also minds. The awareness of ourselves as subjects of experience opens up a world of new possibilities for understanding our own behaviour and the behaviour of others in terms of desires and beliefs, and for implanting and manipulating these (Baron-Cohen, 1995; Frith & Frith, 1999). It has been described as the acquisition of a "theory of mind". Once we realise that others, like ourselves, have a limited, personal perspective on the world we can choose to inform, misinform and influence them in a host of entertaining and profitable ways. This "awareness of awareness" is the penultimate sense (5) of self-consciousness. The degree to which animals other than man possess this awareness is debated.

Finally, we use "self-consciousness" to refer to our self-knowledge in its broadest sense (6)—one's knowledge of oneself as the hero of a personal narrative, deeply conditioned by one's circumstances and cultural background: Contrast our self-knowledge at 6, 16 and 60 or the conceptions of self in a medieval monk and a contemporary scientist. The capacity to relive our past in a form of "mental time-travel" constitutes the "autonoetic awareness" which Endel Tulving has identified as the distinctively human intellectual achievement (Tulving, 1985). Self-depiction is a central focus of art, another distinctively human activity.

What of the relationship between consciousness and self-consciousness? The implication of the past few paragraphs is that it would be unwise to give a general answer to this question, one needs first to specify the senses of consciousness and self-consciousness one has in mind. Two contrasting, controversial, but influential ideas about this relationship deserve a mention here, although space prevents me from pursuing them further. First, the notion, linked to the phenomenological tradition, that some form of pre-reflective self-awareness or "ipseity" is presupposed by even simple forms of perceptual awareness (when I look at the glass I experience "my seeing the glass"). Second, the idea that awareness is summoned into being by self-awareness, specifically by the acquisition of a theory of mind, the idea at the core of some "top-down" theories of consciousness (Humphrey, 1978).

## CONSCIOUSNESS NARROW VERSUS CONSCIOUSNESS BROAD

The third distinction can be introduced via the etymology of "consciousness". The Latin "conscientia", the root of our "consciousness", was formed by the combination of "cum", meaning "with", and "scio", meaning "know" (Lewis, 1960). In its narrow, or strong, sense, conscientia meant knowledge shared with another, often guilty knowledge of the kind one might share with a fellow conspirator. By metaphorical extension it could refer to "knowledge shared with oneself", But alongside this "strong" usage, conscientia was sometimes used in a broad, or weak, sense, in which it meant, simply, knowledge.

The tension between these two senses lives on, I suspect, in our current use of "consciousness". We sometimes reserve the word for mental states, the contents of which we can "share" fully with ourselves. For example, I am currently conscious of the book lying on my desk: I could describe it to you, read its cover, reach out and pick it up. In other words I can report my visual awareness of the book, and use it to guide a range of actions. This is full-blooded awareness, consciousness "narrow" and "strong". Yet we are often inclined to attribute consciousness to creatures who lack the full repertoire of "conscious" behaviour: alinguistic animals, prelinguistic infants, dysphasic adults, for example. We are even tempted to attribute consciousness in a certain sense in cases in which its absence in the strong sense is precisely the focus of our interest. For example, consider experiments in which a person's improving performance in a psychological task reveals that they must be learning a rule (or a "grammar") governing the task, yet they are unable to explain how they are improving their performance, unable to articulate the rule (Berns, Cohen, & Mintun, 1997). There is an inclination to say that 'in some sense' they must have become conscious of the rule even though, in another sense, they are learning it unconsciously. The first sense here is consciousness "broad" or "weak", consciousness as knowledge.

At the "broad" or "weak" extremes of this spectrum lie a range of processes which we normally regard as quintessentially "unconscious": for example, blindsight (Weiskrantz, 1998) and its analogues blind touch and blind smell (Sobel et al., 1999), priming by neglected stimuli (Rees et al.,

2000), priming by masked stimuli (Dehaene et al., 1998), the processing of "unseen" visual stimuli in experiments using binocular rivalry (Kanwisher, 2000) or binocular extinction (Moutoussis & Zeki, 2002) or in states of impaired awareness, like the vegetative and minimally conscious states (Laureys, Berre, & Goldman, 2001). Examples like these create an opportunity for neuroscientists to contrast the features of "conscious" and "unconscious" neural processing (Baars, 2002). These contrasts (see Table 2) are

TABLE 2
"Contrastive analysis": Studies comparing conscious and unconscious brain activity

| *Study (context)* | *Comparison* | *Results* |
|---|---|---|
| Laureys et al., 2000 (Vegetative state) | Vegetative state vs recovery | Increase in cortical metabolic rate and restoration of connectivity with recovery |
| John et al., 2001 (Anaesthesia) | Anaesthesia vs awareness | Loss of gamma band activity and cross-cortical coherence under anaesthesia |
| Sahraie et al., 1997 (Blindsight) | Aware vs unaware mode of perception in blindsight patient GY | Aware mode associated with DLPF and PS activation, unaware with medial F and subcortical |
| Dehaene, 1998 (Backward masking) | Perceived numbers vs backward masked but processed numbers | Unreported numbers underwent perceptual, semantic and motor processing similar but less intense to reported numbers |
| Kanwisher, 2000 (Binocular rivalry) | Attention to "face" or "place" when stimuli of both kinds are simultaneously in view, or perception of face or place during binocular rivalry | Activity in FFA and PPA locked to presence or absence of *awareness* of face and place |
| Moutoussis & Zeki, 2002 (Invisible stimuli) | Perceived vs "invisible" but processed faces/houses | Similar but less intense activation of FFA and PPA by Invisible stimuli |
| Engel et al., 2000 (Binocular rivalry) | Perception of one or other of a pair of rivalrous stimuli | Firing of cells processing currently perceived stimulus better synchronised than firing of cells processing suppressed stimulus |
| Tononi & Edelman, 1998 (Binocular rivalry) | Perception of high vs low frequency flicker during binocular rivalry | More widespread and intense activation by perceived stimulus |
| Petersen et al., 1998 (Task automatisation) | Effortful verb generation task vs performance after training | LPF, ant cing and cerebellar activitation shifts to left perisylvian activation with training |

Key: ant cing = anterior cingulate; DLPF = dorsolateral prefrontal cortex; FFA = fusiform face area: LPF = lateral prefrontal cortex; medial F = medial frontal cortex; PPA = parahippocampal place area; PS = prestriate.

in their early days but so far indicate that several plausible candidates can influence the chances that a given stream of neural processing will give rise to awareness: The amplitude and duration of the associated activity, its degree of synchronisation, its site (for example, cortical or subcortical) and its neural "reach" or connectivity.

The most popular current model of conscious processing proposes that it occurs when individually unconscious modules of cognitive function—conceived of in either psychological or anatomical terms—join forces and communicate. In Baars' Global Workspace Theory (Baars, 2002) and Dehaene's Neuronal Workspace Model (Dehaene & Naccache, 2003), information becomes conscious when it is broadcast widely through the brain, allowing forms of cognitive performance which are otherwise unattainable. Dehaene suggests, for example, that these include the bridging of delays, inhibition of habitual responses, the planning, evaluation and monitoring of novel strategies and higher level semantics. Whether awareness really depends on a qualitatively distinct style of neural processing or rather is a straightforward function of variables such as amplitude and site is a major empirical question for the next decade. Studies of the recovery of awareness in patients with coma, vegetative or minimally conscious states, should help to resolve this central issue.

## CONSCIOUSNESS INNER VERSUS CONSCIOUSNESS OUTER

Some readers will have a nagging sense that the distinction between broad and narrow senses of consciousness in the last section misses the real point of interest. It fails to capture the essential difference between conscious and unconscious processes. Whether information is conscious, you may want to say, does not depend at all upon whether we can report or act upon it. It simply depends on whether it gives rise to "an experience"—whether there is something it feels like to be conscious of the information (Nagel, 1979). And for any neural process, however one discovers this, there either is or there is not an associated experience. This notion, that consciousness is a determinate, private, invisible and crucially important internal process or event is the "inner" concept of consciousness.

I suspect that this notion is the dominant current conception of consciousness, widely shared, by scientists as well as non-scientists. It suggests the following kind of picture of brain–mind interaction: Certain types of process in the brain "generate" consciousness, rather as, in the tale of the Arabian Nights, rubbing Aladdin's magic lamp conjures up the genie. The product of the process, consciousness, is, indeed, rather like the genie, magical and evanescent (although consciousness is even less visible than the genie). We tend to think that this picture of consciousness is simply obvious, necessitated by a range of basic facts about experience and the brain. For example, dreams, hallucinations, mental imagery and brain stimulation experiments teach us that certain kinds of brain activity are all that is needed to produce experience. The resulting experience looks nothing like the brain activity which causes it and must therefore be different in kind from it, a stream of autonomous mental events which arises from the physical ones in the brain.

This widespread conception of consciousness implies that awareness is a deeply private matter, inaccessible to observation by third parties (Zeman, 2004). On this view, awareness casts an "inner light" on a private performance. In a patient just regaining awareness we imagine the light casting a faltering glimmer, which grows steadier and stronger as a richer awareness returns. We sometimes imagine a similar process of illumination at the phylogenetic dawning of awareness, when animals with simple nervous systems first became conscious. We wonder whether a similar light might one day come to shine in artificial brains. But, bright or dim, the light is either on or off; awareness is present or absent—and only the subject of awareness knows for sure. The light of awareness is invisible to all but its possessor.

This inner concept creates some real difficulties for the "science of consciousness". It implies that its chief focus of interest lies beyond the reach of scientific observation. If so we may never be able to integrate consciousness fully into scientific theory. If we cannot cash the language of consciousness in the currency of neuroscience, we will neither be able to provide a deeply satisfying explanation of how matter creates mind, nor to give an intuitive account of how mind—our desires and intentions—influences matter. The most we can hope for are correlations, identifying the bare mysterious fact that certain neural processes give rise to certain kinds of experience which themselves play no part in the explanation of behaviour. This inner view creates an explanatory gap that seems unbridgeable. Things, in brief, look bad for the science of consciousness.

Given the gravity of this impasse, we have reason to backtrack, to consider the possibility that we might have been mistaken about the nature of consciousness, and perhaps even about its contents. This journey back through our assumptions is bound to be a tough one, as it tends to strike us as being so obvious that our experience is as it seems to be, and also obvious, in the light of what we know of neuroscience, that the brain generates experience. So, if we backtrack, does any alternative offer itself?

One alternative emerges quite naturally when we ask ourselves how we establish that others, including patients in states of impaired awareness, are conscious. We do so by interacting with them, by engaging with their behaviour. When we do this, when we communicate or dance or play with other people, we are left with no genuine doubt about their consciousness. This prompts the thought that experience might not arise from the brain in the way we normally envisage. Perhaps, rather than viewing it as a mysterious emanation from the brain, we should think of it as a sophisticated form of interaction with the world, an elaborate process of exploration. This is the "outer" conception of consciousness. If there is something to it, our current efforts to account for consciousness may be excessively "neurocentric" (Zimmer, 2004). Perhaps we need to broaden the horizon of our explanation, to consider the mind as "embodied, embedded and extended" (Broks, 2003)—embodied in the wider frame of our biological being, embedded in the culture in which it has developed, extended in space and time through which our transactions with the physical world proceed.

To many of us this is an alien, disturbing view of consciousness, a theory which snuffs out its essence. Yet there are grounds for doubting that our grasp of the contents and nature of experience is as firm as we usually take it to be. The evidence from work on change blindness & Noe, 2001) and inattentional blindness suggests that our "internal representation" of our visual surroundings is less rich than we normally take it to be, shaking our certainty about the contents of our experience. Evidence from sensory substitution experiments (O'Regan & Noe, 2001) suggests that the "visual" properties of visual experience may be conferred by the manner in which visual behaviour explores the world rather than by the "specific nerve energy" of the normal visual pathways, undermining our usual understanding of how experience arises from the brain.

Neither the inner nor the outer concept of consciousness alone seems to be fully equal to our needs, yet it is not clear how we should reconcile them. Which of these concepts you prefer, the picture of consciousness "inside the head" or the picture of consciousness "at large" in the world, will determine your view of the final distinction I shall draw, between the "hard" and the "easy" questions of consciousness.

## HARD VERSUS EASY QUESTIONS OF CONSCIOUSNESS

If you are drawn to the inner notion of consciousness, to the picture of experience as an entirely private, invisible mental process, you will have the sense that there is a gulf, an apparently unbridgeable gulf, between all that we can learn about the brain from science and the subjective essence of awareness. However, if you are attracted by the idea that it may be possible to reconstrue the concept of awareness in terms of complex interactions with the world, you will be more optimistic about the prospects for a science of consciousness.

The distinction between the "hard" and "easy" questions of consciousness was drawn by the philosopher David Chalmers to highlight the difference between explaining the neural events which mediate conscious behaviour and the (allegedly) more mysterious process by which those events give rise to awareness (Chalmers, 1996), "how the water of the physical brain is turned into the wine of experience" in the words of another philosopher, Colin McGinn (1991). Given the inner notion of consciousness this distinction becomes an important one: Science promises to solve the hard but not the easy question. Given the outer view, the distinction collapses: Explain how the brain facilitates conscious behaviour, and consciousness is explained.

## CONCLUSION

I have tried to give a guide, in this chapter, to the ambiguous concepts of consciousness and awareness. I began with the uncontroversial distinction between the two key colloquial senses of consciousness, the relatively objective notion of wakefulness and the more subjective concept of awareness. I outlined some key findings in neuroscience which have illuminated consciousness in these two senses: They include the discoveries that conscious states have electrical correlates which can be recorded from the surface of the scalp; that these are regulated by pharmacologically specific structures in the brainstem, thalamus and basal forebrain; and a multitude of findings which support the general principle that the features of experience will correspond to features of neural processing. We made a detour via self-consciousness, teasing apart six related but separable senses of the term. Returning to the main topic of consciousness, we identified a spectrum of senses that extends between consciousness "narrow" and consciousness "broad"—consciousness in its strong sense of knowledge shared with oneself, available for report and the control of voluntary action, and consciousness in its broad sense of "knowledge" pure and simple. I reviewed the evidence that underpins global workspace theory, from contrasts between neural processes that do and do not give rise to consciousness. We then examined the intuition that what really matters to us when we are deciding whether a person or a state is conscious is simply the occurrence of "experience", not the possibility of report or deliberate action: On this "inner" conception of consciousness, experience is conceived as an immaterial, invisible and private process. I contrasted this to an "outer" conception which regards "consciousness" as shorthand for intelligent behaviour. Finally we saw that those who are wedded to the inner conception are likely to see the science of consciousness as confronted by an insurmountable challenge—to solve the "hard" problem of consciousness, bridging the explanatory gap between the physical and the mental—while for those who accept the outer conception there is no worrying gap between the two.

The complexities of the concepts of consciousness and awareness have practical import: In scientific work we need to be clear which concept of consciousness we hope to understand; in clinical work we need to be clear about what kind of awareness we are hoping to restore; in communicating with

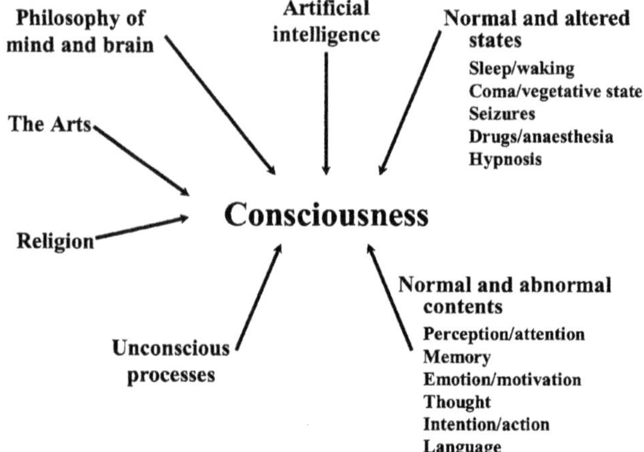


**Figure 8.** Sources of evidence for the study of consciousness.

relatives we sometimes need to convey the subtleties of consciousness, bringing home the message, for example, that recovery from coma is often a gradual and sometimes sadly incomplete affair, not the sudden restitution of the soul. Much of what we know about the science of consciousness derives from clinical studies of brain injured patients. Collaborative research, applying the tools of neuroscience to the analysis of brain injury, has the potential to provide continuing insights into this fundamental biological and cultural capacity.

The topic of consciousness is so rich because it lies at the intersection of several intellectual domains (Figure 8), including some, in the humanities, which focus on the experiences of subjects, and others, in the sciences, which highlight processes in objects. The study of the arts, of religion and philosophy all have their contribution to make alongside the study of the brain and its biology. This richness creates a risk of confusion and cross-purposes alongside the possibility of cross-fertilisation. We should keep this rich but potentially confusing context in the back of our minds as we navigate around the disorders of awareness.

## REFERENCES

Aserinsky, E., & Kleitman, N. (1955). Two types of ocular motility occuring during sleep. *Journal of Applied Physiology*, *8*, 1–10.

Baars, B. J. (2002). The conscious access hypothesis: Origins and recent evidence. *Trends in Cognitive Sciences*, *6*, 47–52.

Baron-Cohen, S. (1995). *Mindblindness*. Cambridge: MIT Press.

Bassetti, C., Vella, S., Donati, F., Wielepp, P., & Weder, B. (2000). SPECT during sleep-walking. *Lancet*, *356*, 484–485.

Beninger, R. J., Kendall, S. B., & Vanderwolf, C. H. (1974). The ability of rats to discriminate their own behaviour. *Canadian Journal of Psychology*, *28*, 79–91.

Berger, H. (1929). Uber das elektrenkephalogramm des Menschen. *Archives of Psychiatry*, *87*, 527–570.

Berns, G. S., Cohen, J. D., & Mintun, M. A. (1997). Brain regions responsive to novelty in the absence of awareness. *Science*, *276*, 1272–1275.

Berrios, G. E., & Markova, I. S. (2003). The self and psychiatry: A conceptual history. In T. Kircher & A. David (Eds.), *The self in neuroscience and psychiatry*. Cambridge: Cambridge University Press.

Broks, P. (2003). *Into the silent land*. London: Atlantic Books.

Chalmers, D. J. (1996). *The conscious mind*. Oxford: Oxford University Press.

Dehaene, S., & Naccache, L. (2003). Towards a cognitive neuroscience of consciousness: Basic evidence and workspace framework. *Cognition*, *79*, 1–37.

Dehaene, S., Naccache, L., Le Clec, H. G., Koechlin, E., Mueller, M., & Dehaene-Lambertz, G. (1998). Imaging unconscious semantic priming. *Nature*, *395*, 595–600.

Dement, W., & Kleitman, N. (1957). Cyclic variations in EEG during sleep and their relation to eye movements, body motility, and dreaming. *Electroencephalography and Clinical Neurophysiology*, *9*, 673–690.

Engel, A. K., Fries, P., Roelfsema, P. R., Konig, P., & Singer, W. (2000). *Temporal binding, binocular rivalry, and consciousness*. Available from: http://www.phil.vt.edu/ASSC/engel/engel.html.

Ffytche, D. H., Howard, R. J., Brammer, M. J., David, A., Woodruff, P., & Williams, S. (1998). The anatomy of conscious vision: An fMRI study of visual hallucinations. *Nature Neuroscience*, *1*, 738–742.

Frith, C. D., & Frith, U. (1999). Interacting minds—a biological basis. *Science*, *286*, 1692–1695.

Gallop, G. G. (1970). Chimpanzees: Self-recognition. *Science*, *167*, 86–87.

Hampton, R. R. (2001). Rhesus monkeys know when they remember. *Proceedings of the National Academy of Science, USA*, *98*, 5359–5362.

Hobson, J. A., & Pace-Schott, E. F. (2002). The cognitive neuroscience of sleep: Neuronal systems, consciousness and learning. *Nature Reviews Neuroscience*, *3*, 679–693.

Humphrey, N. (1978). Nature's psychologists. *New Scientist*, *78*, 900–903.

Ishai, A., Ungerleider, L., & Haxby, J. V. (2000). Distributed neural systems for the generation of visual images. *Neuron*, *28*, 979–990.

Jennett, B. (2005). *The vegetative state* (1st ed.). Cambridge: Cambridge University Press.

John, E. R., Prichep, L. S., Kox, W., Valdes-Sosa, P., Bosch-Bayard, J., Aubert, E., Tom, M., diMichele, F., & Gugino, L. D. (2001). Invariant reversible QEEG effects of anesthetics. *Consciousness and Cognition*, *10*, 165–183.

Kanwisher, N. (2000). Neural correlates of changes in perceptual awareness in the absence of changes in the stimuls. *Towards a science of consciousness*, Abstr. No. 164.

Kanwisher, N. (2001). Neural events and perceptual awareness. *Cognition*, *79*, 89–113.

Laureys, S., Berre, J., & Goldman, S. (2001). Cerebral function in coma, vegetative state, minimally conscious state, locked-in syndrome and brain death. In J. L. Vincent (Ed.), *Yearbook of intensvie care and emergency medicine* (pp. 386–396). Berlin: Springer.

Laureys, S., Faymonvillem, M.-E., Degueldre, C., Delfiore, G., Damas, P., Lambermont, B., Janssens, N., Aerts, J., Franck, G., Luxen, A., Moonen, G., Lamy, M., & Maquet, P. (2000). Auditory processing in the vegetative state. *Brain*, *123*, 1589–1601.

Lewis, C. S. (1960). *Studies in words*. Cambridge: Cambridge University Press.

Llinas, R., & Ribary, U. (1993). Coherent 40-Hz oscillation characterizes dream state in humans. *Proceedings of the National Academy of Science, USA*, *90*, 2078–2081.

Mahowald, M. W., & Schenck, C. H. (1992). Dissociated states of wakefulness and sleep. *Neurology*, *42*, 44–51.

McGinn, C. (1991). *The problem of consciousness*. Oxford: Basil Blackwell.

Moruzzi, G., & Magoun, H. W. (1949). Brain stem reticular formation and the activation of the EEG. *Electroencephalography and Clinical Neurophysiology, 1*, 455–473.

Moutoussis, K., & Zeki, S. (2002). The relationship between cortical activation and percpetion investigated with invisible stimuli. *Proceedings of the National Academy of Science, USA, 99*, 9527–9532.

Nagel, T. (1979). What is it like to be a bat? In *Mortal Questions* (pp. 165–180). Cambridge: Cambridge University Press.

O'Regan, J. K., & Noe, A. (2001). A sensorimotor account of vision and visual consciousness. *Behavioural Brain Science, 24*, 939–973.

Petersen, S. E., van Mier, H., Fiez, J. A., & Raichle, M. E. (1998). The effects of practice on the functional anatomy of task performance. *Proceedings of the National Academy of Science, USA, 95*, 853–860.

Rees, G., Wojciulik, E., Clarke, K., Husain, M., Frith, C., & Driver, J. (2000). Unconscious activation of visual cortex in the damaged right hemisphere of a parietal patient with extinction. *Brain, 123(Pt 8)*, 1624–1633.

Reiss, D., & Marino, L. (2001). Mirror self-recognition in the bottlenose dolphin: A case of cognitive convergence. *Proceedings of the National Academy of Science, USA, 98*, 5937–5942.

Robbins, T. W., & Everitt, B. J. (1995). Arousal systems and attention. In M. S. Gazzaniga (Ed.), *The cognitive neurosciences* (pp. 703–720). Cambridge: MIT Press.

Sahraie, A., Weiskrantz, L., Barbur, J. L., Simmons, A., Williams, S. C., & Brammer, M. J. (1997). Pattern of neuronal activity associated with conscious and unconscious processing of visual signals. *Proceedings of the National Academy of Science, USA, 94*, 9406–9411.

Schenck, C. H., Bundlie, S. R., Ettinger, M. G., & Mahowald, M. W. (1986). Chronic behavioural disorders of human REM sleep: A new category of parasomnia. *Sleep, 9*, 293–308.

Shiel, A., Horn, S. A., Wilson, B. A., Watson, M. J., Campbell, M. J., & McLellan, D. L. (2000). The Wessex Head Injury Matrix (WHIM) main scale: A preliminary report on a scale to assess and monitor patient recovery after severe head injury. *Clinical Rehabilitation, 14*, 408–416.

Smith, J. D., Shields, W. E., & Washburn, D. A. (2003). The comparative psychology of uncertainty monitoring and metacognition. *Behavioural Brain Science, 26*, 317–339.

Sobel, N., Prabhakaran, V., Hartley, C. A., Desmond, J. E., Glover, G. H., Sullivan, E. V., & Gabrieli, J. D. (1999). Blind smell: Brain activation induced by an undetected air-borne chemical. *Brain, 122(Pt 2)*, 209–217.

Teasdale, G., & Jennett, B. (1974). Assessment of coma and impaired consciousness. A practical scale. *Lancet, 2*, 81–84.

Tononi, G., & Edelman, G. M. (1998). Consciousness and complexity. *Science, 282*, 1846–1851.

Tulving, E. (1985). Memory and consciousness. *Canadian Psychology, 26*, 1–12.

Weiskrantz, L. (1998). *Blindsight: A case study and implications* (2nd ed.). Oxford: Clarendon Press.

Working Party of the Royal College of Physicians (2003). *The Vegetative State: Guidance on Diagnosis and Management*. London: Royal College of Physcians of London.

Zeki, S. (1990). A century of cerebral achromatopsia. *Brain, 113(Pt 6)*, 1721–1777.

Zeki, S. (1991). Cerebral akinetopsia (visual motion blindness): A review. *Brain, 114(Pt 2)*, 811–824.

Zeman, A. (2001). Consciousness. *Brain, 124*, 1263–1289.

Zeman, A. (2003). *Consciousness: A user's guide*. London: Yale University Press.

Zeman, A. (2004). Theories of visual awareness. In C. A. Heywood, D. A. Milner, & C. Blakemore (Eds.), *The roots of visual awareness* (pp. 321–329). Amsterdam: Elsevier.

Zimmer, C. (2004). *Soul made flesh*. New York: Free Press.

NEUROPSYCHOLOGICAL REHABILITATION
2006, 16 (4), 377–396

# Visual restoration in cortical blindness: Insights from natural and TMS-induced blindsight

Tony Ro[1,2] and Robert Rafal[3]

[1]*Department of Psychology, Rice University, Houston, TX, USA*
[2]*Department of Physical Medicine and Rehabilitation, Baylor College of Medicine, Houston, TX, USA*
[3]*Wolfson Institute for Clinical and Cognitive Neuroscience, School of Psychology, University of Wales, Bangor, UK*

Unilateral damage to visual cortex of the parietal or occipital lobe can cause the patient to be unaware of contralesional visual information due to either hemispatial neglect or hemianopia. It is now known that both neglect and hemianopia result from the disruption of a dynamic interaction between cortical visual pathways and more phylogenetically primitive visual pathways to the midbrain. We consider the therapeutic implications of these cortical–subcortical interactions in the rehabilitation of hemianopia. We start with the pheonmenon of "blindsight", in which patients with hemianopia can be shown, by implicit measures of visual detection or discrimination, to process visual information without conscious awareness. Some variants of blindsight have been postulated to recruit subcortical processes, while others may reflect compensatory optimisation of processing of spared visual cortex. Both mechanisms may offer opportunities for innovative strategies for rehabilitation of visual field defects. We relate the neural mechanisms that have been proposed to underlie blindsight to those that have been suggested to underlie the recovery of visual function after rehabilitation. It is suggested that the similarity and overlap of the neural processes supporting blindsight and recovery of visual function might provide insights for effective rehabilitation strategies for restoring visual functions.

Correspondence to: E-mail: tro@rice.edu *or* r.rafal@bangor.ac.uk


http://www.psypress.com/neurorehab DOI:10.1080/09602010500435989

## INTRODUCTION

In this article, we use the term unawareness to refer to the lack of a subjective perceptual experience of a visual event, regardless of whether or not that event has been processed by the visual system. Metaphorically, and along the lines of various models of consciousness that have been advanced, visual information that we are unaware of is therefore information that is not on a global workspace, is not on the stage of a Cartesian theatre, or does not have fame in the brain (Dehaene & Naccache, 2001; Dennett, 2001). Unilateral damage to the primary visual cortex, or to the visual association cortex, often causes the patient to become unaware of contralesional visual information because that information is no longer processed by neural structures essential for the generation of visual awareness.

Lesions of posterior association cortex frequently cause the syndrome of hemispatial neglect. Unawareness, in this case is due to inattention. The loss of awareness is not sharply demarcated in retinotopic co-ordinates but, rather, is contralesional to the focus of attention—regardless of where the unattended object is in the visual field (Behrmann & Moscovitch, 1994; Behrmann & Tipper, 1994; Driver, Baylis, & Rafal, 1993; Driver & Halligan, 1991; Posner, Walker, Friedrich, & Rafal, 1987). By contrast, complete destruction of the primary visual cortex (or geniculostriate afferents in the optic radiations) results in hemianopia. Since the primary visual cortex in the occipital lobe, which receives the majority of retinal efferents via the lateral geniculate nucleus of the thalamus, is retinotopically organised (Holmes, 1918; Hubel & Wiesel, 1977; Tootell, Silverman, Switkes, & De Valois, 1982), focal lesions to any given part of it lead to a corresponding retinotopically determined scotoma (Holmes, 1918).

Under certain circumstances, distinguishing between neglect and hemianopia can prove challenging. Assessments and diagnoses of patients may also be complicated by the fact that many patients may present with both neglect and hemianopia or may have a complex form of a visual disorder that may be a hybrid between the two (e.g., see case report by Nadeau & Heilman, 1991). Nonetheless, some differences are typically apparent between patients with a pure hemianopia and a pure form of neglect. With confrontation testing, for example, both neglect as well as hemianopic patients will systematically miss visual events presented to their contralesional fields. However, patients with neglect will more frequently miss a contralesional visual stimulus when presented simultaneously with an ipsilesional one. Furthermore, detailed neuropsychological testing can be utilised to reveal several other visual performance differences between these types of patients. Whereas neglect patients will fail to explore and detect lines or objects on the contralesional side of space, hemianopic patients can compensate for their deficit by moving their eyes contralesionally to bring previously undetected stimuli into their seeing field. Performance of neglect and heminopic patients on line bisection tasks also clearly differs, usually with only neglect patients showing ipsilesional biases on bisection performance (Halligan & Marshall, 1988; but see Ferber & Karnath, 2001).

Hemianopia and neglect also differ in terms of their prognosis for recovery and compensation. While most patients with hemispatial neglect improve, and many recover, hemianopia is usually permanent. Nevertheless, patients with hemianopia often compensate spontaneously (Zihl, 2000)—and a persistent hemianopia is less disabling than persisting neglect. This is, perhaps, surprising when one considers that, unlike hemianopia in which damage to primary visual cortex completely eliminates the processing (even unconscious processing) of all but the most simple visual features, this is not the case in patients with hemispatial neglect. Indeed, it has been shown that in spite of the dramatic exclusion from consciousness of neglected stimuli, perceptual processing of them can proceed to the level of semantic classification (Berti & Rizzolatti, 1992; McGlinchey-Berroth et al., 1993) and that preattentive vision parses the scene to extract figure from ground (Driver et al., 1993), group objects and define their primary axes (Driver, Baylis, Goodrich, & Rafal, 1994), and prioritize the location of objects that are not perceived consciously for subsequent orienting (Danziger, Kingstone, & Rafal, 1998). Indeed, not only is semantic information encoded outside of awareness, but it has been shown that selection for awareness occurs at the latest stage of information processing just prior to response (Baylis, Driver, & Rafal, 1993; Rafal et al., 2002).

By contrast, hemianopic deficits traditionally had been considered to be complete and irreversible in humans. Even in selected patients in whom processing without awareness has been demonstrated (we consider this phenomenon of blindsight later), it has for the most part been limited to processing only of simple visual features. Nevertheless, studies in non-human primates have shown evidence of some recovery of function with experience and training (Cowey, 1967; Mohler & Wurtz, 1977). Here we describe some of the mechanisms that may be responsible for the demonstrated recovery of visual function in humans and focus on the mechanisms responsible for blindsight and the potential for exploiting them therapeutically in rehabilitating visual function after damage to the occipital cortex.

## Restoration of vision after cortical blindness: The Sprague effect

A cardinal principle guiding rehabilitation is that lesion-induced deficits may not be understood simply in terms of the absence of a putative function that is normally mediated by the lesioned tissue. Rather, the pathological behaviour reflects the re-organisation of dynamic interactions of the region with other interconnected structures. In the case of blindness due to lesions of visual cortex, we need to consider the remote effects of the lesion on midbrain visual circuits. The geniculostriate pathway is a recent development in evolution, emerging only in mammals. In sub-mammalian vertebrates, all visual input to the brain is via the optic tectum of the midbrain. This pathway mediates reflexive orienting—the visual grasp reflex—to visual signals and the basic processing of visual stimuli.

In mammals the optic tectum is referred to as the superior colliculus (SC); and the fact that visual cortex lesions cause complete loss of visual awareness indicates that the retinotectal pathway, in humans, does not normally mediate conscious visual experience. Nevertheless, the primary visual cortex is directly connected to the SC, and the parietal lobes are connected to it via the pulvinar nucleus of the thalamus. Loss of visual awareness after lesions of either primary visual cortex or visual association cortex reflects dysfunction throughout this cortico–subcortical network.

Sprague first demonstrated that visual orienting is mediated by a dynamic interaction between the cerebral cortex and the midbrain pathways for reflexive orienting (Sprague, 1966). In a classic experiment, cats were rendered blind in one visual field by unilateral extirpation of occipital and parietal cortex. It was then shown that orienting towards the contralesional field was restored if the opposite superior colliculus was removed. This finding indicates that loss of vision after lesions of visual cortex reflects dysfunction not only of the damaged cortex, but also the remote disruption of subcortical visual pathways that might otherwise afford some recovery of visual function. This pioneering work gave us the first clues to how recovery from blindness might be facilitated.

### Two approaches to rehabilitation of blindness due to lesions of visual cortex

This review focuses on the recovery of vision in heminaopia, and considers two potential strategies. The first is to optimise function of the unlesioned subcortical pathways through procedures that facilitate or release the subcortically mediated visual grasp reflex—thereby bringing the stimulus to the sighted region of the fovea. This might be termed the "bottom-up" approach. The second strategy is to train patients to strategically search into the region of the scotoma—the "top-down" approach.

We begin by considering the phenomenon of "blindsight"—the demonstration of visual processing in the absence of awareness—and then consider how this phenomenon might inform rational approaches to rehabilitation.

## BLINDSIGHT IN HEMIANOPIC PATIENTS

Blindsight refers to the above chance performance of cortically blind patients on forced-choice visual discrimination tasks despite being unaware of the visual stimulation (for review, see Stoerig & Cowey, 1997; Weiskrantz, Warrington, Sanders, & Marshall, 1974). Patients with blindsight can, for example, accurately localise visual stimuli with hand or eye movements and/or discriminate different types of visual events (e.g., shape, wavelength) well above chance, but without any awareness.

Three major explanations have been postulated for this residual vision. These are not mutually exclusive; each may apply in some patients but not in others (Morland et al., 2004):

*1. Extrageniculate mediation through subcortical pathways.* Visual information transmitted through the retinotectal pathway, or some other subcortical pathway (e.g., retino-pulvinar (Williams, Azzopardi, & Cowey, 1995), is projected to extrastriate visual cortex, and is sufficient to drive visually guided behaviour without awareness. Based on the demonstration of accurate localisation with saccadic eye movements, a function that involves oculomotor processes of the superior colliculus, it has been suggested that the retinotectal or secondary visual pathway may mediate some residual visual functions in patients exhibiting blindsight (Perenin & Jeannerod, 1975; Poppel, Held, & Frost, 1973; Weiskrantz et al., 1974). Furthermore, the retinotectal pathway projects through the pulvinar into the dorsal stream of the extrastriate cortex (Kaas & Huerta, 1988), which has been suggested to be involved with vision for action in the absence of awareness (Goodale & Milner, 1992; Milner & Goodale, 1995). Consistent with this anatomy, in addition to generating accurate visually guided saccades to unseen targets, patients with visual field deficits and blindsight have also been shown to accurately point towards visual stimuli presented within their scotoma (Blythe, Kennard, & Ruddock, 1987; Perenin & Jeannerod, 1975, 1978; Weiskrantz et al., 1974).

*2. Geniculoextrastriate mediation.* Direct projections from the lateral geniculate to extrastriate cortex may be sufficient for some visual discrimination—and even for some "sensation" that patients do not experience as actually "seeing". This mechanism has been postulated, for example, to mediate some discrimination of wavelength, since collicular neurons do not have colour opponency (Stoerig & Cowey, 1989, 1991). This mechanism also may account for the Riddoch effect (Sincich, Park, Wohlgemuth, & Horton, 2004)—a sensation of motion that some hemianopics report (Zeki & Ffytche, 1998).

*3. Partial sparing of primary visual cortex, with sufficient preservation of cortical processing for stimuli to reach objective but not subjective threshold.* (Fendrich, Wessinger, & Gazzaniga, 1992; Wessinger, Fendrich, & Gazzaniga, 1997). This explanation, positing "islands" of spared cortex, has been ruled out in some blindsight patients based on behavioural/perimetric (Kentridge, Heywood, & Weiskrantz, 1997) and neuroimaging (Barbur, Watson, Frackowiak, & Zeki, 1993; Stoerig, Kleinschmidt, & Frahm, 1998; Zeki & Ffytche, 1998) findings, but may nonetheless be responsible for blindsight in some patients.

Whether blindsight may be due to superior colliculus function or remnants of spared cortex, or some combination thereof, there is one clear difference between these two accounts of blindsight: while only a small minority of patients with occipital cortex damage may have some sparing of cortical tissue, the majority of patients with occipital cortex damage, including those with spared cortex, have intact superior colliculi. Therefore, according to the retinotectal account, most patients should exhibit blindsight, but the reported prevelance of it has traditionally been relatively rare (Blythe et al., 1987; Marzi, Tassinari, Aglioti, & Lutzemberger, 1986). However, a more recent study in progress with a larger group of patients and with more extensive probes for unconscious processing suggests that the majority of patients may have blindsight (Sahraie, personal communication), providing some support for a retinotectal account of blindsight.

Despite claims of cortical involvement in blindsight, and even though not all patients with visual cortical damage may exhibit it, there has been a large body of evidence implicating superior colliculus involvement in different forms of blindsight. For example, Rafal et al. (1990) tested three patients, each with a dense homonymous hemianopia, to examine whether extrageniculate vision may be responsible for unconscious processing (i.e., blindsight). In that study, the patients made saccadic eye movements or manual button-press responses under monocular conditions to seen targets on the ipsilesional side of space. On half of the trials, a distractor was presented in the contralesional, blind hemifield. Although the patients never reported seeing these distractors in their blind hemifield, their saccadic latencies to the seen target were significantly delayed in comparison to the no distractor trials (see Figure 1). Furthermore, this effect was more robust for distractors in the temporal hemifield, which has more projections into the superior colliculus than the nasal hemifield (but see Williams et al., 1995). Based on this asymmetry, as well as the known contributions of the superior colliculus in generating saccadic eye movements (Kaas & Huerta, 1988; Munoz & Wurtz, 1995; Posner & Cohen, 1980; Robinson & McClurkin, 1989), it was concluded that the retinotectal pathway leading to the superior colliculus was involved with the unconscious processing of distractors. A more recent study, however, failed to replicate this unconscious distractor effect in a larger group of hemianopic patients (Walker et al., 2000), suggesting that this indirect measure of blindsight may not be as robust and detectable in all patients with visual cortex damage and sparing of the superior colliculus.

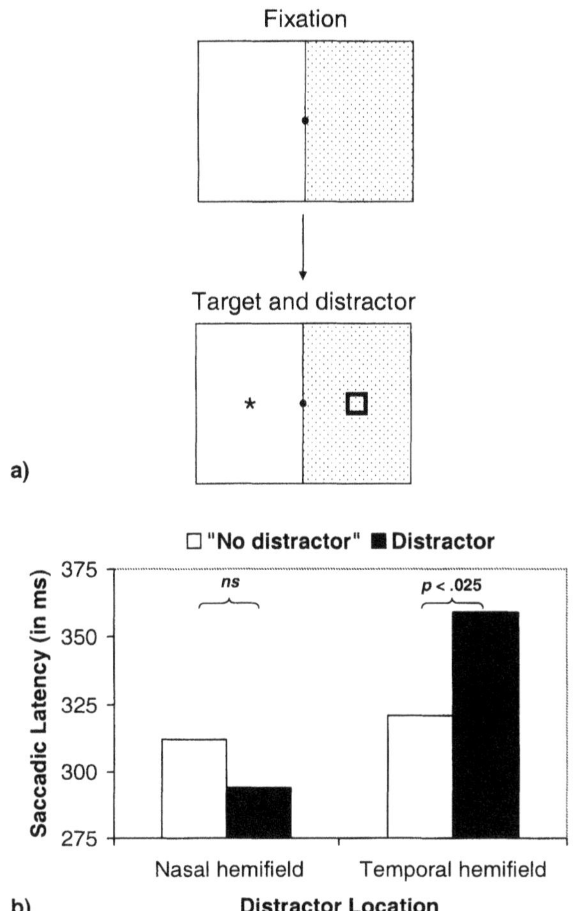


**Figure 1.** (a) The stimuli used in the study by Rafal et al. (1990) examining the effects of unseen remote distractors on target responses in hemianopic patients. Following fixation, the patients were asked to move their eyes to a target presented in the normal hemifield while distractors were presented in the blind hemifield depicted here by the stippled region. (b) The saccadic latencies for conditions with distractors in the nasal (left) and temporal (right) hemifields averaged across three patients. Note that the "no distractor" trials contained a distractor that was presented after the saccade was made.

Furthermore, using a similar type of task, but only requiring a button press response rather than a localisation task, Marzi and colleagues demonstrated a redundancy gain (i.e., faster simple detection responses to targets in the good hemifield when a simultaneous stimulus was placed in the hemianopic hemifield), but only in a small proportion of patients (Marzi et al., 1986; Tomaiuolo et al., 1997). This facilitation from unseen redundant stimuli also has been proposed to be a function of subcortical mechanisms. However, if such were the case, it is again unclear why not all patients with visual cortex damage show this redundancy gain effect. One possibility may be that with stimuli presented into a scotoma of a patient, there are both inhibitory (i.e., distractor effects) in addition to facilitatory (i.e., redundancy gain) effects and the net results of slower or faster reaction times may be dependent on the task, with some tasks showing the former, whereas others showing the latter or a null effect.

Additional evidence for retinotectal involvement in blindsight, and validating the naso-temporal asymmetry as a marker for collicular mediation, was demonstrated in a different type of target localisation task by Dodds and colleagues (Dodds, Machado, Rafal, & Ro, 2002). This study examined a patient with a homonymous hemianopia as a result of visual cortex damage from a stroke. In a forced-choice location discrimination task, the patient demonstrated a higher proportion of correct verbal guesses of the location of visual targets (i.e., more blindsight) when the target stimuli to be discriminated were projected to the temporal hemifield under monocular viewing conditions as compared to nasal hemifield conditions. This result is important in that it suggests that retinotectal function may be assessed in non-oculomotor tasks (i.e., without saccadic eye or reaching hand movements) and may have the ability to influence verbal reports and awareness.

## EXPLORATION OF BLINDSIGHT USING TRANSCRANIAL MAGNETIC STIMULATION

Inconsistencies of blindsight in studies of hemianopic patients may have to do with methodological differences, patient selection, or many other potential factors. We have been examining whether transcranial magnetic stimulation (TMS) (for reviews on TMS, see Hallett, 2000; Jahanshahi & Rothwell, 2000; Robertson, Theoret, & Pascual-Leone, 2003; Walsh & Cowey, 2000) might be used to consistently induce blindsight-like behaviour in normal observers. If possible, these TMS-induced visual dysfunctions might provide an additional and converging means for studying blindsight. Further, because the extent and chronicity of the "virtual" lesion created by TMS is under experimental control, extraneous factors such as diaschesis and/or reorganisation of brain function would play minimal roles in any measured blindsight effects.

In the first study, the unconscious distractor effect paradigm used by Rafal et al. was modified and adapted so that TMS could be used to induce a transient blindness of the distractor in otherwise normal seeing observers (Ro, Shelton, Lee, & Chang, 2004). Since the TMS pulse primarily affects cortical surface structures rather than deeper tissue, the extent of the scotoma induced by TMS is limited to approximately 1 degree of visual angle in the fovea. In these studies, saccadic eye movements or manual button presses were made to targets appearing in one of four peripheral locations (see Figure 2). On the critical trials, a TMS pulse was given that induced visual suppression of a near foveal distractor. When the participants were unaware of these distractors, as assessed after each trial, we found that saccadic eye movement latencies were nonetheless delayed by these unconscious distractors. Importantly, this unconscious distractor effect was not present when the participants were making indirect button press responses on a keypad placed in front of them. Thus, a form of blindsight was induced with TMS and was similar to that observed in patients with naturally occurring lesions.

In another TMS study, we have also demonstrated spared discrimination processes independent of saccadic eye movements (Boyer, Harrison, & Ro, 2005). In both experiments of this study, the visual cortex was first localised with TMS by finding a coil position on the posterior brain that, when stimulated, induced a transient scotoma. After visual cortex localisation, participants were asked to judge the orientation of a bar in one experiment or the colour of a disk in the other experiment, each of which was presented within the scotoma. The participants were asked to only report that the orientation of the bar or the colour was perceived when he or she was aware of the orientation or colour of the stimuli. Otherwise, the participants were asked to guess the orientation of the bar or the colour of the disk and to provide a confidence rating. Our results showed that even though the participants were unaware of the orientation or colour of the stimulus, they nonetheless guessed significantly above chance on the orientation of the bar and the colour of the disk. Interestingly, some of our participants reported "having a sense" of the orientation of the bar much like patients with Type II blindsight who often "felt" that something was presented, but were unable consciously to perceive it (cf., Poppel et al., 1973; Weiskrantz et al., 1974; Zeki & Ffytche, 1998). Perhaps as a consequence of this sense or feeling, confidence ratings in our experiments were highly correlated with their accuracy performance on these judgement tasks, suggesting that their subjective experiences may have been influenced by unconscious processes.

These TMS results demonstrating spared orientation and colour processing without primary visual cortex demonstrate that TMS can be used to induce more traditional forms of blindsight (i.e., above-chance discrimination) and provide further support for the existence of a geniculoextrastriate pathway that bypasses V1 and awareness (Sincich et al., 2004; Stoerig & Cowey, 1989, 1991). Since both orientation and colour cannot be effectively discriminated by the superior colliculus, the most plausible pathway supporting these visual discriminatory behaviours without V1 and awareness may be a direct

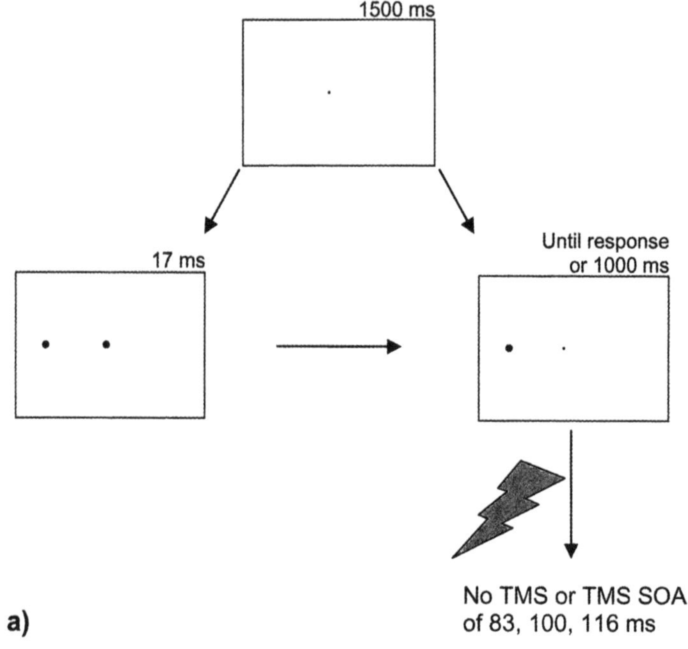


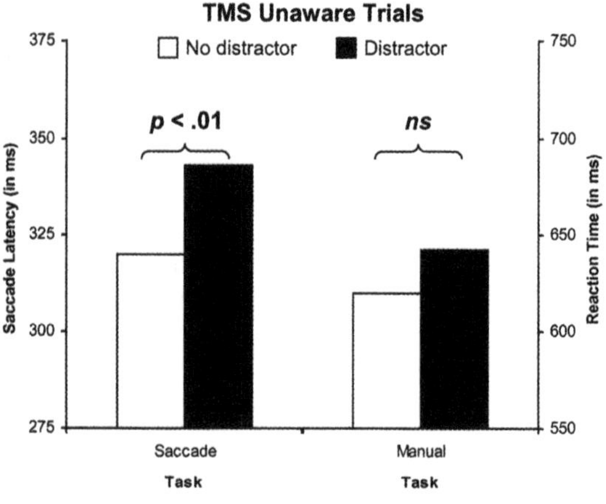


**Figure 2.** (a) The stimuli used in the TMS study by Ro et al. (2004) examining the effects of unseen distractors on target responses. On half of the trials, a distractor was presented along with the peripheral target (downward left arrow), whereas on the other half of the trials no distractor was presented (downward right arrow). (b) The saccadic latencies for trials with unconscious distractors were significantly slower than trials without a distractor, but no difference was measured in the manual button press task.

geniculate pathway into area V4 of extrastriate cortex, which contains a high proportion of feature-selective and colour-opponent cells (Desimone, Schein, Moran, & Ungerleider, 1985; Gallant, Braun, & Van Essen, 1993; Zeki, 1980). Along with previous anatomical tracer studies that have provided evidence for the existence of this lateral geniculate nucleus to V4 pathway (Fries, 1981; Yukie & Iwai, 1981), our results suggest that this pathway may also play a functional role in direct visual stimulus attribute processing without any awareness.

Taken together, these studies using TMS and patients with visual cortical damage strongly suggest that intact retinotectal and/or geniculoextrastriate functioning may be crucial and responsible for some forms of blindsight. These findings further suggest that recruitment or training of these retinotectal and/or geniculoextrastriate pathways may be advantageous in the restoration of visual function after primary visual cortex damage. As most patients with visual cortex damage and resulting cortical blindness will have an intact superior colliculus, it might be possible to train or encourage patients to advantageously utilise their retinotectal functions, and perhaps even remnant extrastriate processes when still intact, to enhance visual awareness.

## RETINOTECTAL FUNCTIONS VS. REORGANISATION/ RECOVERY OF VISUAL CORTEX

Based on this selective review of blindsight, we now consider its therapeutic implications; specifically, that the mechanisms supporting blindsight may also be promoted to rehabilitate and restore some vision after visual cortex damage. Studies in non-human primates suggest that the mechanism for the recovery of visual function after damage to the primary visual cortex may be a function of the superior colliculus in the midbrain (Mohler & Wurtz, 1977; Zihl & von Cramon, 1979). Mohler and Wurtz, for example, demonstrated recovery of visual orienting to stimuli presented within a practised region of a surgically induced scotoma in monkeys. Subsequent to this recovery, a lesion placed in the homologous visual representation of the ipsilateral superior colliculus eliminated this recovery effect. This demonstration of reorganisation and restoration of visual function in monkeys, as well as findings suggesting superior colliculus contributions to blindsight (see above), suggest that similar reorganisation might be seen in humans after occipital cortex damage, despite the notions that recovery of visual function is unlikely due to the hard-wired nature of the visual system.

Interestingly, a subset of patients with blindsight report being subjectively aware of the presence of some visual information, but do not experience any visual phenomena. This form of blindsight, referred to as Type II blindsight (e.g., see Cowey, 2004), may indicate that some patients may be able to access and interpret some of the unconscious processing of visual information and consequent behaviours through other visual processing mechanisms, such as the coding within the superior colliculus for reflexive eye movements towards "unseen" events. Thus, training patients to compensate for their visual deficits by relying on known properties of the extrageniculostriate pathways may prove to be a fruitful endeavour for restoring visual loss. Although there have been many attempts at rehabilitating cortical blindness, including what we refer to as peripheral techniques, such as the use of prisms to redirect light from blind regions of space (Peli, 2000; Rossi, Kheyfets, & Reding, 1990), our focus here is on the rehabilitation of visual function through central means and their relations to blindsight. Specifically, we focus on the methods that have examined the rehabilitation of visual function by attempts to induce the reorganisation and/or utilisation of different brain structures and functions with training or instruction.

The earliest approaches to restitution were based on bottom-up stimulation, in which detection or eye movement responses were made to visual signals presented in the blind field. One form of visual field loss rehabilitation examined by Zihl involves repeated stimulation within and specifically near the borders of blind regions of a patient's scotoma (Zihl & von Cramon, 1979). Another form of rehabilitation employs saccadic eye movement training (Kerkhoff, Munssinger, & Meier, 1994; Zihl, 1980, 1981; Zihl & von Cramon, 1985). Patients are repeatedly presented with visual targets within their scotoma and are instructed to generate saccadic eye movements to these "unseen" targets. As mentioned above, the ability of patients with visual field deficits as a consequence of post-geniculate damage to make accurate saccadic eye movements has been repeatedly demonstrated (e.g., see Poppel et al., 1973, and the above section on blindsight; Weiskrantz et al., 1974). This may involve the recruitment of the superior colliculus in the visual processing of stimuli presented within the scotoma. Interestingly, this repeated saccadic eye movement or localisation training leads to increases in perimetric maps of visual field size. Thus, by perhaps promoting the use of retinotectal vision, visual field sizes may be increased. As with the rehabilitation techniques involving repeated stimulation and detection of peripheral targets placed in the scotoma (see below for more details), however, eccentric fixation may also be responsible for the reported perimetrically measured visual field increases following this form of training.

Kasten, Sabel, and their colleagues have reported a new method of potentially rehabilitating visual loss using what they refer to as visual restitution training (Kasten, Poggel, & Sabel, 2000; Kasten, Wust, Behrens-Baumann, & Sabel, 1998). Conveniently for patients as well as therapists, these training procedures are implemented on standard computers and can be done in the comfort of the patient's own home. The technique presents a stimulus, dynamically changing in size, near the fovea in the sighted visual field. The stimulus is slowly moved across the midline until it disappears in the scotoma. The disappearance is signalled by the patient, at which point the stimulus is moved back into the sighted field; and the process successively repeated. By systematically working at the boundaries of the scotoma, it was shown that the boundary of the scotoma could be moved and the field of vision expanded. In a subsequent study, the effects were shown to generalise to chromatic stimuli (Kasten et al., 2000).

It has been suggested that these types of rehabilitation procedures involving stimulation of blind regions in a patient's visual field, especially the borders, leads to increased sensitivity in detecting the presence of lights within the trained region by restoring the function of cortical tissue, such as islands of spared cortex (Fendrich et al., 1992; Wessinger et al., 1997), or in this particular case the shores of dysfunctional tissue surrounding the lesion. Unfortunately, however, this restoration of vision has been questioned, inconsistent, and simply may be a consequence of eccentric fixations or other methodological shortcomings (e.g., see Balliet, Blood, & Bach-y-Rita, 1985) or may only be possible in certain types of patients (Pambakian & Kennard, 1997). Furthermore, it is unclear whether these presumed expansions of visual fields for simple detection of stimuli might provide lasting functional benefits and improvements in more complex, real-life visual tasks.

Although more recent studies have attempted to control fixation by implementing tasks at fixation (Kasten et al., 1998, 2000), many of these tasks involve the detection of a change in colour of the fixation point, which is sufficiently simple and could likely have been accurately performed with modest degrees of eccentric fixation. Furthermore, since the restorative effects were much more pronounced when the patients knew where the targets would appear, and the recovery expanded the borders by an average of only a few degrees, fixating a position a few degrees towards the scotoma might well be responsible for the seemingly expanded visual field while also still allowing for accurate performance on the central "fixation" task. These highly promising techniques therefore require further verification with systematic means of measuring and controlling fixation (e.g., by using a Purkinje eye tracker and image stabilisation methods as in the studies by Fendrich and colleagues, 1992).

Schendel and Robertson (2004) demonstrated increases in visual field size and detection when a hemianopic patient placed his arm near the visual stimuli. Their patient with a homonymous hemianopia was better able to detect visual targets when his contralesional hand was placed near the source of visual stimulation. Studies in non-human primates demonstrate visual fields of cells in premotor cortex that are anchored to the hand (Graziano, Yap, & Gross, 1994). This finding suggests that projections to the premotor cortex, perhaps through the superior colliculus and dorsal processing stream, may be involved with the increased detection with an outstretched hand. Although a central target detection task was required in an attempt to ensure fixation, eye movements were not directly monitored and image stabilisation methods were not used, as with the studies by Kasten and colleagues. Thus, it is also unclear whether Schendel and Robertson's results might have been due to eccentric fixations that were larger when the contralesional hand was outstretched in space. The less than perfect accuracy rates on the central fixation task suggest that deviated gaze may have played some role in their effects.

The studies reviewed thus far may all be considered "bottom-up" strategies in which visual (and proprioceptive in the case of Schendel & Robertson, 2004), stimulation is used to "pull" the patient's attention and eye movements into the scotoma. Most rely on a collicularly mediated visual grasp reflex. However, subcortical pathways may not be spared in some patients; another approach is then needed. Pambakian et al. (Pambakian & Kennard, 1997; Pambakian, Mannan, Hodgson, & Kennard, 2004) used a visual search task that encourages patients to strategically explore their blind field to find a specific visual feature in a cluttered display. Not only did search performance improve after training in many patients, there was also a demonstration of sustained improvement in tasks of daily living.

One of us (Rafal) has had the opportunity to observe the effectiveness of this approach in a patient treated by Sophie Hayward and Carolyn Young in conjunction with Alidz Pambakian. This 29-year-old woman had sustained a severe traumatic brain injury 12 years earlier. She posed an unusual clinical challenge that highlights the importance of tailoring therapy based on the particular circumstances of each individual patient. Hemiparesis and diplopia had recovered, but she was left with persistent hemianopia—for which she had not compensated at all, and which left her with severe visual disability. A magnetic resonance imaging scan revealed that there was not only occipital lobe damage, but also lesions in the pulvinar nucleus of the thalamus and the dorsal midbrain. This case is instructive in demonstrating that subcortical pathways are involved in spontaneous compensation for hemianopia. Given subcortical damage in this patient, it seemed unlikely that a "bottom-up" strategy (e.g., saccadic training) would be effective. She was treated using the protocol developed by Pambakian and Kennard (1997) and showed gratifying improvement in her visual capabilities in everyday activities.

## SUBCORTICAL CONTRIBUTIONS TO BLINDSIGHT: IMPLICATIONS FOR VISUAL REHABILITATION

The projections into the superior colliculus continue on through the pulvinar into the dorsal visual processing stream of the brain (Goodale & Milner,

1992; Kaas & Huerta, 1988; Milner & Goodale, 1995). Thus, by training patients to generate saccadic eye or reaching hand movements into the scotoma, the patients might frequently detect targets with a considerable degree of accuracy and may even allow the patients to become aware of stimuli within their impaired visual field. Consistent with this notion, the accuracy in localising targets with saccadic eye movements only becomes possible in some patients when the patients are explicitly made aware of this possibility (Zihl, 1981). Thus, restoration of vision may be more prominent if patients are not only made aware of this possibility, but may also prevent the formation of learned nonuse (Ro et al., in press; Taub, Harger, Grier, & Hodos, 1980; Taub, Heitmann, & Barro, 1977), which occurs when patients attempt to compensate for deficits by relying only upon intact function, such as with frequent head movements or eye movements into the blind region for conscious visual processing. In the case of visual cortex damage, patients with visual field loss may experience learned nonuse of their extrageniculate vision due, perhaps, to the initial lack of conscious awareness of the processing occurring in spared visual areas of the brain. However, instructions to the patients to attempt to process and guess about information within their blind hemifields may be highly beneficial for inducing some recovery of vision.

In addition to being involved with oculomotor function and likely responsible for various blindsight phenomena, the superior colliculus has also been demonstrated to be directly involved with the reflexive orienting of attention (Kustov & Robinson, 1996; Rafal et al., 1988; Robinson & Kertzman, 1995). A study of one hemianopic patient has demonstrated an intact inhibition of return (IOR)—a delay in detecting visual targets at previously cued locations that has been suggested to influence attentional and oculomotor processes (see Klein, 2000 for a review). In that study, IOR was generated by a cue within the hemianopic field of a patient and assessed by taking advantage of the environmentally-based aspect of the IOR phenomenon (Danziger, Fendrich, & Rafal, 1997). The patient then moved his eyes so that a cue and a target presented at the same location in space were presented successively onto blind and seeing portions of the retina (see Figure 3). The same magnitude of IOR was measured in the blind and seeing portions in this one patient, suggesting that attentional and visuomotor processes remained intact within the blind region. An elegant study by Kentridge, Heywood, and Weiskrantz (1999) has further implicated a role of the superior colliculus in unconscious visual processing and attentional orienting by demonstrating that unseen visual events nonetheless induced an attentional orienting response to specific locations in an impaired field of a hemianopic patient.

Based on such evidence, and the strong relationship between attention and consciousness, it is conceivable that patients with visual field deficits

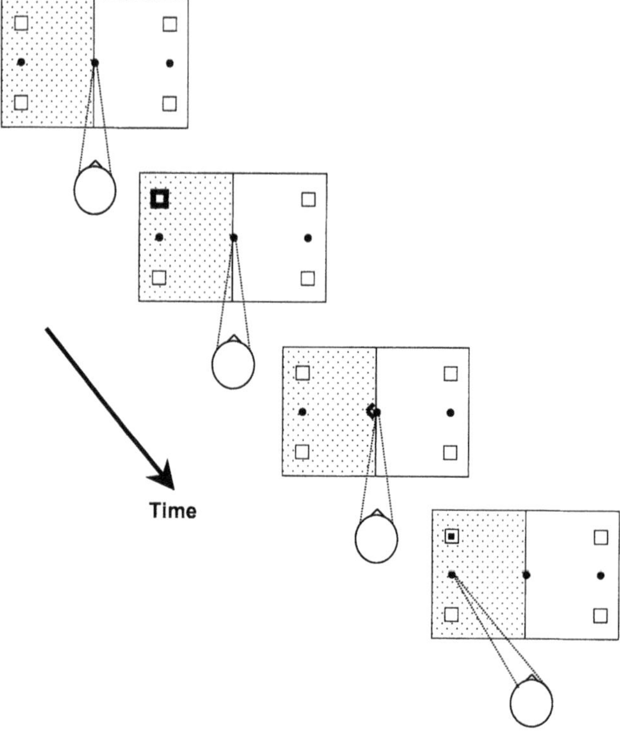


**Figure 3.** The stimuli used by Danziger et al. (1997) examining IOR in the left hemianopic field of a patient with right visual cortex damage. Following central fixation by the patient, a cue was presented in one of the four boxes. Following the cue, the patients were instructed to move their eyes to the fixation point within the hemifield indicated by a central arrow. A target then appeared at the previously cued spatial location, as shown in this illustration, or in the uncued location within the same hemifield.

consequent to primary visual cortex damage might be able to use such reflexive attentional orienting mechanisms of the superior colliculus and blindsight to eventually influence visual awareness. Anecdotal reports from patients suggest that although there is unawareness of visual events, they sometimes have the sense or impression that something was presented, which may be a function of reflexive orienting and may influence their ability to localise and discriminate at above chance levels (i.e., show blindsight). Thus, systematic explorations for enhancing visual awareness through retinotectal functions warrant further exploration. With insights from what we have learned from blindsight and by further examining residual vision in patients with visual field deficits, further clues for effective means of rehabilitating vision might then be provided.

## REFERENCES


Balliet, R., Blood, K. M., & Bach-y-Rita, P. (1985). Visual field rehabilitation in the cortically blind? *Journal of Neurology, Neurosurgy, and Psychiatry, 48*, 1113–1124.

Barbur, J. L., Watson, J. D., Frackowiak, R. S., & Zeki, S. (1993). Conscious visual perception without V1. *Brain, 116*(Pt 6), 1293–1302.

Baylis, G., Driver, J., & Rafal, R. (1993). Extinction and stimulus repetition. *Journal of Cognitive Neuroscience, 5*, 453–466.

Behrmann, M., & Moscovitch, M. (1994). Object-centered neglect in patients with unilateral neglect: Effects of left-right coordinates of objects. *Journal of Cognitive Neuroscience, 6*, 1–16.

Behrmann, M., & Tipper, S. P. (1994). Object-based visual attention: Evidence from unilateral neglect. In M. Moscovitch (Ed.), *Attention and performance. XIV: Conscious and nonconscious processing and cognitive functioning* (pp. 351–376). Hillsdale, NJ: Lawrence Erlbaum.

Berti, A., & Rizzolatti, G. (1992). Visual processing without awareness: Evidence from unilateral neglect. *Journal of Cognitive Neuroscience, 4*, 345–351.

Blythe, I. M., Kennard, C., & Ruddock, K. H. (1987). Residual vision in patients with retrogeniculate lesions of the visual pathways. *Brain, 110*(Pt 4), 887–905.

Boyer, J., Harrison, S., & Ro, T. (2005). Unconscious processing of orientation and color without primary visual cortex. *Proceedings of the National Academy of Sciences, 102*, 16875–16879.

Cowey, A. (1967). Perimetric study of field defects in monkeys after cortical and retinal ablations. *Quarterly Journal of Experimental Psychology, 19*, 232–245.

Cowey, A. (2004). The 30th Sir Frederick Bartlett lecture. Fact, artefact, and myth about blindsight. *Quarterly Journal of Experimental Psychology, 57A*, 577–609.

Danziger, S., Fendrich, R., & Rafal, R. D. (1997). Inhibitory tagging of locations in the blind field of hemianopic patients. *Consciousness and Cognition, 6*, 291–307.

Danziger, S., Kingstone, A., & Rafal, R. (1998). Reflexive orienting to signals in the neglected visual field. *Psychological Science, 9*, 119–123.

Dehaene, S., & Naccache, L. (2001). Towards a cognitive neuroscience of consciousness: Basic evidence and a workspace framework. *Cognition, 79*, 1–37.

Dennett, D. (2001). Are we explaining consciousness yet? *Cognition, 79*, 221–237.

Desimone, R., Schein, S. J., Moran, J., & Ungerleider, L. G. (1985). Contour, color and shape analysis beyond the striate cortex. *Vision Research, 25*, 441–452.

Dodds, C., Machado, L., Rafal, R., & Ro, T. (2002). A temporal/nasal asymmetry for blindsight in a localisation task: Evidence for extrageniculate mediation. *Neuroreport, 13*, 655–658.

Driver, J., Baylis, G. C., Goodrich, S. J., & Rafal, R. D. (1994). Axis-based neglect of visual shapes. *Neuropsychologia, 32*, 1353–1365.

Driver, J., Baylis, G., & Rafal, R. (1993). Preserved figure–ground segmentation and symmetry perception in a patient with neglect. *Nature, 360*, 73–75.

Driver, J., & Halligan, P. W. (1991). Can visual neglect operate in object-centered coordinates? An affirmative single case study. *Cognitive Neuropsychology, 8*, 475–494.

Fendrich, R., Wessinger, C. M., & Gazzaniga, M. S. (1992). Residual vision in a scotoma: Implications for blindsight [see comments]. *Science, 258*, 1489–1491.

Ferber, S., & Karnath, H. O. (2001). How to assess spatial neglect—line bisection or cancellation tasks? *Journal of Clinical and Experimental Neuropsychology, 23*, 599–607.

Fries, W. (1981). The projection from the lateral geniculate nucleus to the prestriate cortex in macaque monkeys. *Proceedings of the Royal Society of London B, 213*, 73–86.

Gallant, J. L., Braun, J., & Van Essen, D. C. (1993). Selectivity for polar, hyperbolic, and Cartesian gratings in macaque visual cortex. *Science, 259*, 100–103.

Goodale, M. A., & Milner, A. D. (1992). Separate visual pathways for perception and action. *Trends in Neurosciences, 15*, 20–25.

Graziano, M. S. A., Yap, G. S., & Gross, C. G. (1994). Coding of visual space by premotor neurons. *Science, 266*, 1054–1057.

Hallett, M. (2000). Transcranial magnetic stimulation and the human brain. *Nature, 406*, 147–150.

Halligan, P. W., & Marshall, J. C. (1988). How long is a piece of string? A study of line bisection in a case of visual neglect. *Cortex, 24*, 321–328.

Holmes, G. (1918). Disturbances of vision by cerebral lesions. *British Journal of Ophthalmology, 2*, 353–384.

Hubel, D. H., & Wiesel, T. N. (1977). Ferrier lecture. Functional architecture of macaque monkey visual cortex. *Proceedings of the Royal Society of London B Biological Science, 198*, 1–59.

Jahanshahi, M., & Rothwell, J. (2000). Transcranial magnetic stimulation studies of cognition: an emerging field. *Experimental Brain Research, 131*, 1–9.

Kaas, J. H., & Huerta, M. F. (1988). The subcortical visual system of primates. In H. Steklis & J. Erwin (Eds.), *Comparative primate biology: Vol. 4. Neurosciences* (pp. 327–391). New York: Wiley-Liss.

Kasten, E., Poggel, D. A., & Sabel, B. A. (2000). Computer-based training of stimulus detection improves color and simple pattern recognition in the defective field of hemianopic subjects. *Journal of Cognitive Neuroscience, 12*, 1001–1012.

Kasten, E., Wust, S., Behrens-Baumann, W., & Sabel, B. A. (1998). Computer-based training for the treatment of partial blindness. *Natural Medicine, 4*, 1083–1087.

Kentridge, R. W., Heywood, C. A., & Weiskrantz, L. (1997). Residual vision in multiple retinal locations within a scotoma: Implications for blindsight. *Journal of Cognitive Neuroscience, 9*, 191–202.

Kentridge, R. W., Heywood, C. A., & Weiskrantz, L. (1999). Attention without awareness in blindsight. *Proceedings of Biological Science, 266*, 1805–1811.

Kerkhoff, G., Munssinger, U., & Meier, E. K. (1994). Neurovisual rehabilitation in cerebral blindness. *Archives of Neurology, 51*, 474–481.

Klein, R. (2000). Inhibition of return: What, where, when, why and how. *Trends in Cognitive Sciences, 4*, 138–147.

Kustov, A. A., & Robinson, D. L. (1996). Shared neural control of attentional shifts and eye movements. *Nature, 384*, 74–77.

Marzi, C. A., Tassinari, G., Aglioti, S., & Lutzemberger, L. (1986). Spatial summation across the vertical meridian in hemianopics: A test of blindsight. *Neuropsychologia*, 24, 749–758.

McGlinchey-Berroth, R., Milberg, W. P., Verfaellie, M., Alexander, M., & Kilduff, P. T. (1993). Semantic processing in the neglected visual field: Evidence from a lexical decision task. *Cognitive Neuropsychology, 10*, 79–108.

Milner, A. D., & Goodale, M. A. (1995). *The visual brain in action* (Vol. 27). Oxford; New York: Oxford University Press.

Mohler, C. W., & Wurtz, R. H. (1977). Role of striate cortex and superior colliculus in visual guidance of saccadic eye movements in monkeys. *Journal of Neurophysiology, 40*, 74–94.

Morland, A. B., Le, S., Carroll, E., Hoffmann, M. B., & Pambakian, A. (2004). The role of spared calcarine cortex and lateral occipital cortex in the responses of human hemianopes to visual motion. *Journal of Cognitive Neuroscience, 16*, 204–218.

Munoz, D. P., & Wurtz, R. H. (1995). Saccade-related activity in monkey superior colliculus. I. Characteristics of burst and buildup cells. *Journal of Neurophysiology, 73*, 2313–2333.

Nadeau, S. E., & Heilman, K. M. (1991). Gaze-dependent hemianopia without hemispatial neglect. *Neurology, 41*, 1244–1250.

Pambakian, A. L., & Kennard, C. (1997). Can visual function be restored in patients with homonymous hemianopia? *British Journal of Ophthalmology*, *81*, 324–328.

Pambakian, A. L., Mannan, S. K., Hodgson, T. L., & Kennard, C. (2004). Saccadic visual search training: A treatment for patients with homonymous hemianopia. *Journal of Neurology, Neurosurgery and Psychiatry*, *75*, 1443–1448.

Peli, E. (2000). Field expansion for homonymous hemianopia by optically induced peripheral exotropia. *Optometry and Vision Science*, *77*, 453–464.

Perenin, M. T., & Jeannerod, M. (1975). Residual vision in cortically blind hemifields. *Neuropsychologia*, *13*, 1–7.

Perenin, M. T., & Jeannerod, M. (1978). Visual function within the hemianopic field following early cerebral hemidecortication in man—I. Spatial localization. *Neuropsychologia*, *16*, 1–13.

Poppel, E., Held, R., & Frost, D. (1973). Residual visual function after brain wounds involving the central visual pathways in man. *Nature*, *243*, 295–296.

Posner, M. I., & Cohen, Y. (1980). Attention and the control of movements. In J. Requin (Ed.), *Tutorials in motor behavior* (pp. 243–258). Amsterdam: North Holland.

Posner, M. I., Walker, J. A., Friedrich, F. J., & Rafal, R. D. (1987). How do the parietal lobes direct covert attention? *Neuropsychologia*, *25*, 135–146.

Rafal, R., Danziger, S., Grossi, G., Machado, L., & Ward, R. (2002). Visual detection is gated by attending for action: Evidence from hemispatial neglect. *Proceedings of the National Academy of Science USA*, *26*, 26.

Rafal, R. D., Posner, M. I., Friedman, J. H., Inhoff, A. W., & Bernstein, E. (1988). Orienting of visual attention in progressive supranuclear palsy. *Brain*, *111*, 267–280.

Rafal, R., Smith, J., Krantz, J., Cohen, A., & Brennan, C. (1990). Extrageniculate vision in hemianopic humans: Saccade inhibition by signals in the blind field. *Science*, *250*, 118–121.

Ro, T., Noser, E., Boake, C., Wallace, R., Gaber, M., Bernstein, M., Speroni, A., De Joya, A., Burgin, S. W., Zhang, L., Grotta, J., & Levin, H. (in press). Functional reorganization and recovery after constraint induced movement therapy in acute stroke: Case reports. *Neurocase*.

Ro, T., Shelton, D., Lee, O. L., & Chang, E. (2004). Extrageniculate mediation of unconscious vision in transcranial magnetic stimulation-induced blindsight. *Proceedings of the National Academy of Science USA*, *101*, 9933–9935.

Robertson, E. M., Theoret, H., & Pascual-Leone, A. (2003). Studies in cognition: The problems solved and created by transcranial magnetic stimulation. *Journal of Cognitive Neuroscience*, *15*, 948–960.

Robinson, D. L., & Kertzman, C. (1995). Covert orienting of attention in macaques. III. Contributions of the superior colliculus. *Journal of Neurophysiology*, *74*, 713–721.

Robinson, D. L., & McClurkin, J. W. (1989). The visual superior colliculus and pulvinar. *Reviews of Oculomotor Research*, *3*, 337–360.

Rossi, P. W., Kheyfets, S., & Reding, M. J. (1990). Fresnel prisms improve visual perception in stroke patients with homonymous hemianopia or unilateral visual neglect. *Neurology*, *40*, 1597–1599.

Schendel, K., & Robertson, L. C. (2004). Reaching out to see: Arm position can attenuate human visual loss. *Journal of Cognitive Neuroscience*, *16*, 935–943.

Sincich, L. C., Park, K. F., Wohlgemuth, M. J., & Horton, J. C. (2004). Bypassing V1: A direct geniculate input to area MT. *Nature Neuroscience*, *7*, 1123–1128.

Sprague, J. M. (1966). Interaction of cortex and superior colliculus in mediation of peripherally summoned behavior in the cat. *Science*, *153*, 1544–1547.

Stoerig, P., & Cowey, A. (1989). Wavelength sensitivity in blindsight. *Nature*, *342*, 916–918.

Stoerig, P., & Cowey, A. (1991). Increment-threshold spectral sensitivity in blindsight. Evidence for colour opponency. *Brain*, 1487–1512.

Stoerig, P., & Cowey, A. (1997). Invited review. Blindsight in man and monkey. *Brain*, *120*, 535–559.

Stoerig, P., Kleinschmidt, A., & Frahm, J. (1998). No visual responses in denervated V1: High-resolution functional magnetic resonance imaging of a blindsight patient. *Neuroreport*, *9*, 21–25.

Taub, E., Harger, M., Grier, H. C., & Hodos, W. (1980). Some anatomical observations following chronic dorsal rhizotomy in monkeys. *Neuroscience*, *5*, 389–401.

Taub, E., Heitmann, R. D., & Barro, G. (1977). Alertness, level of activity, and purposive movement following somatosensory deafferentation in monkeys. *Annals of the New York Academy Science*, *290*, 348–365.

Tomaiuolo, F., Ptito, M., Marzi, C. A., Paus, T., & Ptito, A. (1997). Blindsight in hemispherectomized patients as revealed by spatial summation across the vertical meridian. *Brain*, *120*(Pt 5), 795–803.

Tootell, R. B., Silverman, M. S., Switkes, E., & De Valois, R. L. (1982). Deoxyglucose analysis of retinotopic organization in primate striate cortex. *Science*, *218*, 902–904.

Walker, R., Mannan, S., Maurer, D., Pambakian, A. L., & Kennard, C. (2000). The oculomotor distractor effect in normal and hemianopic vision. *Proceedings of the Royal Society of London B Biological Science*, *267*, 431–438.

Walsh, V., & Cowey, A. (2000). Transcranial magnetic stimulation and cognitive neuroscience. *Nature Reviews Neuroscience*, *1*, 73–79.

Weiskrantz, L., Warrington, E. K., Sanders, M. D., & Marshall, J. (1974). Visual capacity in the hemianopic field following a restricted occipital ablation. *Brain*, *97*, 709–728.

Wessinger, C. M., Fendrich, R., & Gazzaniga, M. S. (1997). Islands of residual vision in hemianopic patients. *Journal of Cognitive Neuroscience*, *9*, 203–221.

Williams, C., Azzopardi, P., & Cowey, A. (1995). Nasal and temporal retinal ganglion cells projecting to the midbrain: Implications for "Blindsight". *Neuroscience*, *65*, 577–586.

Yukie, M., & Iwai, E. (1981). Direct projection from the dorsal lateral geniculate nucleus to the prestriate cortex in macaque monkeys. *Journal of Comparative Neurology*, *201*, 81–97.

Zeki, S. (1980). The representation of colours in the cerebral cortex. *Nature*, *284*, 412–418.

Zeki, S., & Ffytche, D. H. (1998). The Riddoch syndrome: Insights into the neurobiology of conscious vision. *Brain*, *121*(Pt 1), 25–45.

Zihl, J. (1980). Blindsight: Improvment of visually guided eye movements by systematic practice in patients with cerebral blindness. *Neuropsychologia*, *18*, 71–77.

Zihl, J. (1981). Recovery of visual functions in patients with cerebral blindness. Effect of specific practice with saccadic localization. *Experimental Brain Research*, *44*, 159–169.

Zihl, J. (2000). *Rehabilitation of visual disorders after brain injury*. UK: Psychology Press Ltd.

Zihl, J., & von Cramon, D. (1979). Restitution of visual function in patients with cerebral blindness. *Journal of Neurology, Neurosurgery and Psychiatry*, *42*, 312–322.

Zihl, J., & von Cramon, D. (1985). Visual field recovery from scotoma in patients with postgeniculate damage. A review of 55 cases. *Brain*, *108*(Pt 2), 335–365.

NEUROPSYCHOLOGICAL REHABILITATION
2006, 16 (4), 397–414

# Self-awareness after acquired and traumatic brain injury

Laura J. Bach[1,2] and Anthony S. David[2]

[1]*Lishman Brain Injury Unit, Maudsley Hospital, London,* [2]*Department of Psychological Medicine, Institute of Psychiatry, London, UK*

Self-awareness deficits are common after acquired and (traumatic) brain injury (ABI), particularly in social behaviour, yet the underlying cognitive and neuroanatomical structures supporting social self-awareness are not fully understood. This paper reviews the current literature on prevalence, type and severity of self-awareness deficits in ABI. Neuropsychological and neuroanatomical models are reviewed and theoretical frameworks are examined. We summarise results of a case-control comparison of 20 ABI patients with and 20 ABI patients without behavioural disturbance. Our research found that lack of social self-awareness predicts behavioural disturbance in acquired and traumatic brain injury independent of cognitive and executive function. Theory of mind ability was related to self-awareness and a possible role for metacognition and affective processes in self-awareness is discussed to account for social self-awareness deficits.

## INTRODUCTION

A common sequel of acquired brain injury is impaired self-awareness of deficits (Stuss & Anderson, 2004). Self-awareness deficits in brain injury have been reported as ranging from 45% to 97% in patients with traumatic brain injury (TBI) (Sherer et al., 1998a) depending on severity of injury

Correspondence should be addressed to Laura Bach, Lishman Brain Injury Unit, Maudsley Hospital, Denmark Hill, London. SE5 8AZ. Tel: +44(0)20 7 919 3217. Fax: +44(0)20 7 919 2087. E-mail: l.bach@iop.kcl.ac.uk

We are grateful to and would like to thank Dr. Simon Fleminger for his clinical input and all the patients, families and carers for their participation in the study.



http://www.psypress.com/neurorehab DOI:10.1080/09602010500412830

(Freeland, 1996). The variability of reported prevalence rates is bound to reflect varying assessment measures.

Self-awareness deficits in TBI may be different from other conditions. In TBI aetiology is acute, due to a road traffic accident, assault or a fall for example, with little or no time for adjustment in comparison to the slow progression found in neurodegenerative diseases such as Alzheimer's or Parkinson's. Secondly, it is well documented that TBI is highest in young people, peaking at 15–24 years of age (Kraus, Rock, & Hemyari, 1990) and most common in males (Kraus, 1993). Within this group other pre-injury factors such as risk-taking behaviour, substance/alcohol abuse and cognitive deficits are common (Kreutzer, Witol, & Marwitz, 1996) confounding interpretation of outcome. Furthermore, TBI has been noted not only as a risk factor for psychopathology but also as a risk factor for acquiring additional psychopathology (Van Reekum et al., 1996). This paper reviews some of the major issues surrounding self-awareness (definitions, phenomenology, theoretical models and their relationship to behavioural dysfunction, measures of self-awareness and methodological issues). Finally, we report new data that examine the relationship between self-awareness and behavioural disturbance.

## Definitions

A major difficulty in attempting to understand the construct of self-awareness is its complexity, both at the semantic and operational level. Definitions of self-awareness or insight, the term more commonly used in the psychiatric literature, are not simple (David, 1990) and often the terms self-awareness and insight are used interchangeably. Slack, imprecise and ambiguous terms continue to confuse research results leading to theoretical and empirical obfuscation (Marková & Berrios, 2000). However, systematic studies of self-awareness have emerged, which provide for greater precision of definition (David, Buchanan, Reed, & Almeida, 1992). The authors of this paper define self-awareness in operational terms, "as a process by which an individual is able to rate their behavioural responses (physical, somatic, cognitive, and affective) in accordance with ratings with some objective standard, usually from an informant, who knows the individual well." Discrepancy ratings are subject to a number of flaws, e.g., informant bias, patient's level of cognitive function. Nevertheless, definitions of self-awareness based on discrepancy ratings are most commonly used when examining self-awareness in brain injury patients (Prigatano, 1992; Teasdale et al., 1997). There are very few studies aimed specifically at examining the performance of normal subjects and few studies use normal controls. Teasdale et al. (1997), in a large, multicultural sample, using discrepancy ratings, found that brain injury patients consistently performed worse than controls (i.e., showed larger discrepancy ratings) and Leathem, Murphy, and Flett (1998) reported variability in the accuracy of normal subjects' ratings compared to relative reports for specific items of emotional control (controlling laughing and crying) where relatives tend to under-rate these behaviours compared to the subject.

## Phenomenology

Self-awareness deficits in brain injury can be observed in relation to a wide variety of impairments and phenomena, ranging from observable physical/motor problems to a range of more subjective cognitive deficits (e.g., poor memory) and finally behavioural disturbance, (e.g., apathy, disinhibition, inappropriate behaviours, etc.) (Prigatano, 1992). Deficits of social self-awareness pose a particular difficulty in terms of assessment due to their complexity, ambiguity, cultural relativism and the current lack of empirical measures of social behaviour. Behavioural disturbance may be the result of cognitive deficits and studies need to control for this aspect when investigating social self-awareness deficits.

One of the most intriguing features of deficits involving self-awareness is the presence of striking dissociations between different aspects of awareness. For example, reduced self-awareness for behavioural deficits in comparison to physical deficits in brain injury patients (Prigatano & Altman 1990),

## Models of self-awareness

A number of theoretical models have been proposed to explain impairments of self-awareness in brain injury patients: hierarchical descriptive, executive, frontal, and psychological. None of the models is able to adequately account for the self-awareness deficits seen following brain injury. Crosson, Poeschel Barco, and Velozo (1989) described a three tiered hierarchical approach. The first level refers to intellectual awareness and involves an ability to understand that a mental or physical function is impaired (awareness for a memory deficit). The second level, emergent awareness, refers to the ability to recognise problems as they are occuring (e.g., to be aware that one has a memory deficit and that one has difficulty while remembering things). The third level, anticipatory awareness, is the ability to anticipate or predict that a problem will or might occur before an activity has commenced (e.g., to be aware one has a memory deficit and have difficulty remembering things, and also understand that this may result in difficulties with remembering appointments). A practical advantage of this descriptive model is that it can be adapted to target training for rehabilitation. However, its major difficulty is that it reflects purely descriptive constructs of self-awareness deficits rather than providing any explanatory basis for the deficit.

Executive models of self-awareness have been developed which focus on the disruption of hypothetical higher order executive processes of self-monitoring and control (Schacter, 1990; Stuss & Levine, 2002), many of which are linked to integrity of the frontal lobes. These accounts are not without problems (inability to explain self-awareness deficits in the case of unilateral neglect, following non-frontal or right hemisphere damage, McGlynn & Schachter, 1989). However, there remains compelling evidence, both anecdotal and from empirical studies, that supports frontal lobe involvement in self-awareness deficits (Stuss & Levine, 2002).

## Psychological models

Psychological models focus on conceptual constructs such as denial which is considered as an adaptive coping mechanism for trauma and stress (Prigatano, 1999; Weinstein & Khan, 1955). The relationship between denial and distress, however, is complex since the two often coincide: distress could be a product of lack of denial; alternatively denial may only modify distress to a limited extent suggesting that either explicit or even implicit self-awareness still occurs. The denial model appears to describe merely degrees of distress rather than provide any explanatory cognitive framework. Overall, a psychological model has limited appeal for explanation of behavioural and social awareness deficits in brain injury where acknowledgement of a behavioural deficit frequently occurs alongside the behavioural transgression.

## Measurement of awareness of deficit in people with brain injury

A large number of scales exist to assess self-awareness in patients with brain injury. These range in design from self-report questionnaires to semi-structured interviews. The most common method for measurement of self-awareness employs discrepancy scores. Discrepancy ratings involve comparing self-ratings of competencies by patients and ratings by informants, usually for a variety of domains (physical, cognitive, emotional, social). The discrepancy between ratings provides a measure of level of self-awareness. Self versus other difference ratings measures are the most common (Fleming, Strong, & Ashton, 1996). Limitations of discrepancy ratings include possible rater bias and heterogeneity in participant samples, including variation in level of cognitive function and time since injury as well as cultural differences (Prigatano, Ogano, & Amakusa, 1997). Discrepancies between relatives' and professionals' ratings have also been noted (Fordyce & Roueche, 1986). A pertinent criticism of patient–professional ratings is that, in some cases, professionals often only obtain only a limited and short sample (snapshot) of a patient's abilities.

In normal individuals it has been reported that rating questionnaires are vulnerable to factors such as misreading items, variable interpretation of items and failure to consistently apply items to general times and situations (McCrae, Stone, Fagan, & Foster, 1998). Clare et al. (2004) raise issues of the influence of context on patient responses, i.e., experimental demand characteristics and patient expectations. Further issues concern determination of scaling severity, cut-off values and a striking lack of normative data (see Clare et al., 2004, for review).

Comparison of patients' self-ratings with objective test performance assumes that this method is free from informant biases and can thus provide a valid measure of actual functioning. However, there is a disappointing lack of correlation between objective test measures and self-/clinical ratings of awareness in patients with TBI (Leathem et al., 1998; Prigatano & Altman, 1990; Sherer et al., 1998b). Furthermore many standard neuropsychological tests lack ecological validity, and clinical experience demonstrates that TBI patients may perform poorly on these measures, yet functionally, perform well in familiar everyday settings and vice versa. Additionally, testing may be time-consuming and fatiguing for patients, with problems of patient motivation and resistance to testing.

As yet there is no consensus on the best method of measurement. Recent studies have attempted to directly compare different methods in brain injury patients (Fleming Strong, & Ashton, 1998). Little or only partial agreement between methods was found in brain injury patients (Bogod Mateer, & MacDonald, 2003; Fischer, Trexler, & Gauggel, 2004; Sherer et al., 1998b).

## Type and rates of self-awareness deficits in TBI

Using the Patient Competency Rating Scale (PCRS; Prigatano & Fordyce, 1986) it is found that TBI patients tend to overestimate their abilities compared to relatives' ratings, particularly for social and emotional competencies (Allen & Ruff, 1990; Fordyce & Roueche, 1986). However cultural variations have been reported (Prigatano & Leathem, 1993). Overestimation of competencies has been observed for spontaneous complaints (Santos, Castro-Caldas, & De Sovsa, 1998) and in the acute setting (Newman, Garmoe, Beatty, & Ziccardi, 2000). In general, the reporting rate for different symptom types, by brain injury patients, was not related to severity of injury (Port, Willmott, & Charlton, 2002; Sbordone, Seyranian, & Ruff, 1998).

## Self-awareness and severity of injury

The majority of studies have found that severity of brain injury as measured by the Glasgow Coma Scale (GCS) or the duration of post-traumatic amnesia (PTA) shows little association with self-awareness defined as patient–informant discrepancy ratings (Allen & Ruff, 1990; Port et al., 2002; Ranseen, Bohaska, & Schmidt, 1990). A few studies suggest a weak association with PTA duration and GCS score (Leathem et al., 1998; Prigatano et al., 1998). It is conceivable that inconsistency within the literature may be due to methodological difficulties, for example different methods for assessing PTA and for assessment of self-awareness.

## Self-awareness and chronicity

Nothwitstanding problems with assessment measures persistent deficits of self-awareness in TBI are well documented (for a review see Prigatano, 1992). Many TBI patients show severe lack of self-awareness early on in the recovery process with increasing awareness during the first six months to one year post-injury (Fleming & Strong, 1999), although increased awareness may continue well past this time (Godfrey, Partridge, Knight, & Bishara, 1993). For brain injury patients with chronic deficits of self-awareness, improvement in self-awareness over time is often limited (Newman et al., 2000; Ranseen et al., 1990).

## Self-awareness and neuropsychology

Overall there is little evidence to support an association between self-awareness and general intellectual functioning in normal subjects. Clinical observations (see later), do not support such a relationship in the majority of studies of patients in the post-acute setting, also. As McGlynn and Schachter (1989) remark, there are reports of many patients with intact IQ who show disturbed self-awareness. Furthermore there has been little evidence to suggest a link with specific cognitive processes (Prigatano, 2005) and our own studies support this finding.

It is a commonly held view that deficits in executive function are associated with reduced behavioural/social self-awareness. To date, there has been a disappointing lack of any strong correlational evidence to support this, consistent with our own research (see below). There are many accounts of patients with impaired behavioural/social self-awareness who are able to perform well on standard executive function tests (Stuss & Levine, 2002). Moreover, no specific neuropsychological pattern has been identified (Lanham et al., 2000; Prigatano et al., 1998; Ranseen et al., 1990). There are reported deficits on experimental paradigms assumed to be sensitive to decision-making (Bechara, 2004) and this is an area which may be fruitful for investigating awareness deficits (see our work below).

## Self-awareness and rehabilitation/outcome after TBI

Diminished awareness is recognised as a limiting factor in functional recovery and rehabilitation outcome (Prigatano, 1992) and has been observed for a range of different treatment interventions including direct therapist feedback, experiential feedback, psychotherapy, self-rating comparison, in vivo demonstration and education (for review see Sherer, et al., 1998c). A number of studies indicate that individuals who report greater awareness of their deficits (as observed by the rehabilitation team) show better treatment outcome (for a review see Deaton, 1986) and the same patients also show a more successful return to work not only in the short term (Ben-Yishay, Silver, Piasetsky, & Rattok, 1987) but also in the long term (Ezrachi et al., 1991). The relationship between awareness and outcome is however not straightforward,. Acknowledgement of deficits is no guarantee of a good outcome (Fleming, 1999) and increased emotional distress is common (Godfrey Knight, & Partridge, 1996, Godfrey et al., 1993).

Not only is current level of self-awareness a marker for motivation but also premorbid personality characteristics and coping patterns need to be taken into account (Brooks 1991; Fordyce, Roveche, & Prigatano, 1983; Malia, 1997). For example, Fordyce et al. (1983) point out that premorbid dysfunctional coping skills may be detrimental to outcome. The challenge here would be the ability of the patient to accept and learn new coping strategies, made complex by the cognitive capacity for new learning.

## INVESTIGATION OF SELF-AWARENESS AND BEHAVIOURAL DISTURBANCE AND ACQUIRED BRAIN INJURY

The current relationship between self-awareness, behaviour and cognition remains unclear. It has been postulated that appropriate social behaviour is dependent on the ability to understand others' thoughts, desires and intentions, commonly referred to as theory of mind (ToM) (Baron-Cohen, 1989; Happé et al., 1994). Any model of social awareness deficits would need to encompass ToM processing, arguably at some higher level of awareness (Stuss & Anderson, 2004). To date this has been overlooked but is one area that we in our recent research have investigated as a factor mediating self-awareness in brain injury. In addition we also endeavoured to explore the role of cognitive mechanisms deemed sensitive to particular areas of frontal damage such as orbitofrontal cortex.

The overall aim of our recent research was to explore the putative correlates of behavioural disturbance in acquired brain injury: cognitive, theory of mind and self-awareness. Secondary aims included an examination of the nature of the relationship between behavioural disturbance, reduced self-awareness and theory of mind ability, given that behavioural disturbance, lack of self-awareness and theory of mind deficits have all been associated with frontal dysfunction, and investigation of personality traits assumed to reflect poor mentalising ability.

In the findings reported below we attempted to investigate these relationships in a series of studies using a modified PCRS as the primary measure of self-awareness on patients referred to a specialist neuropsychiatry brain injury service, the Lishman Unit, at the Maudsley Hospital, South London.

Particular questions of interest were:

- Self-awareness deficits are commonly seen in behaviourally disturbed brain injury patients, so does lack of social self-awareness predict social behavioural disturbance?
- What is the nature of the relationship between executive function, theory of mind and social self-awareness?
- What is the relationship between social behavioural disturbance and cognition?
- What is the role of theory of mind ability in social behavioural disturbance — does it predict social behavioural disturbance?

The main hypotheses were:

- ABI patients categorised as behaviourally disturbed would show significantly greater lack of social self-awareness compared to ABI patients who are not behaviourally disturbed.
- ABI patients categorised as behaviourally disturbed would be impaired on theory of mind tasks and would be impaired relative to non-behaviourally disturbed ABI patients.
- Theory of mind performance would predict level of social self-awareness.
- Performance on a decision-making task would be associated with level of social self-awareness.

### Self versus other ratings of behaviour

The modified PCRS included items targeted specifically on mentalising ability as a purer measure of psychosocial function, for example, "How much of a problem do I have in understanding jokes?" and "How much of a problem do I have being tactful?" Our aim was to investigate a number of putative factors which have previously been linked to psychosocial impairments in other disorders such as autism (Happé et al., 1994) and patients with orbitofrontal damage (Damasio, 1996).

## SAMPLE

A consecutive series of 47 head injury patients were entered into the study with their major carer. Seven (14%) were excluded; two participants due to severe depression, one subject because of non-confirmation of brain injury, one participant revealed a history of developmental learning disability, one participant was later found to have a history of alcoholism, and one participant failed to comply with testing. Thirty-one participants had a traumatic brain injury and nine participants had suffered a cerebral vascular accident. Participants were classified as behaviourally disturbed ($n = 20$) or non-behaviourally disturbed ($n = 20$) using the selected items assumed to reflect social mentalising ability from the Neurobehavioural Rating Scale (NRS; Levin et al., 1987) and those formed the basis of a case-control comparison (see Appendix I for items). Participants were required to score at least "mild" on a minimum of five out of seven of these selected items. Participants were assessed on a range of cognitive measures, which included general intellectual function, memory, attention, and a variety of executive tests, including tests of everyday problem-solving. The two groups were well matched for age, education, premorbid ability, verbal IQ and verbal memory. Table 1 describes demographics, IQ and cognitive scores for the two groups.

We assessed performance on a gambling task previously reported as sensitive to poor decision-making and behavioural disturbance in ventromedial frontal patients (Bechara, Tranel, Damasio, & Damasio, 1996). Consistent with previous research we found a lack of relationship between self-awareness and cognitive function and executive measures. There was no association with gambling performance. A striking observation, however, was the marked relationship between self-awareness and behaviour, independent of cognition, severity of brain injury or location of brain damage. Indeed behaviourally disturbed patients significantly overestimated their

TABLE 1
Means, standard deviations, ranges and $p$ values of age, years of education, premorbid IQ, verbal IQ and cognitive function for the BEH and NBEH groups

| | *Behavioural* ($n = 20$) | | | *Non-behavioural* ($n = 20$) | | | |
|---|---|---|---|---|---|---|---|
| *Demographic* | *Mean* | *SD* | *Range* | *Mean* | *SD* | *Range* | *P* value |
| Age (years) | 37.6 | 13.7 | 19–62 | 38.4 | 12.4 | 21–62 | 0.89 |
| Years of education | 12.2 | 1.7 | 10–16 | 13.0 | 2.8 | 8–20 | 0.34 |
| NART-R estimated WAIS-R FIQ | 101.4 | 14.9 | 74–121 | 105.9 | 10.6 | 87–122 | 0.28 |
| Verbal IQ | 93.2 | 16.1 | 72–139 | 98.7 | 18.8 | 75–132 | 0.33 |
| Memory | 23.9 | 10.8 | 5–43 | 30.4 | 21.8 | 8–114 | 0.25 |
| Verbal fluency | 28.6 | 10.9 | 12–56 | 29.8 | 9.5 | 12–45 | 0.1 |
| Trail making test | 125.5 | 66.7 | 55–286 | 122.6 | 55.2 | 42–226 | 0.1 |
| PAS total ToM score | 9.3 | 9.7 | $-7 \pm 35$ | 0.3 | 8.3 | $-16 \pm 14$ | – |
| PAS-total behaviour score | 6.8 | 5.7 | $-2 \pm 16$ | 0.6 | 5.6 | $-12 \pm 14$ | – |

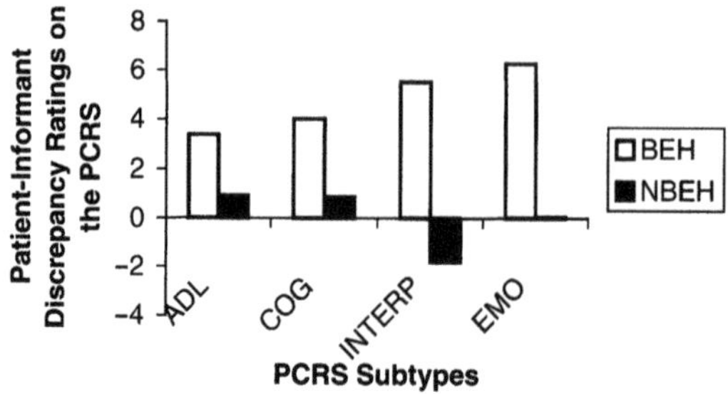


**Figure 1.** Histograms of patient-informant discrepancy ratings on the four subtypes of the PCRS for the BEH and NBEH groups. PCRS subtype include competencies in ADL = Activities of Daily Living (e.g., washing, dressing), COG = Cognitive (e.g., memory, attention), INTERP = Interpersonal (e.g., acting appropriately around friends), EMO = Emotional (e.g., crying, laughing). BEH = Behaviourally disturbed group, NBEH = Non-behaviourally disturbed group.

level of psychosocial functioning compared to other domains (see Figure 1) and ability to understand others thoughts and feelings (see Figure 2) as scored against their relatives' ratings on the PCRS. The majority (80%) of behaviourally disturbed participants overestimated their social functioning compared to less than half (45%) in the non-behavioural group.

## THEORY OF MIND

Self-awareness of one's own competencies, and in particular one's competency for social interaction and mentalising ability, is thought to reflect the ability to form abstract representations of the self and to be able to manipulate this in working memory in order to compare representations of competencies with external feedback (Frith, 1996). Theory of Mind (ToM) refers to the ability to form mental representations about the beliefs, intentions and desires of others (Premack & Woodruff, 1978) and the ability to decouple

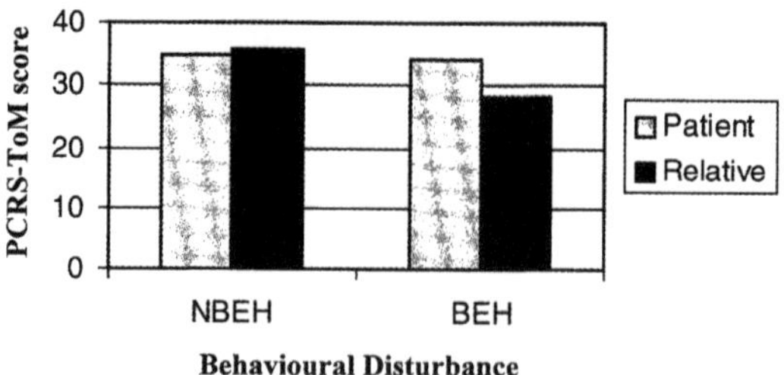


**Figure 2.** Perceived ratings of competency by patients and relatives on the PCRS-ToM. Total PCRS-ToM score = patient self-ratings/informant ratings of the patient on the 9 PCRS-ToM questions. BEH = Behaviourally disturbed group, NBEH = Non-behaviourally disturbed group.

these beliefs from one's own reality. We postulated that appropriate social behaviour is predicated on the ability to understand others' thoughts, desires and intentions, commonly referred to as theory of mind (ToM) (Baron-Cohen, 1989; Happé, 1994). Participants' ability to understand mental states was assessed using both verbal (stories) and non-verbal (cartoons) theory of mind tasks (see Happé, 1994; Happé, Brownell, & Winner, 1999); for example, the ability to infer a mental state cause for a protaganist's utterances or actions, such as a lie or double-bluff (see Appendix I for examples). There was a modest significant relationship between social self-awareness and performance on the theory of mind stories ($r = -.421$, $p < .01$) and a weaker significant relationship between social self-awareness and performance on the theory of mind cartoons ($r = -.329, p < .05$). ToM stories score uniquely and significantly predicted self-awareness group membership ($p < .05$). Poor mentalising ability was found to be a significant risk for overestimating both general and social/mentalising competencies. These results are intriguing as they suggest a relationship between self-awareness and metacognitive processing although it is acknowledged that many of our subjects performed at ceiling on the ToM tasks thus constraining conclusions. Use of more sensitive measures may possibly detect more subtle deficits. For example, faux pas is assumed to reflect higher level mentalising ability and incorporates both an affective and cognitive component. It requires an understanding of not just another person's mental state but also the ability to understand that something you say or do may hurt the feelings of another person. Stone et al. (1998) found that patients with orbitofrontal cortex damage were impaired on this measure but were able to pass first and second order ToM tasks. Theory of mind ability was found to be associated with verbal IQ and memory and to a limited number of executive function tests in contrast to a lack of correlation between cognitive and social self-awareness measures. Logistic regression analysis identified ToM performance as a predictor of overestimating social self-awareness, lending further support to the notion that social awareness may be mediated by different or higher level metacognitive processes.

## PERSONALITY CHANGE AND AWARENESS

A third study investigated the relationship between self-awareness and personality traits assumed to reflect poor mentalising behaviour. Personality traits included aloof, mentalising traits (callous, distrustful, egocentric, lack of empathy, literal, resourceless, tactless, undemonstrative, unimaginative and unresponsive) and behavioural traits (aggressive, anxious, impulsive, irresponsible, rigid). Traits were assessed by a key informant, usually a relative, using the Personality Assessment Schedule modified to include these traits (PAS; Tyrer & Alexander, 1979). Higher scores mean more abnormal traits were endorsed. Level of self-awareness was found to predict the overall level of mentalising ability and the number of behavioural personality traits rated as present by informants. This was found for both general and social self-awareness as measured by discrepancy ratings on the PCRS (see Table 1 for total PAS scores).

Overall, it was found that people with behavioural disturbance following brain injury showed significantly less self-awareness compared to those without behavioural disturbance. However behavioural problems were not specifically associated with type of self-awareness (i.e., brain injury patients with behaviour problems showed impaired self-awareness for both general and social/mentalising self-awareness). Theory of mind ability was found to be a significant predictor for level of social self-awareness. A detailed report of the empirical work in this paper will be published separately.

## CONCLUSIONS AND SUMMARY

The range of theoretical models for explaining self-awareness are unsatisfactory as they fail to adequately identify the individual and collective cognitive mechanisms responsible for the different types of self-awareness. The Schachter (1990) and Agnew and Morris (1998) models are geared towards an explanation of mainly mnemonic functions. We found that executive models alone failed to account for empirical findings over a range of executive functions, which included tasks specifically designed to tap higher order planning and problem-solving abilities, suggesting a widespread cognitive heterogeneity of self-awareness. The underlying basis for most of these models rests on deficits in comparative systems and self-monitoring ability and possible impairment of semantic memory update. It is perhaps surprising that we found a lack of association between social/mentalising self-awareness and executive measures. Reasons for this may be that (1) current theoretical models are incorrect and inadequate (likely), (2) current executive measures lack sensitivity for everyday social functioning (probable), or (3) other estimates of poor self-awareness are imperfect (probable). We should also add that our sample is relatively small and hence we have limited statistical power to detect group differences. Additionally our sample included a minority of stroke patients (7), making conclusions for TBI patients somewhat constrained. Stroke patients were included as we were interested in patients with acquired brain injury, not just traumatic brain injury. The initial power calculation using Cohen's d statistic (Cohen, 1988) indicated that a sample size of 20 patients in each group was sufficient to detect any group differences at a significance level of $p = .05$ and effect size = 0.6. Forty participants were deemed appropriate to detect any significant differences between the groups, with 80% power. According to

Cohen (1988) an effect size of 0.6 is regarded as a medium effect able to discriminate between groups of this size and for tests of 80% power.

Our own research findings described in this paper suggest a role for metacognitive processing, although the role of mentalising ability requires further investigation. We found theory of mind ability was associated with of social self-awareness, and that theory of mind ability and self-awareness of personality traits were related to social self-awareness even though mentalising ability was independent of self-awareness of personality traits. In support of this a recent study by McDonald and Flanagan (2004) has reported an association between mentalising ability and social perception. This suggests that mentalising and social self-awareness may reflect either similar cognitive mechanisms or that a separate cognitive process (metacognition) may be involved.

A noteable finding was that theory of mind ability was intact in our brain injury patients, indicating that behavioural disturbance can occur despite seemingly preserved theory of mind ability. Both groups passed ToM stories and cartoons and performed at a comparable level to controls. Behavioural disturbance can therefore occur despite intact theory of mind ability. There is a possibility that ToM ability in adults is retrieved via semantic systems, which may be spared in brain injury, rather than as a result of on-line processing.

From a review of the literature, demographic factors and general intellectual functioning, including memory, appear to be unrelated to self-awareness deficits. Further light on the nature of self-awareness deficits in brain injury may be shed from studies of emotional processing (Bramham et al., 2006; Hornak et al., 1996; McDonald & Flanagan, 2004), which indicate an association between impaired emotion recognition and social behaviour and perception in patients with frontal lobe damage. Bramham et al. (personal communication) for example, investigated social and emotional functioning in 34 neurosurgical patients with orbitofrontal (OFC) damage and 34 patients with non-OFC damage. There was a significant difference between groups for emotion expression recognition and measures of empathy but no difference for general level of self-awareness into behaviour. Further investigation of mentalising, self-awareness and emotion processing is required to determine whether affective cognitive mechanisms have a role in self-awareness processing.

A major issue highlighted in this review is the inadequate role of neuropsychology and the extent to which it is able to measure self-awareness. This failure may be due to self-awareness being incorrectly defined in terms of cognitive processes. We speculate that social/mentalising self-awareness may be domain-specific and may be mediated by metacognitive processes, perhaps theory of mind and affective processing. Future studies should focus on broader yet reliable measures which encompass these processes.

In summary, following acquired and traumatic brain injury we found:

- Level of self-awareness is unrelated to severity (PTA/GCS) of brain injury.
- Premorbid and current intellectual functioning are not strongly related to level of self-awareness.
- Cognitive and executive functions are not strongly related to level of self-awareness.
- Current neuropsychological measures may be insensitive tools for the assessment of self-awareness.
- Self-awareness is an important risk factor for behavioural disturbance. ABI patients with behavioural and personality problems rate their social competency significantly more highly than do their relatives.
- Metacognitive, behavioural and affective indices may provide more sensitive measures of lack of self-awareness and future studies should address this.

## REFERENCES


Agnew, S. K., & Morris, R. G. (1998). The heterogeneity of anosognosia for memory impairment in Alzheimer's disease: A review of the literature and a proposed model. *Aging and Mental Health*, *2*, 7–19.

Allen, C. C., & Ruff, R. M. (1990). Self-rating versus neuropsychological performance of moderate versus severe head-injured patients. *Brain Injury*, *4*, 7–17.

Baron-Cohen, S. (1989). The autistic child's theory of mind: A case of specific developmental delay. *Journal of Child Psychology and Psychiatry*, *30*, 285–287.

Bechara, A. (2004). The role of emotion in decision-making: Evidence from neurological patients with orbitofrontal damage. *Brain and Cognition*, *55*, 30–40.

Bechara, A., Tranel, D., Damasio, H., & Damasio, A. R. (1996). Failure to respond autonomically to anticipated future outcomes following damage to prefrontal cortex. *Cerebral Cortex*, *6*, 215–225.

Ben-Yishay, Y., Silver, S. M., Piatsetsky, E., & Rattok, J. (1987). Relationship between employability and vocational outcome after intensive holistic cognitive rehabilitation. *Journal of Head Trauma and Rehabilitation*, *2*, 35–48.

Bogod, N., Mateer, C. A., & MacDonald, S. W. S. (2003). Self-awareness after traumatic brain injury: A comparison of measures and their relationship to executive function. *Journal of the International Neuropsychological Society*, *9*, 450–458.

Bramham, J., Morris, R. G., Hornak, J., Rolls, E. T., Bullock, P., & Polkey, C. E. (2006). Emotional and social functioning following neurosurgical lesions to the orbitofrontal or dorsolateral prefrontal cortex.

Brooks, N. (1991) The head injured family. *Journal of Clinical and Experimenal Neuropsychology*, *13*, 155–188.

Clare, L., Wilson, B. A., Carter, G., Roth, I., & Hodges, J. R. (2004). Awareness in early-stage Alzheimer's disease: Relationship to outcome of cognitive rehabilitation. *Journal of Clinical and Experimental Neuropsychology*, *26*, 215–226.

Cohen, J. (1988). *Statistical power analysis for the behavioral sciences* (2nd ed.). New York: Academic Press.

Crosson, B., Poeschel Barco, P., & Velozo, C. A. (1989). Awareness and compensation in post acute head injury rehabilitation. *Journal of Head Trauma Rehabilitation, 4*, 46–54.

Damasio A. R. (1996). The somatic marker hypothesis and the possible functions of the prefrontal cortex. *Philosophical Transactions of the Royal Society of London–Series B: Biological Sciences, 351*, 1413–1420.

David, A. S. (1990). Insight and psychosis. *British Journal of Psychiatry, 156*, 798–808.

David, A. S., Buchanan, A., Reed, A., & Almeida, O. (1992). The assessment of insight in psychosis. *British Journal of Psychiatry, 161*, 599–602.

Deaton, A. V. (1986). Denial in the aftermath of traumatic head injury: Its manifestations, measurement and treatment. *Rehabilitation Psychology, 31*, 231–240.

Ezrachi, O., Ben-Yishay, Y., Kay., Diller, L., & Rattok, J. (1991). Predicting employment in traumatic brain injury following neuropsychological rehabilitation. *Journal of Head Trauma Rehabilitation, 6*, 71–84.

Fischer, S., Trexler, L. E., & Gauggel, S. (2004). Awareness of activity limitations and prediction of performance in patients with brain injuries and orthopaedic disorders. *Journal of the International Neuropsychological Society, 10*, 190–199.

Fleming, J. M. (1999). Self-awareness of deficits: Issues for brain injury rehabilitation. *Proceedings from the 21st Annual Brain Impairment Conference, Brisbane, Australia.*

Fleming, J. M., & Strong, J. (1999). A longitudinal study of self-awareness functional deficits underestimated by persons with brain injury. *Occupational Therapy Journal of Research, 19*, 3–17.

Fleming, J. M., Strong, J., & Ashton, R. (1996). Self-awareness of deficits in adults with traumatic brain injury: How best to measure? *Brain Injury, 10*, 1–15.

Fleming, J. M., Strong, J., & Ashton, R. (1998). Cluster analysis of self-awareness levels in adults with traumatic brain injury and relationship to outcome. *Journal of Head Trauma Rehabilitation, 13*, 39–51.

Fordyce, D. J., & Roueche, J. R. (1986). Changes in perspectives of disability among patients, staff and relatives during rehabilitation of brain injury. *Rehabilitation Psychology, 31*, 217–229.

Fordyce, D. J., Roueche, J. R., & Prigatano, G. P. (1983). Enhanced emotional reactions in chronic head trauma patients. *Journal of Neurology, Neurosurgery and Psychiatry, 46*, 620–624.

Freeland, J. (1996). Awareness of deficits: A complex interplay of neurological, personality, social and rehabilitation factors. *Magazine, 4*, 32–34.

Frith, C. (1996). Brain mechanisms for 'having a theory of mind'. *Journal of Psychopharmacology, 10*, 9–15.

Godfrey, H. P. D., Knight, R. G., & Partridge, F. M. (1996). Emotional adjustment following traumatic brain injury: A stress-appraisal-coping formulation. *Journal of Head Trauma and Rehabilitation, 11*, 29–40.

Godfrey, H. P. D., Partridge, F. M. Knight, R. G., & Bishara, S. (1993). Course of insight disorder and emotional dysfunction following closed head injury: A controlled cross-sectional follow-up study. *Journal of Clinical and Experimental Neuropsychology, 15*, 503–515.

Happé, F. (1994). An advanced theory of mind: Understanding of story character's thoughts and feelings by able, autistic, mentally handicapped and normal children. *Journal of Autism and Developmental Disorders, 24*, 129–154.

Happé, F., Brownell, H., & Winner, E. (1999). Acquired 'theory of mind' impairments following stroke. *Cognition, 70*, 211–240.

Hornak, J., O'Doherty, J. Bramham, J., Rolls, E. T., Morris, R. G.,. Bullock, P. R., & Polkey, C. E. (1996). Reward-related reversal learning after surgical excision in orbito-frontal or dorsolateral prefrontal cortex in humans. *Journal of Cognitive Neuroscience, 16*, 463–478.

Kraus, J. F. (1993). Epidemiology of head injury. In P. R. Coopes (ed.), *Head injury* (3rd ed., pp. 1–25). Baltimore, MD: Williams and Wilkins.

Kraus, J. F., Rock, A., & Hemyari, P. (1990). Brain injuries among infants, children, adolescents and young adults. *American Journal of Disorders in Childhood, 144*, 684–691.

Kreutzer, J. S., Witol, A. D., & Marwitz, J. H. (1996). Alcohol and drug abuse among young persons with traumatic brain injury. *Journal of Learning Disabilities, 29*, 643–651.

Lanham, R. A. Jr., Weisenburger, J. E., Schwab, K. A., & Rosner, M. M. (2000). A longitudinal investigation of the concordance between individuals with traumatic brain injury and family or friend ratings on the Katz adjustment scale. *Journal of Head Trauma and Rehabilitation, 15*, 1123–1138.

Leathem, J. M., Murphy, L. J., & Flett, R. A. (1998). Self- and informant-ratings on the patient competency rating scale in patients with traumatic brain injury. *Journal of Clinical and Experimental Neuropsychology, 20*, 694–705.

Levin, H. S., High, W. M., Goethe, K. E., Sisson, R. A., Overall, J. E., Rhoades, H. M., Eisenberg, H. M., Kalisky, Z., & Gary, H. E. (1987). The neurobehavioural rating scale: Assessment of the behavioural sequelae of head injury by the clinician. *Journal of Neurology, Neurosurgery and Psychiatry, 50*, 183–193.

Malia, K. (1997). Insight after brain injury: What does it mean? *Journal of Cognitive Rehabilitation, May/June*, 10–16.

Marková, I. S., & Berrios, G. E. (2000). Insight into memory deficits. In G. E. Berrios and J. R. Hodges (Eds.), *Memory disorders in psychiatric practice* (pp. 204–233). Cambridge: Cambridge University Press.

McCrae, R. R., Stone, S. V., Fagan, P. J., & Costa, P. T. (1998). Identifying causes of disagreement between self-reports and spouse ratings. *Journal of Personality, 66*, 285–313.

McDonald, S., & Flanagan, S. (2004). Social perception deficits after traumatic brain injury: Interaction between emotion recognition, mentalizing ability and social communication. *Neuropsychology, 18*, 572–579.

McGlynn, S. M., & Schacter, D. L. (1989). Unawareness of deficits in neuropsychological syndromes. *Journal of Clinical and Experimental Neuropsychology, 11*, 143–205.

Newman, A. C., Garmoe, W., Beatty, P., & Ziccardi, M. (2000). Self-awareness of traumatically brain injured patients in the acute in-patient setting. *Brain Injury, 14*, 333–344.

Port, A., Willmott, C., & Charlton, J. (2002). Self-awareness following traumatic brain injury and implications for rehabilitation. *Brain Injury, 16*(4), 277–289.

Premack, D., & Woodruff, G. (1978). Does the chimpanzee have a theory of mind? *Behavioral and Brain Sciences, 1*, 515–526.

Prigatano, G. P. (1992). Personality disturbances associated with traumatic brain injury. *Journal of Consulting and Clinical Psychology, 60*, 360–368.

Prigatano, G. P. (1999). Diller Lecture. Impaired awareness finger tapping and rehabilitation outcome after brain injury. *Rehabilitation Psychology*, 145–159.

Prigatano, G. P. (2005). Disturbances of self-awareness and rehabilitation of patients with traumatic brain injury. *Journal of Head Trauma and Rehabilitation, 20*, 19–29.

Prigatano, G. P., & Altman, I. M. (1990). Impaired awareness of behavioural limitations after traumatic brain injury. *Archives of Physical Medicine and Rehabilitation, 71*, 1058–1063.

Prigatano, G. P., Altman, I. M., & O'Brien, K. (1990). Behavioural limitations that traumatic brain-injured patients tend to underestimate. *Clinical Neuropsychologist, 4*, 162–176.

Prigatano, G. P., Bruna, O., Mataro, M., Munoz, J. M., Fernandez, S., & Junque, C. (1998). Initial disturbances of consciousness and resultant impaired awareness in Spanish patients with traumatic brain injury. *Journal of head Trauma Rehabilitation, 13*, 29–38.

Prigatano, G. P., & Fordyce, D. J. (1986). Cognitive dysfunction and social adjustment after brain injury. In G. P. Prigatano, D. J. Fordyce, H. K. Zeiner, J. R. Roueche, M. Pepping & B. C. Wood (eds.), *Neuropsychological Rehabilitation after Brain Injury*. Baltimore: Johns Hopkins University Press.

Prigatano, G. P., & Leathem, J. M. (1993). Awareness of behavioural limitations after traumatic brain injury: A cross-cultural study of New Zealand Maoris and non-Maoris. *Clinical Neuropsychologist, 7*, 123–135.

Prigatano, G. P., Ogano, M., & Amakusa, B. (1997). A cross-sectional study on impaired self-awareness in Japanese patients with brain dysfunction. *Neuropsychiatry, Neuropsychology and Behavioral Neurology, 10*, 135–145.

Ranseen, J. D., Bohaska, L. A., & Schmidt, F. A. (1990). An investigation of agnosia following traumatic head injury. *International Journal of Clinical Neuropsychology, 9*, 145–148.

Santos, M. E., Castro-Caldas, A., & De Sousa, L. (1998). Spontaneous complaints of long-term traumatic brain-injured subjects and their close relatives. *Brain Injury, 12*, 759–767.

Sbordone, R. J., Seyranian, G. D., & Ruff, R. M. (1998). Are the subjective complaints of traumatically brain injured patients reliable? *Brain Injury, 12*, 505–515.

Schacter, D. I. (1990). Toward a cognitive neuropsychology of awareness: Implicit knowledge and anosognosia. *Journal of Clinical and Experimental Neuropsychology, 12*, 155–178.

Sherer, M., Bergloff, P., Levin, E. High, Jr., W. M., Oden, K. E., & Nick, T. G. (1998a). Impaired awareness and employment outcome after traumatic brain injury. *Journal of Head Trauma Rehabilitation, 13*, 52–61.

Sherer, M., Boake, C., Levin, E., Silver, B. V., Ringholx, G., & High, Jr. M. (1998b). Characteristics of impaired awareness after traumatic brain injury. *Journal of the International Neuropsychological Society, 4*, 380–387.

Sherer, M., Oden, K., Bergloff, P., Levin, E., & High Jr., W. M. (1998c). Assessment and treatment of impaired awareness after brain injury: Implications for community integration. *NeuroRehabilitation, 10*, 25–37.

Stone, V. E., Baron-Cohen, S., & Knight, R. T. (1998). Frontal lobe contributions to theory of mind. *Journal of Cognitive Neuroscience, 10*, 640–656.

Stuss, D. T., & Anderson, V. (2004). The frontal lobes and theory of mind: Developmental concepts from adult focal lesion research. *Brain and Cognition, 55*, 69–83.

Stuss, D. T., & Levine, B. (2002). Adult clinical neuropsychology: Lessons from studies of the frontal lobes. *Annual Review of Psychology, 53*, 401–433.

Teasdale, T. W., Christensen, A. L., Willmes, K., Deloche, G., Braga, L., Stachowiak, F., Vendrell, J. M., Castro-Caldoas, A., & Leclercq, M. (1997). Subjective experience in head-injured patients and their close relatives: A European Brain Injury Questionnaire study. *Brain Injury, 11*, 543–563.

Tyrer, P., & Alexander, J. (1979). Classification of personality disorder. *British Journal of Psychiatry, 135*, 163–167.

Van Reekum, R., Bolago, I., Finlayson, M. A., Garner, S., & Links, P. S. (1996). Psychiatric disorders after traumatic brain injury. *Brain Injury, 10*, 19–327.

Weinstein, E. A., & Kahn, R. L. (1955). *Denial of illness: Symbolic and physiological aspects*. Springfield, IL: Charles C. Thomas.

# APPENDIX I

## Items of the NRS classified as socially/behaviourallydisturbed:

emotional withdrawal, disinhibition, hyperactivity-agitation, inaccurate insight, hostility-uncooperativeness, decreased initiative-motivation, suspiciousness.

## Example 1 ToM story (Liar)

Simon is a big liar. Simon's brother Jim knows this, he knows that Simon never tells the truth! Now yesterday Simon stole Jim's ping-pong bat, and Jim knows Simon has hidden it somewhere, though he can't find it. He's very cross. So he finds Simon and he says, "Where is my ping-pong bat? You must have hidden it either in the cupboard or under your bed, because I've looked everywhere else. Where is it, in the cupboard or under the bed?" Simon tells him the bat is under his bed.

Question: Why will Jim look in the cupboard for the bat?

## Example 2 ToM story (Double Bluff)

During the war, the Red army captures a member of the Blue army. They want him to tell them where his army's tanks are; they know they are either by the sea or in the mountains. They know that the prisoner will not want to tell them, he will want to save his army, and so he will certainly lie to them. The prisoner is very brave and very clever, and he will not let them find his tanks. The tanks are really in the mountains. Now when the other side ask him where his tanks are, he says, "They are in the mountains".

NEUROPSYCHOLOGICAL REHABILITATION
2006, 16 (4), 415–438

# An integrated biopsychosocial approach to understanding awareness deficits in Alzheimer's disease and brain injury

Tamara Ownsworth[1], Linda Clare[2], and Robin Morris[3]

[1]*Division of Occupational Therapy, School of Health and Rehabilitation Sciences, The University of Queensland, St Lucia, Australia*
[2]*School of Psychology, University of Wales Bangor, Gwynedd, UK*
[3]*Neuropsychology Unit, Department of Psychology, Institute of Psychiatry, London, UK*

Considerable emphasis has been placed upon cognitive neuropsychological explanations of awareness disorders in brain injury and Alzheimer's disease (AD), with relatively few models acknowledging the role of psychosocial factors. The present paper explores clinical presentations of unawareness in brain injury and AD, reviews the evidence for the influence of psychosocial factors alongside neuropsychological changes, and considers a number of key issues that theoretical models need to address, before going on to discuss some recently-developed models that offer the potential for developing a comprehensive biopsychosocial account. Building on these developments, we present a framework designed to assist clinicians to identify the specific factors contributing to an individual's presentation of unawareness, and illustrate its application with a case example.

Correspondence should be sent to Dr Tamara Ownsworth, School of Psychology, Griffith University Mt Gravatt Campus, Nathan 4111, Queensland, Australia.

A University of Queensland Travel Award for International Collaborative Research and a National Health and Medical Research Council Public Health Fellowship jointly supported the preparation of this paper.



http://www.psypress.com/neurorehab DOI:10.1080/09602010500505641

# INTRODUCTION

Awareness disorders are common following neurological injury and illness, and a range of different explanations has been proposed to account for these. Neurocognitive explanations highlight the nature of brain pathology as the origin of awareness deficits, particularly with regard to lesion location and cognitive dysfunction (McGlynn & Schacter, 1989). Psychological theories, however, recognise the possible contribution of premorbid personality style and the motivated use of psychological defence mechanisms such as denial in blocking unpleasant thoughts from awareness (Gainotti, 1993; Weinstein, Friedland, & Wagner, 1994). Other explanations suggest that in some cases, or to some degree, unawareness of illness or injury might be socially constructed, or a product of social and environmental factors (Clare, 2004b; Weinstein & Kahn, 1955). Some forms of unawareness, such as those related to sensory, perceptual and motor deficits, would appear to be satisfactorily explained in terms of neurological impairment (McGlynn & Schacter, 1989). However, other manifestations of unawareness, for example, those seen in the long-term sequelae of brain injury or during the gradual onset of Alzheimer's disease (AD), may represent a more complex interplay between neurocognitive, psychological and socio-environmental factors (Prigatano & Weinstein, 1996).

Theoretical models of unawareness may therefore have greater clinical utility in these contexts if they allow for the possibility of integrating neurological, psychological and socio-environmental levels of explanation. Here we will review the evidence regarding clinical presentations of unawareness in brain injury and AD, and consider a number of key issues that theoretical models need to address, before going on to discuss some recently-developed models that offer the potential for developing a comprehensive account. Finally, building on this work, we will present a framework designed to assist clinicians to identify the specific factors contributing to an individual's presentation of unawareness, and illustrate its application with a case example.

# KEY ISSUES IN UNDERSTANDING AWARENESS DEFICITS

## Clinical presentations of unawareness

It is broadly acknowledged that many individuals with brain injury and AD lack awareness of their changes in functioning. Clinical presentations of unawareness have been characterised in terms of "partiality", "specificity" and "extension" (Schacter & Prigatano, 1991), and although based primarily upon clinical observations, this nonetheless provides one approach for understanding awareness deficits. Partiality refers to the degree of unawareness that is evident for a particular deficit. Prigatano (1999) distinguished between complete syndromes, in which no awareness is demonstrated for a particular functional impairment, and partial syndromes in which individuals display limited awareness of their impairment. Specificity relates to the degree to which awareness varies across different functional domains. Awareness deficits may be domain-specific (i.e., restricted to a particular function, for example, motor skills) or global in nature (i.e., a general lack of awareness extending across a range of abilities) (Marcel, Tegner, & Nimmo-Smith, 2004; Toglia & Kirk, 2000). Extension refers to the type or aspect of awareness that can be compromised. For example, an individual may demonstrate knowledge that a deficit exists but show poor appreciation of the consequences of this deficit, or be unable to self-monitor and identify the problem as it occurs in daily living (Crosson et al., 1989).

Disorders of awareness may differ according to the nature of brain pathology in terms of the type, severity, time course or onset and extent of injury (Prigatano & Weinstein, 1996). General clinical observations of individuals with brain injury suggest that immediately after an injury many grossly overestimate their abilities across a broad range of functions. Level of awareness typically increases with time since injury with many developing relatively accurate awareness of their impaired functioning, while others demonstrate ongoing partial or complete unawareness syndromes (Fleming & Strong, 1999; Godfrey, Partridge, Knight, & Bishara, 1993; Prigatano, 1999). Research indicates that individuals are more likely to acknowledge motor and sensory impairments than changes in cognitive, social and emotional functioning (Fleming & Strong, 1999; Hibbard & Gordon, 1992; Toglia & Kirk, 2000).

Investigations of neurocognitive correlates of unawareness have generally produced mixed findings. While there is some empirical support from the brain injury literature concerning the role of general cognitive disturbance (e.g., Nathanson, Bergman, & Gordon, 1952), many investigations of brain injury have failed to find a relationship between degree of awareness deficits and generalised cognitive impairment, based upon measures of global cognitive functioning, memory, attention and language (Burgess et al., 1998; Fleming, Strong, & Ashton, 1998; McKinlay & Brooks, 1984; Prigatano, Altman, & O'Brien, 1990). Deficits in awareness have been observed in individuals with intact intellectual functioning following brain injury (McGlynn & Schacter, 1989). The evidence for an association between level of unawareness and severity of injury is also mixed. Although Prigatano (1999) presented a series of studies that report significant correlations, a similar number of studies fail to support the view that individuals with severe brain injuries are more likely to underestimate their problems than individuals with mild or moderate injuries (Allen & Ruff, 1990; Anderson & Tranel, 1989; Fleming et al., 1998; Sbordone, Seyranian, & Ruff, 1998). This suggests, therefore, the need to consider more specific mechanisms underlying awareness deficits following brain injury.

In relation to AD, some researchers have suggested that unawareness of impairments is a clinical feature of the disorder (e.g., Feher et al., 1991; Green, Goldstein, Sirockman, & Green, 1993). However, the proportion of individuals deemed unaware varies considerably from study to study (Clare, 2004a, b). Empirical studies of AD fail to support the view that generalised cognitive impairment underlies awareness deficits. In the early stages of AD, level of awareness appears variable. The evidence indicates that some individuals with AD may display awareness deficits during the early stage of the illness while their general cognitive functioning is relatively intact, but conversely others may display no apparent awareness deficits even when general cognitive functioning is compromised. In some cases, level of awareness has been shown to increase over time, even as the illness itself continues to progress (e.g., Weinstein, 1991; Weinstein et al., 1994). Any relationship between illness severity and unawareness is not straightforward, and while some studies report associations between greater severity and lower awareness, others have found no association (Clare, 2004b). Although unawareness is thought to be more common in the advanced stages of AD, some individuals in a later stage of AD have been found to recognise and acknowledge various impairments related to their illness (e.g., Mayhew, Acton, Yauk, & Hopkins, 2001). The same mixed pattern of findings is evident with regard to awareness and duration of illness or stage of progression. The evidence generally suggests there is considerable variation in the level of awareness of deficits displayed by people with AD at each stage of its progression (for comprehensive overviews, see Clare 2004b; Aalten et al., in press).

Some initial evidence to support the role of the frontal lobes in awareness was based upon case studies of individuals with frontal lobe pathology who demonstrated awareness deficits (see reviews by Agnew & Morris, 1998; McGlynn & Schacter, 1989). More systematic studies assessing cerebral perfusion found that hypoperfusion in the right dorsolateral frontal lobe was associated with awareness deficits for individuals with AD (Reed, Jagust, & Coulter, 1994; Starkstein et al., 1995). During the last 15 years various researchers have examined the relationship between measures of executive functioning and indices of awareness. An association between level of awareness and measures of executive functioning has been found in studies of individuals with AD (Mangone et al., 1991; Michon et al., 1994; Starkstein et al., 1993). Similarly, studies have identified a relationship between level of awareness and performance on measures of executive functioning for individuals with brain injury. Aspects of executive functioning related to level of awareness include reasoning (Malec, Machulda, & Moessner, 1997; Ownsworth, McFarland, & Young, 2002), idea generation or fluency (Burgess et al., 1998; Ownsworth & Fleming, in press), mental flexibility

(Burgess et al., 1998; Trudel, Tryon, & Purdum, 1998) and self-regulation and error behaviour (Bogod, Mateer, & Macdonald, 2003; Burgess et al., 1998; Ownsworth & Fleming, in press). Recent research by Marcel et al. (2004) found that unawareness or anosognosia for hemiplegia was associated with the ability to flexibly evaluate one's own performance on a task, rather than actual performance on the test. These findings led to the suggestion that awareness of deficits requires individuals to re-calibrate their judgement based upon direct personal experience with a deficit, or make a "self-relevant adjustment" (Vuilleumeir, 2004).

Overall, the literature indicates that theoretical models need to account for different manifestations of unawareness that vary according to the nature of brain pathology, functional domain, type and degree of unawareness.

## Integrating different levels of explanation

Various frameworks consider the interaction between biological, psychological and social influences on unawareness (Allen & Ruff, 1990; Clare, 2004a; Langer & Padrone, 1992; Marková & Berrios, 2000; Prigatano & Weinstein, 1996). For example, Prigatano and Weinstein (1996) proposed that the way in which people with brain injury adapt to and represent their disabilities is influenced by an interaction between the nature of brain pathology (neurocognitive factors), the meaning of the disability as determined by premorbid experiences, personality and values (psychological factors), and the milieu or environment in which the behaviour is elicited or observed (socio-environmental factors). Recent explorations of unawareness in people with AD similarly highlight the role of psychological appraisal and social influences (Marková & Berrios, 2000; Clare, 2004a; Seiffer, Clare, & Harvey, in press).

Researchers suggest that individuals' reaction to injury or illness generally appears to reflect a relative contribution of premorbid personality characteristics or coping strategies, and post-injury responses to trauma (Clare, 2003, 2004a; Ownsworth & McFarland, 2004; Weinstein & Kahn, 1955). Although it is recognised that individuals can employ a range of psychological defence mechanisms, the term "denial" is most commonly referred to in the literature as the main psychological reaction contributing to awareness deficits (Prigatano, 1999). An individual's response to an injury or illness is also influenced to some extent by the social environment in which behaviours are elicited and interpreted (Clare, 2003, 2004a; Prigatano & Weinstein, 1996). Consequently, it is clinically important to try to identify the relative contribution of these factors to a given individual's presentation of unawareness.

Only a small number of studies have explored the role of psychological and socio-environmental factors in unawareness for individuals with brain injury and AD, in terms of emotional adjustment, personality and coping style and socio-cultural context. It must be acknowledged that it is very difficult to determine the extent to which awareness deficits are mediated by neurocognitive mechanisms, related to psychological denial, avoidance or selective non-disclosure, and/or influenced by socio-environmental variables. For example, it is possible that in early-stage AD and after brain injury neurological changes influence the nature of subjective experience and emotional processing, such that psychological processes are directly affected. Neurologically mediated changes in emotional and personality functioning following brain injury have been well documented (Gainotti, 1993; Ownsworth & Oei, 1998). Furthermore, there is evidence to suggest that people with early-stage AD demonstrate deficits on emotional processing tasks, which do not appear to be due to a primary problem in emotional processing but can be largely attributed to the secondary effects of other cognitive impairments (Zaitchik & Albert, 2004). Thus, it can be difficult to understand what self-report measures truly reflect. Of course, self-report measures are only one approach used, in combination with reports from significant others, behavioural observation and objective tests, to investigate factors underlying awareness deficits.

Various studies have found that level of unawareness is associated with time since injury, emotional status and motivation following brain injury (Allen & Ruff, 1990; Fleming et al., 1998; Godfrey et al., 1993). Godfrey et al. (1993) found that the development of awareness is most pronounced between approximately 6 and 12 months post-injury and is associated with increased emotional distress. It was suggested that acknowledging the impact of deficits too early in recovery would mean accepting major changes that affect personal control, independence and self-esteem, which is likely to have aversive emotional consequences. Therefore, individuals initially cling to the hope of returning to their previous status (Godfrey et al., 1993). Coping strategies such as denial are believed act as a buffer to emotional distress and give individuals time to develop more effective coping strategies (Gainotti, 1993). The availability of accurate and meaningful feedback and concrete life experiences serves to promote realistic self-appraisal over time (Toglia & Kirk, 2000). These findings suggest that, in some cases, unawareness might be related to denial, and/or a lack of relevant information or opportunities to observe post-injury changes.

The role of denial in determining awareness deficits in AD was emphasised by Weinstein et al. (1994). They argued that denial of impairments was strongly related to pre-existing personality traits such as having high expectations of oneself, being conscientious with a strong work ethic, and viewing illness as a sign of weakness. Cotrell and Lein (1993), exploring awareness and denial in people with AD by interviewing their carers, found that reactions ranged from realism through minimisation of problems to complete denial of difficulty, with individual responses closely linked to pre-existing coping styles. Clare (2002, 2003), using an interpretive phenomenological method, found evidence for a range of emotional responses and coping strategies among people with early-stage AD, which were consistent with pre-existing personality characteristics. Seiffer et al. (in press) found evidence for a relationship between the personality variable of conscientiousness and level of unawareness in early-stage dementia, and between attitudes to emotional expression and the adoption of an avoidant coping style in managing the threat of dementia. This study identified a distinction between denial operating at an unconscious level and avoidant coping operating at a more conscious level. Cheston, Jones, and Gilliard (2003) described the impact of group psychotherapy on assimilation and integration of the experience of developing dementia, suggesting that expression of explicit awareness of the diagnosis or its implications could be influenced through this form of intervention.

Similar to AD, personality characteristics found to relate to awareness deficits following brain injury include perfectionism, denial of personal inadequacies, defensiveness and being highly work-oriented (Prigatano & Weinstein, 1996). Based upon clinical observations, Prigatano (1999) identified that individuals with partial awareness of their deficits might demonstrate a range of coping methods, and distinguished between "non-defensive" strategies that reflect premorbid characteristics and "defensive" strategies that are used to protect against emotional distress. Ownsworth et al. (2002) empirically investigated the role of denial in unawareness using self-report measures of defensiveness and minimisation. The findings suggested that although individuals with defensive personality characteristics might be unwilling to disclose negative information about themselves, they are often aware of their deficits and develop a range of adaptive coping strategies. Similarly, individuals who minimise or under-report their symptoms may also demonstrate effective use of other compensatory strategies. Thus, these individuals may downplay their deficits in particular contexts but adjust their lives accordingly. However, individuals displaying impaired executive functioning and either form of denial demonstrated significantly lower levels of awareness and strategy behaviour, suggesting that these individuals may rely excessively on minimisation or defensiveness as a main way of coping (Ownsworth et al., 2002). Research by Kortte, Wegner, and Chwalisz (2003) found that defensive denial in the first 12 months post-injury, as measured by a clinician rating scale (Prigatano & Klonoff, 1998), was associated with greater use of avoidant coping strategies and that use of these strategies was associated with depression. This finding challenges the view that denial acts as a buffer to emotional distress (Gainotti, 1993) and suggests that persisting denial can be maladaptive when it hinders the adjustment process and the development of effective coping strategies.

The tendency to overestimate behavioural competency generally appears to be universal. However, various socio-cultural variables appear to influence how individuals respond to questions about their injury or illness (Gainotti, 1975; Prigatano, 1999). A study of Japanese individuals with brain injury found that, unlike American individuals, participants overestimated their self-care skills but not their social or emotional control abilities (Prigatano, Ogano, & Amakusa, 1997). This finding was attributed to cultural values in which independence is highly valued in Japan. A New Zealand study identified that Maori individuals describe themselves as less competent behaviourally than non-Maoris with English ancestry (Prigatano & Leathem, 1993). Prigatano (1999) suggested that individuals' responses to questions might be influenced by their ability to assess what is relevant to their culture. Severe injuries, which can lead to diffuse brain damage affecting the fronto-temporal regions, might reduce individuals' capacity to be aware of "any socially relevant impairment in a given culture" (Prigatano, 1999, p. 278). However, this interesting explanation, which specifically links neural processes with the socio-cultural context, requires further investigation.

A number of studies of AD and brain injury have indicated that unawareness, in some cases, or to some degree, may be socially constructed. In particular, the nature of assessment methods influences individuals' responses and, thus, resulting opinions formed about awareness. For example, Sherer et al. (1998) identified that individuals' responses to specific questions about their injury-related impairments were more consistent with their relatives' reports than their responses to global questions. Marcel et al. (2004) found that responses to questions framed in the third person reflected greater awareness of hemiplegia than questions framed in the first person. In relation to AD, Derouesné et al. (1999) and Kaszniak and Christenson (1996) have noted that results from different methods of assessing unawareness are not closely correlated, and that the presence and degree of awareness deficits elicited varies according to the assessment methods used. This might go some way, therefore, to explaining some of the anomalies in the literature. The implications of these findings are that clinicians' interpretations of unawareness need to be based on consideration of the extent to which selected assessment tasks have provided the opportunity for individuals to demonstrate awareness of their deficits.

Overall, there is a small but growing body of research which highlights the psychological and socio-environmental factors potentially contributing to individuals' presentations of unawareness. These developments suggest that it would be useful if models of unawareness were able to account for the possible ways in which biological, psychological and social factors interact for a given individual.

## Awareness indicators and objects of awareness

In general, our understanding of awareness phenomena is greatly influenced by how the theoretical construct of awareness has been measured in research and clinical practice. It should be remembered that indices of awareness derived from available measures can only be a partial reflection of the phenomenon of awareness for any given individual (Marková et al., in press). Indications of awareness or, conversely, unawareness, can be inferred from a diverse range of behaviours which include verbal reports, ability to set realistic goals, use of compensatory strategies, compliance with rehabilitation or treatment (e.g., medication), predictions of performance on a task and recognition of errors during performance (Fleming, Strong, & Ashton, 1996; Godfrey et al., 1993; Hart, Giovannetti, Montgomery, & Schwartz, 1998; Ownsworth, McFarland, & Young, 2000; Sohlberg et al., 1998; Trosset & Kaszniak, 1996). However, the most common approaches to measuring unawareness in people with brain injury and AD include the discrepancy method based upon self-ratings and informant ratings, and clinician rating methods (see reviews by Clare, 2004b; Clare, Marková, Verhey & Kenny, in press; Simmonds & Fleming, 2003). In view of the range of different indicators of awareness, it is clearly problematic for clinicians to provide an opinion that an individual's awareness is intact or absent on the basis of a single score or sample of behaviour. More specifically, such basic assessment methods may not capture the complexity and structure of the theoretical construct of unawareness.

Marková and Berrios (2001) proposed that unawareness varies according to the "object of insight" that is assessed and, as such, is determined by the conceptual framework underlying a particular assessment approach. While object of insight appears similar to specificity, or the degree to which awareness deficits vary across functional domains (Schacter & Prigatano, 1991), object of insight is a broader concept that shapes the type of unawareness elicited in clinical practice and investigated in empirical studies. For example, a review by Clare et al. (in press) identified that the objects of insight most typically selected by researchers to investigate unawareness in people with AD include memory difficulty and its impact and implications, self-care and ADL difficulties, impairment of cognitive functioning and phenomenological experience. Other studies focus on more specific aspects of unawareness, such as awareness of driving behaviour (Cotrell & Wild, 1999) or awareness of ability to manage finances (Van Weilingen et al., 2004). Many general conclusions about unawareness in brain injury and AD are made on the basis of a single assessment of a specific object of awareness and, consequently, provide only a limited perspective on unawareness phenomena. However, selected studies have employed multidimensional assessment procedures that used two or more awareness indicators for a particular object of awareness, therefore providing a richer approach (Clare et al., in press). For example, in one study, unawareness of memory functioning in a group of people with early-stage AD was assessed using participant/informant discrepancy, self-rating/objective task performance discrepancy and phenomenological accounts of subjective experience (Clare, 2002, 2003; Clare et al., 2002, 2004; Clare, Roth, & Pratt, in press). In general, theoretical models may have greater clinical utility if they can accommodate variations in unawareness relating to different objects and indicators of awareness, and guide the development of enhanced measurement approaches to capture the complexity of the phenomenon of unawareness.

## Explicit and implicit manifestations of awareness

Investigations of unawareness have traditionally placed most emphasis upon what people say, which is not always reflected in how people behave (Krefting, 1989). This point relates to an issue that is commonly raised in the literature, namely, the distinction between explicit and implicit awareness. Overall, research has yet to develop systematic approaches for distinguishing between implicit and explicit processes related to unawareness. However, empirical research suggests that information about one's self that is only partially registered in consciousness can influence ongoing experience (Kihlstrom & Tobias, 1991; Schacter, 1990) and, therefore, the implicit/explicit distinction warrants exploration. Various authors distinguish between disorders of awareness of sensory input such as blindsight (i.e., patients are aware that they cannot see but may not be aware of their residual spatial ability), and lack of awareness of impairment or reflective consciousness, such as where patients are unaware of cortical blindness (McGlynn & Schacter, 1989; Zeman, 2001). A few notable studies have developed approaches to examine implicit manifestations of awareness, which were inferred from responsivity on tasks. In one study that focused on lack of awareness of sensory input, Bologna and Camp (1997) found that individuals with advanced AD who lacked explicit self-recognition of their own reflection in a mirror nonetheless showed behaviours indicating that self-recognition might have occurred at an implicit level.

Andersson, Gundersen, and Finset (1999) examined awareness of deficits using psychophysiological measures to monitor autonomic reactivity of individuals with brain injury while they were engaged in therapeutic interaction that required them to describe the effects of their injury. The individuals rated by clinicians as having reduced awareness were found to experience low autonomic reactivity, which was interpreted as evidence of organic factors underlying awareness deficits. The authors predicted that individuals displaying denial would experience increased autonomic activity during therapeutic interaction, thus indicating implicit awareness of deficits, although this remains to be investigated. General clinical examples of implicit awareness in the literature include patients who do not verbally acknowledge deficits but show avoidance of tasks related to their impaired functioning, or display compensatory behaviours such as use of memory strategies (McGlynn & Schacter, 1989). However, one concern with interpreting such behaviour as evidence of implicit awareness is that some individuals who do not verbally report their deficits may actually be fully aware of their existence but choose not to disclose these deficits (Ownsworth et al., 2002). Conversely, other individuals display awareness of deficits through their verbal reports but show poor recognition of related difficulties during performance and a failure to use compensatory strategies (Giovanetti, Libon, & Hart, 2002; Hart et al., 1998; Toglia & Kirk, 2000).

In general, because there is little systematic research evidence, only limited conclusions can be drawn about the relationship between explicit and implicit awareness states in AD and brain injury and how these relate to the nature or degree of unawareness. However, it may be beneficial for future research to be guided by theoretical models that have the potential to distinguish between implicit and explicit awareness manifestations.

## The process of developing awareness

Awareness of deficits following brain injury has been represented as a pyramid with hierarchical and interdependent levels (Crosson et al., 1989). This model proposes that the development of "intellectual awareness", or basic knowledge of impairment, provides the foundation for developing the capacity to recognise a problem when it occurs, or "emergent awareness". The ability to acknowledge impairment and recognise difficulties during performance is viewed as the prerequisite for "anticipatory awareness", which is the ability to predict when problems will occur in the future (Crosson et al., 1989). Toglia and Kirk (2000) identified various limitations of the pyramid model, including an inability to explain how the levels of awareness work together and to account for discrepancies in behaviour across skill domains and situations. They developed a comprehensive dynamic interactional model (CDIM), which proposes that gaining awareness involves a dynamic process of restructuring self-knowledge. Similar to the pyramid framework, the CDIM differentiates between "knowledge" that exists prior to a task and "on-line awareness", which is activated during tasks and situations. However, according to this model, dynamic interactions occur between individuals' pre-existing or stored knowledge, beliefs, affective states and on-line awareness, which lead to variations in awareness, also dependent upon the task and situation. While no systematic or experimentally validated approach was outlined to distinguish between these factors, the CDIM framework emphasises the dynamic and interactive relationship between internal and external influences in determining level of awareness and changes in awareness over time, and suggests that the process of developing awareness needs to be reflected in theoretical models.

## Overview and summary

The preceding discussion has highlighted a number of key issues that require consideration in attempting to understand awareness disorders. These can serve as a guide when evaluating the comprehensiveness and applicability of cognitive neuropsychological models. It is important to acknowledge here that some models aiming to explain very specific focal types of awareness deficit will not necessarily need to address these issues. Although beyond the scope of the present review, some theories argue that various forms of unawareness relating to selective neurological deficits result directly from underlying brain pathology (for a detailed review see McGlynn & Schacter, 1989), and as previously noted this may in certain cases provide sufficient explanation. Here, however, our focus is on the broader context of awareness deficits seen after brain injury and in the early stages of AD. The review has considered some key characteristics that would help to ensure a comprehensive and clinically useful account of awareness deficits in AD or brain injury. First, such theoretical models need the potential to explain different presentations of unawareness according to the nature of brain pathology, functional domain, type and degree of unawareness. Second, models should allow for the possibility of integrating neurological and psychosocial levels of explanation. Third, models need to accommodate variations in awareness due to different objects and indicators of awareness. Fourth, models might profitably have the potential to distinguish between implicit and explicit manifestations of awareness, although as noted previously there is little empirical evidence available to date in this domain. Finally, theoretical models need to explain the process of developing awareness or re-structuring self-knowledge over time.

# EXPLANATORY MODELS AND FRAMEWORKS

Here we will consider how recent theoretical models have attempted to address these key issues. We will discuss firstly a comprehensive cognitive neuropsychological model of awareness deficits, and secondly a biopsychosocial framework for understanding awareness deficits.

## A cognitive neuropsychological model

A range of cognitive neuropsychological models has attempted to account for awareness deficits, including those of Prigatano and colleagues

(Prigatano, 1999; Prigatano et al., 1990) and Stuss and colleagues (Stuss, 1991; Stuss & Benson, 1986; Stuss, Picton, & Alexander, 2001). Here, we will focus on Schacter's (1990) Dissociable Interactions and Conscious Experience (DICE) model together with its recent elaborations by Morris and colleagues (Agnew & Morris, 1998; Morris & Hannesdottir, 2004). The DICE model (McGlynn & Schacter; 1989; Schacter, 1990) proposes that conscious experiences or "phenomenal awareness" require activation of a specific system called the conscious awareness system (CAS), which interacts with, but is distinct from, language, memory, perception and other cognitive modules. It is hypothesised that domain-specific awareness deficits occur when there is a selective disconnection between the central CAS and a specific module (e.g., sensory input). Such forms of unawareness are more common after right hemisphere or parietal lobe damage (McGlynn & Schacter, 1989; Marcel et al., 2004), but are most likely to develop when the lesion encompasses both frontal and parietal regions (Pia, Neppi-Modona, Ricci, & Berti, 2004). Global awareness deficits for all cognitive domains are predicted to arise from damage to the central CAS, leading to an inability to detect changes across all domains. The DICE model also proposes that CAS has an output link to an executive system responsible for initiating, organising and monitoring complex ideas and actions. Therefore, awareness deficits relating to complex functions such as social, behavioural and personality changes occur following damage to either the executive system or its connection to CAS (McGlynn & Schacter, 1989). The DICE model was further developed by Agnew and Morris (1998) and Morris and Hannesdottir (2004), who presented the Cognitive Awareness Model (CAM) to explain awareness deficits in AD.

Central to the CAM is the notion that appraisal of abilities (and hence of cognitive impairment), is based on perception of success or failure on cognitive tasks or behavioural activity. This appraisal facilitates adaptation by helping to not expose the individual to unnecessary failure, while optimising task activity. Information about success or failure is constantly monitored with the necessary information derived from perceptual input being stored either in short-term or long-term memory, but also consolidated in semantic memory. With regard to the latter, the model refers to the personal data base (PDB), the fund of personal information derived from experience, including information concerning ability or impairment. The trigger for the PDB to be updated is through the output action of a set of comparator mechanisms within the central executive system, which detects a mismatch between the PDB record and the experience of cognitive success or failures. Awareness of failure is generated in an immediate sense, when there is mismatch, with a signal sent to a metacognitive awareness system (MAS), leading to metacognitive output or conscious awareness of poor performance or failure. Additionally, information from the PDB can also be fed into the

MAS to provide the person with awareness of cognitive ability. As an additional component, the comparator systems also provide an output into an implicit mechanism that can guide behavioural responses, without necessarily being accompanied by awareness. This latter mechanism explains why people can adapt their behaviour following response failure, but not necessarily be aware of cognitive failure. The action of this system explains certain phenomena associated with implicit awareness, those concerned with reaction to failure or success. The PDB record is shaped not just by the output of the comparator mechanisms but also by general semantic knowledge, for example the cultural and social experiences of an individual concerning what to expect about ability. Hence, for example, the expectations of other people can produce a sense of success or failure by influencing the content of the PDB.

The CAM was originally used to explain three possible types of anosognosic deficits in relation to memory failure in AD (Agnew & Morris, 1998). Firstly, "mnemonic anosognosia" occurs when the memory impairment itself results in an error of encoding or updating the PDB, and hence creating a permanent record relating to evaluation of self-ability. In this case, memory failure can be detected, and possibily feed through to an implicit mechanism for behavioural change. Secondly, "executive anosognosia" arises due to a breakdown in the executive system or comparator mechanism, in which no mismatch is detected between incoming information and the PDB, hence the meaning of the failure is lost. Thirdly, "primary anosognosia" is due to failure of the MAS in which information concerning impairment is detected and stored, but does not have access to consciousness. In this case the person has only implicit knowledge of memory failure, with the implicit system providing a mechanism by which behavioural adaptation can still take place, but without the person being aware of the reason.

A main feature of the CAM (Morris & Hannesdottir, 2004) is that it explains how cognitive impairment might contribute to awareness deficits at different levels of metacognitive processing. This explanation emphasises that memory impairment may not actually produce an awareness disorder, but might contribute by sustaining unawareness. Additionally, the model explains different types of awareness deficits, implicit and explicit manifestations of each, and the process of developing awareness in which the PDB is a proposed mechanism through which socio-cultural experiences might influence awareness. To date, the model provides a comprehensive account of awareness phenomena for memory deficits in AD, and by extension could account for awareness of other cognitive impairments or functional changes relevant to AD and brain injury. However, the model does not comprehensively account for the role of psychosocial factors and would need to be expanded upon further, or integrated with other accounts in order to fully to achieve this. The model represents a useful advance in that it does propose a mechanism by which psychological factors could operate. There is a need to explain in what way personality, coping style, values and prior experiences may contribute to awareness, other than through the general notion of influencing the contents of semantic memory. Additionally, there is a need to consider the extent to which awareness deficits are socially constructed and shaped by the environment.

## A biopsychosocial model

Various frameworks consider the interaction between biological, psychological and social influences on unawareness (for example, Allen & Ruff, 1990; Langer & Padrone, 1992; Marková & Berrios, 2000). These general frameworks identify the multifaceted nature of awareness disorders and the possible ways in which biological, psychological and social factors interact for a given individual. However, a more comprehensive biopsychosocial model of unawareness is needed to account for varied clinical presentations across a range of presenting problems. This framework needs to encompass key contributions of cognitive neuropsychological models and consider the operation of psychological and social factors in unawareness. Clare (2004a) presented a comprehensive biopsychosocial framework for considering awareness and unawareness in early-stage AD that attempted to address these issues.

This biopsychosocial framework incorporates relevant factors at the biological, psychological and social levels, presented in the context of subjective experience of self. The role of information and knowledge about the illness, and ability to understand this, is also acknowledged. At the biological level, factors include the type of unawareness, as defined in cognitive neuropsychological models (e.g., domain-specific unawareness, executive anosognosia or impaired self-awareness), along with consideration of the possible neurocognitive mechanisms involved (e.g., damage to the conscious awareness system or executive system, or to links between these and other cognitive functions). At the psychological level, factors include denial, coping style (such as avoidant coping or minimisation), and behavioural indications of implicit awareness where explicit awareness is absent, as well as meanings attributed to experience (e.g., the explanations individuals adopt in response to changes or the onset of symptoms or difficulties) and the emotional aspect of experience. At the social level, factors include interactions with family, friends and professionals, dimensions of experience such as stigma or exclusion, and the influence of social and cultural representations of dementia. The model proposes a dynamic interaction between the factors operating at each of the three levels, which influences and is influenced by subjective experience of self. It is suggested that the relative contribution of factors operating at each level will vary across individuals and indeed this would also be the case when comparing different kinds of disorder or disability. Thus, for some individuals with specific, focal awareness deficits, these might predominantly be accounted for by factors at the biological level. In early-stage AD, however, psychological and social factors would typically account for a much greater proportion of any observed awareness deficits. This model goes some way towards achieving a broad explanatory framework, but is presented as a preliminary model with the caveat that further work would be required to delineate more precisely the processes operating within each level and the nature of the interactions between them (Clare, 2004a).

## AN INTEGRATED BIOPSYCHOSOCIAL FRAMEWORK FOR CLINICIANS

Overall, as previously discussed, different studies indicate that psychological and socio-environmental factors appear to contribute to individuals' presentations of unawareness. Building on the developments of the CAM model (Agnew & Morris, 1998; Morris & Hannesdottir, 2004) and the comprehensive biopsychosocial framework for understanding unawareness in AD (Clare, 2004a), and incorporating similar developments in the brain injury field (Ownsworth et al., 2002; Prigatano, 1999; Sherer et al., 1998), a framework is presented in Table 1 that is designed to assist clinicians to identify a particular factor, or combination of factors, that might contribute to an individual's presentation of unawareness. Although this framework does not encapsulate all the contributions of cognitive neuropsychological models, it represents an integration of neurocognitive, psychological and socio-environmental factors, based upon existing empirical evidence and some clinical observations. Unlike cognitive neuropsychological models, this biopsychosocial framework emphasises the interactive role of psychosocial factors in unawareness and explains how variations might occur due to different objects and indicators of awareness. Other socio-environmental factors relate to issues that might either impede the development of awareness, or influence to a degree which individuals report their post-injury impairments in a particular social context. A case description focusing in particular on psychological and socio-environmental factors will be used to support the clinical application of the model presented in Table 1.

### Case description

Ben sustained a mild to moderate traumatic brain injury and was seen for a research assessment at 6 months post-injury and again at 18 months post-injury. During a standardised awareness interview at 6 months post-injury,

TABLE 1

An integrated biopsychosocial framework for understanding awareness disorders in Alzheimer's disease and brain injury

| *Bases for unawareness* | *Area of functioning* | *How awareness deficits might arise* | *Consideration for given individual* |
|---|---|---|---|
| Neurocognitive factors | Knowledge of selective physical, sensory or cognitive changes | Selective disconnection between the conscious awareness system and a specific module: Evidence of dysfunction in the right hemisphere or fronto-parietal region | Apparent/Not apparent |
| | Knowledge of global changes (i.e., cognitive, behavioural and emotional functioning) | Damage to frontal systems or widespread neurological damage: Memory impairment and/or evidence of executive impairment (damage to the conscious awareness system and connections) | Apparent/Not apparent |
| | On-line awareness or self-monitoring of behaviour during performance | A breakdown in the executive system or comparator mechanism: Difficulty identifying errors in performance or re-calibrating self-judgement based upon direct experience with a deficit | Apparent/Not apparent |
| Psychological factors | Partial unawareness: | Non-disclosure of information that is partially or fully recognised due to premorbid personality characteristics or coping methods | |
| | (a) Change in functioning or information about self is viewed as emotionally threatening and would mean accepting major changes that affect personal control, independence and self-esteem; or | (a) Defensive reactions: Denial, avoidance, minimisation, resistance, blaming others, etc. | Apparent/Not apparent |
| | (b) Information about change in self is difficult to make sense of | (b) Non-defensive reactions: The person senses that something is wrong but continues to act as if nothing is wrong and relies on previous ways of thinking and reacting | Apparent/Not apparent |

(*Table continued*)

Table 1 (Continued)

| *Bases for unawareness* | *Area of functioning* | *How awareness deficits might arise* | *Consideration for given individual* |
|---|---|---|---|
| Socio-environmental context | Determined by the assessment context itself: The objects of insight, the type and nature of questions or observations used as awareness indicators | Individuals perceive that they stand to lose rather than gain from disclosing their problems in the specific assessment context; or | Apparent/Not apparent |
| | | Individual have not had relevant information or opportunities to recognise changes in functioning; or | Apparent/Not apparent |
| | | Cultural values influence how individuals answer specific questions about socially relevant impairment; or | Apparent/Not apparent |
| | | The selected assessment tasks have not provided an opportunity for the individuals to display awareness of deficits | Apparent/Not apparent |

which was conducted just prior to discharge from outpatient rehabilitation, Ben reported minimal physical changes and did not acknowledge any of the cognitive or behavioural changes that had been reported by a relative and clinicians. Self-report measures indicated highly defensive personality characteristics and the use of minimisation as a coping strategy (see Ownsworth et al., 2002). A neuropsychological assessment identified mild deficits in attention, memory and language while his general intellectual functioning and executive functions were in the "superior" range for his age. Ben showed frustration during the neuropsychological feedback session and stated that he found the cognitive rehabilitation exercises meaningless, and subsequently failed to attend various appointments.

During a 12-month follow-up interview, however, Ben acknowledged a range of cognitive and behavioural impairments and identified that these were particularly problematic when he returned to work and study. When reminded of his responses on the previous interview Ben commented: "Well, I wouldn't have told you everything then would I?" He explained that although he had been conscious of some degree of cognitive change while attending rehabilitation, he was unsure how significant these impairments would be until he tested his skills in a more demanding and familiar environment (i.e., work and study). Ben also identified that he had been very keen to complete rehabilitation and felt that if he acknowledged these changes at the time of the first assessment his programme might have been extended, thus delaying his goal of returning to work and study.

This case description illustrates the complex interplay of psychological and socio-environmental factors that potentially influence an individual's presentation of awareness deficits and participation in rehabilitation. In particular, Ben displayed a highly defensive personality style, avoidant coping and minimisation. Therefore, it appears that he found the initial assessment about his post-injury changes emotionally threatening. The increased awareness that he displayed during the second interview at the 12-month follow-up may have been related to having relevant opportunities and meaningful life experiences outside the rehabilitation context that allowed him to recognise changes in his functioning. It is also likely that due to his success in returning to study and work he felt less emotionally threatened by discussing these impairments in the context of an interview. To some extent, reliance upon Ben's verbal reports during the initial interview may not have provided sufficient opportunity for him to display awareness of his cognitive changes. Additionally, it appeared that Ben felt he had more to lose than to gain by disclosing his post-injury problems in the initial assessment, which was conducted just prior to discharge from rehabilitation. Overall, this case description highlights the value of exploring individuals' phenomenological or subjective experience to understand factors contributing to unawareness.

### Overview and summary

Overall, the application of the biopsychosocial framework and its implications for rehabilitation needs to be systematically investigated in further research. Additionally, although the present review identified some similarities concerning awareness phenomena in brain injury and AD, the clinical relevance of the framework requires careful consideration for each client group. In particular, the combination of factors contributing to awareness deficits for a younger person with brain injury are likely to be different to those considered relevant for an older person with AD.

## CONCLUSIONS

The findings of the present review indicate that cognitive neuropsychological accounts have the capacity to explain a broad range of awareness phenomena in brain injury and AD, but typically overlook the role of psychosocial factors. Recent developments, however, offer the possibility for greater integration. An integrated biopsychosocial approach for understanding awareness disorders has been proposed and emphasises that unawareness can arise from a complex interaction between neuro-cognitive, psychological and socio-environmental factors. The proposed framework can be used to assist clinicians to identify the specific factor, or set of factors, which might contribute to a given individual's presentation of unawareness. Further research is required to empirically investigate the interaction between different bases of unawareness and examine the clinical relevance of the proposed biopsychosocial approach for different client groups. As previously identified, such research could profitably investigate implicit and explicit manifestations of awareness for individuals with neuropsychologically-based unawareness and/or psychologically-based awareness deficits. Additionally, cross-cultural studies could examine individuals' awareness of socially relevant impairment and their ability to make self-relevant adjustments based upon direct experience.

## REFERENCES


Aalten, P., van Valen, E., Clare, L., Kenny, G., & Verhey, F. (in press). Awareness in dementia: A review of clinical correlates. *Aging and Mental Health.*

Agnew, S. K., & Morris, R. G. (1998). The heterogeneity of anosognosia for memory impairment in Alzheimer's disease: A review of the literature and a proposed model. *Aging and Mental Health, 2*, 7–19.

Allen, C. C., & Ruff, R. M. (1990). Self-rating versus neurophysiological performance of moderate versus severe head-injured patients. *Brain Injury, 4*, 7–17.

Andersson, S., Gundersen, P. M., & Finset, A. (1999). Emotional activation during therapeutic interaction in traumatic brain injury: Effect of apathy, self-awareness and implications for rehabilitation. *Brain Injury*, *13*, 393–404.

Bogod, N. M., Mateer, C. A., & Macdonald, S. W. S. (2003). Self-awareness after traumatic brain injury: A comparison of measures and their relationship to executive functions. *Journal of the International Neuropsychological Society*, *9*, 450–458.

Bologna, S. M., & Camp, C. J. (1997). Covert versus overt self-recognition in late stage Alzheimer's disease. *Journal of the International Neuropsychological Society*, *3*, 195–198.

Burgess, P. W., Alderman, N., Evans, J., Emslie, H., & Wilson, B. A. (1998). The ecological validity of tests of executive function. *Journal of the International Neuropsychological Society*, *4*, 547–558.

Cheston, R., Jones, K., & Gilliard, J. (2003). Group psychotherapy and people with dementia. *Aging and Mental Health*, *7*, 452–461.

Clare, L. (2002). We'll fight it as long as we can: Coping with the onset of Alzheimer's disease. *Aging and Mental Health*, *6*, 139–148.

Clare, L. (2003). Managing threats to self: Awareness in early-stage Alzheimer's disease. *Social Science and Medicine*, *57*, 1017–1029.

Clare, L. (2004a). The construction of awareness in early-stage Alzheimer's disease: A review of concepts and models. *British Journal of Clinical Psychology*, *43*, 155–175.

Clare, L. (2004b). Awareness in early-stage Alzheimer's disease: A review of methods and evidence. *British Journal of Clinical Psychology*, *43*, 177–196.

Clare, L., Marková, I., Verhey, F., & Kenny, G. (in press). Awareness in dementia: A review of assessment methods and measures. *Aging and Mental Health.*

Clare, L., Roth, I. & Pratt, R. (in press). Perceptions of change over time in early-stage Alzheimer's disease, and implications for understanding awareness and coping style. *Dementia.*

Clare, L., Wilson, B. A., Carter, G., Roth, I., & Hodges, J. R. (2002). Assessing awareness in early-stage Alzheimer's disease: Development and piloting of the Memory Awareness Rating Scale. *Neuropsychological Rehabilitation*, *12*, 341–362.

Clare, L., Wilson, B. A., Carter, G., Roth, I., & Hodges, J. R. (2004). Awareness in early-stage Alzheimer's disease: Relationship to outcome of cognitive rehabilitation. *Journal of Clinical and Experimental Neuropsychology*, *26*, 215–226.

Cotrell, V., & Lein, L. (1993). Awareness and denial in the Alzheimer's disease victim. *Journal of Gerontological Social Work*, *19*, 115–132.

Cotrell, V., & Wild, K. (1999). Longitudinal study of self-imposed driving restrictions and deficit awareness in patients with Alzheimer disease. *Alzheimer Disease and Associated Disorders*, *13*, 151–156.

Crosson, B. C., Barco, P. P., Velozo, C. A., Bolseta, M. M., Werts, D., & Brobeck, T. (1989). Awareness and compensation in post-acute head injury rehabilitation. *Journal of Head Trauma Rehabilitation*, *4*, 46–54.

Derouesné, C., Thibault, S., Lagha-Pierucci, S., Baudouin-Madec, V., Ancri, D., & Lacomblez, L. (1999). Decreased awareness of cognitive deficits in patients with mild dementia of the Alzheimer type. *International Journal of Geriatric Psychiatry*, *14*, 1019–1030.

Feher, E. P., Mahurin, R. K., Inbody, S. B., Crook, T. H., & Pirozzolo, F. J. (1991). Anosognosia in Alzheimer's disease. *Neuropsychiatry, Neuropsychology and Behavioural Neurology*, *4*, 136–146.

Fleming, J. M., & Strong, J. (1999). A longitudinal study of self-awareness: Functional deficits underestimated by persons with brain injury. *Occupational Therapy Journal of Research*, *19*, 3–17.

Fleming, J. M., Strong, J., & Ashton, R. (1996). Self-awareness of deficits in adults with traumatic brain injury: How best to measure? *Brain Injury*, *10*, 1–15.

Fleming, J. M., Strong, J., & Ashton, R. (1998). Cluster analysis of self-awareness levels in adults with traumatic brain injury and relationship to outcome. *Journal of Head Trauma Rehabilitation, 13*, 39–51.

Gainotti, G. (1975). Confabulation of denial in senile dementia: An experimental study. *Psychiatric Clinics, 8*, 99–108.

Gainotti, G. (1993). Emotional and psychosocial problems after brain injury. *Neuropsychological Rehabilitation, 3*, 259–277.

Giovannetti, T., Libon, D. J., & Hart, T. (2002). Awareness of naturalistic action errors in dementia. *Journal of the International Neuropsychological Society, 8*, 633–644.

Godfrey, H. P. D., Partridge, F. M., Knight, R. G., & Bishara, S. (1993). Course of insight disorder and emotional dysfunction following closed head injury: A controlled cross-sectional follow-up study. *Journal of Clinical and Experimental Neuropsychology, 15*, 503–515.

Green, J., Goldstein, F. C., Sirockman, B. E., & Green, R. C. (1993). Variable awareness of deficits in Alzheimer's disease. *Neuropsychiatry, Neuropsychology and Behavioural Neurology, 6*, 159–165.

Hart, T., Giovannetti, T., Montgomery, M. W., & Schwartz, M. F. (1998). Awareness of errors in naturalistic action after traumatic brain injury. *Journal of Head Trauma Rehabilitation, 13*, 16–28.

Hibbard, M. R., & Gordon, W. A. (1992). Awareness of disability in patients following stroke. *Rehabilitation Psychology, 37*, 103–120.

Kaszniak, A. W., & Christenson, G. D. (1996). Self-awareness of deficit in patients with Alzheimer's disease. In S. R. Hameroff, A. W. Kaszniak, & A. C. Scott (Eds.), *Towards a science of consciousness: the first Tucson discussions and debates*. Cambridge, MA: MIT Press.

Kihlstrom, J. F., & Tobias, B. A. (1991). Anosognosia, consciousness and the self. In G. P. Prigatano & D. L. Schacter (Eds.), *Awareness of deficits after brain injury: Clinical and theoretical issues* (pp. 198–222). New York: Oxford University Press.

Kortte, K. B., Wegner, S. T., & Chwalisz, K. (2003). Anosognosia and denial: Their relationship to coping and depression in acquired brain injury. *Rehabilitation Psychology, 48*, 131–136.

Krefting, L. (1989). Reintegration into the community after head injury: The results of an ethnographic study. *Occupational Therapy Journal of Research, 9*, 67–83.

Langer, K. G., & Padrone, F. J. (1992). Psychotherapeutic treatment of awareness in acute rehabilitation of traumatic brain injury. *Neuropsychological Rehabilitation, 2*, 59–70.

McGlynn, S. M., & Schacter, D. L. (1989). Unawareness of deficits in neuropsychological syndromes. *Journal of Clinical and Experimental Neuropsychology, 11*, 143–205.

McKinlay, W. W., & Brooks, D. N. (1984). Methodological problems in assessing psychosocial recovery following severe head injury. *Journal of Clinical and Experimental Neuropsychology, 6*, 87–99.

Malec, J. F., Machulda, M. M., & Moessner, A. M. (1997). Differing problem perceptions of staff, survivors, and significant others after brain injury. *Journal of Head Trauma Rehabilitation, 12*, 1–13.

Mangone, C. A., Hier, D. B., Gorelick, P. D., Ganellen, R. J., Langenberg, P., Boarman, R., & Dollear, W. C. (1991). Impaired insight in Alzheimer's disease. *Journal of Geriatric Psychiatry and Neurology, 4*, 189–193.

Marcel, A. J., Tegner, R., & Nimmo-Smith, I. (2004). Anosognosia for plegia: Specificity, extension, partiality and disunity of bodily unawareness. *Cortex, 40*, 19–40.

Marková, I. S., & Berrios, G. E. (2000). Insight into memory deficits. In G. E. Berrios & J. R. Hodges (Eds.), *Memory disorders in psychiatric practice* (pp. 204–233). Cambridge: Cambridge University Press.

Marková, I. S., & Berrios, G. E. (2001). The 'object' of insight assessment: Relationship to insight 'structure'. *Psychopathology, 34*, 245–252.

Marková, I. S., Clare, L., Wang, M., Romero, B., & Kenny, G. (in press). Awareness in dementia; conceptual issues. *Aging and Mental Health.*

Mayhew, P., Acton, G. J., Yauk, S., & Hopkins, B. A. (2001). Communication from individuals with advanced DAT: Can it provide clues to their sense of awareness and well-being? *Geriatric Nursing*, *22*, 106–110.

Michon, A., Deweer, B., Pillon, B., Agid, Y., & Dubois, B. (1994). Relation of anosognosia to frontal lobe dysfunction in Alzheimer's disease. *Journal of Neurology, Neurosurgery and Psychiatry*, *57*, 805–809.

Morris R. G., & Hannesdottir, K. (2004). Loss of 'awareness' in Alzheimer's disease. In R. G. Morris & J. T. Becker (Eds.), *The cognitive neuropsychology of Alzheimer's disease* (pp. 275–296). Oxford: Oxford University Press.

Nathanson, M., Bergman, P. S., & Gordon, G. (1952). Denial of illness. *Archives of Neurology and Psychiatry*, *68*, 380–387.

Ownsworth, T. L., & Fleming, J. (in press). The relative importance of metacognitive skills, emotional status and executive functioning in psychosocial adjustment following acquired brain injury, *Journal of Head Trauma Rehabilitation.*

Ownsworth, T. L., & McFarland, K. (2004). Investigation of psychological and neuropsychological factors associated with clinical outcome following a group rehabilitation programme. *Neuropsychological Rehabilitation, 14*, 535–562.

Ownsworth, T. L., McFarland, K., & Young, R. McD. (2000). Development and standardisation of the Self-regulation Skills Interview (SRSI): A new clinical assessment tool for acquired brain injury. *The Clinical Neuropsychologist*, *14*, 76–92.

Ownsworth, T. L., McFarland, K., & Young, R. McD. (2002). Investigation of factors underlying deficits in self-awareness and self-regulation. *Brain Injury*, *16*, 291–309.

Ownsworth, T. L., & Oei, T. P. S. (1998). Depression after traumatic brain injury: Conceptualisation and treatment considerations. *Brain Injury*, *12*, 735–751.

Pia, L., Neppi-Modona, M., Ricci, R., & Berti, A. (2004). The anatomy of anosognosia for hemiplegia: A meta-analysis. *Cortex*, *40*, 367–377.

Prigatano, G. P. (1999). *Principles of neuropsychological rehabilitation.* New York: Oxford University Press.

Prigatano, G. P., Altman, I. M., & O'Brien, K. P. (1990). Behavioural limitations that brain-injured patients tend to underestimate. *Clinical Neuropsychologist, 4*, 27–33.

Prigatano, G. P., & Klonoff, P. S. (1998). A clinician's rating scale for evaluating impaired self-awareness and denial of disability after brain injury. *Clinical Neuropsychologist, 12*, 56–67.

Prigatano, G. P., & Leathem, J. M. (1993). Awareness of behavioural limitations after traumatic brain injury: A cross-cultural study of New Zealand Maoris and non-Maoris. *Clinical Neuropsychologist*, *7*, 123–135.

Prigatano, G. P., Ogano, M., & Amakusa, B. (1997). A cross-cultural study on impaired self-awareness in Japanese patients with brain dysfunction. *Neuropsychiatry Neuropsychology and Behavioural Neurology*, *10*, 135–143.

Prigatano, G. P., & Weinstein, E. A. (1996). Edwin A. Weinstein's contributions to neuropsychological rehabilitation. *Neuropsychological Rehabilitation, 6*, 305–326.

Reed, B. R., Jagust, W. J., & Coulter, L. (1994). Anosognosia in Alzheimer's disease: Relationships to depression, cognitive function and cerebral perfusion. *Journal of Clinical and Experimental Neuropsychology*, *15*, 231–244.

Sbordone, R. J., Seyranian, G. D., & Ruff, R. M. (1998). Are the subjective complaints of traumatically brain injured patients reliable? *Brain Injury*, *12*, 505–515.

Schacter, D. L. (1990). Toward a cognitive neuropsychology of awareness: Implicit knowledge and anosognosia. *Journal of Clinical and Experimental Neuropsychology*, *12*, 155–178.

Schacter, D. L., & Prigatano, G. P. (1991). Forms of unawareness. In G. P. Prigatano & D. L. Schacter (Eds.), *Awareness of deficit after brain injury: Clinical and theoretical issues* (pp. 258–262). New York: Oxford University Press.

Seiffer, A., Clare, L., & Harvey, R. (in press). The role of personality and coping in relation to awareness of current functioning in early-stage dementia. *Aging and Mental Health.*

Sherer, M., Boake, C., Levin, E., Silver, B. V., Ringholz, G., & High, W. M. (1998). Characteristics of impaired awareness after traumatic brain injury. *Journal of the International Neuropsychological Society, 4*, 380–387.

Simmonds, M., & Fleming, J. M. (2003). Occupational therapy assessment of self-awareness following traumatic brain injury. *British Journal of Occupational Therapy, 66*, 447–453.

Sohlberg, M. M., Mateer, C. A., Penkman, L., Gland, A., & Todis, B. (1998). Awareness intervention: Who needs it? *Journal of Head Trauma Rehabilitation, 13*, 62–78.

Starkstein, S. E., Fedoroff, J. P., Price, T. R., Leiguarda, R., & Robinson, R. G. (1993). Neuropsychological deficits in patients with anosognosia. *Neuropsychiatry, Neuropsychology and Behavioural Neurology, 6*, 43–48.

Starkstein, S. E., Vazquez, S., Migliorelli, R., Teson, A., Sabe, L., Leiguarda, R. (1995). A single-photon emission computed tomographic study of anosognosia in Alzheimer's disease. *Archives of Neurology, 52*, 415–420.

Stuss, D. T. (1991). Disturbance of self-awareness after frontal system damage. In G. P. Prigatano & D. L. Schacter (Eds.), *Awareness of deficit after brain injury: Clinical and theoretical issues* (pp. 63–83). New York: Oxford University Press.

Stuss, D. T., & Benson, D. F. (1986). *The Frontal Lobes.* New York: Raven Press.

Stuss, D. T., Picton, T. W., & Alexander, M. P. (2001). Consciousness, self-awareness and the frontal lobes. In S. Salloway, P. Malloy, & J. Duffy (Eds.), *The frontal lobes and neuropsychiatric illness* (pp. 101–109). Washington DC: American Psychiatric Press.

Toglia, J., & Kirk, U. (2000). Understanding awareness deficits following brain injury. *NeuroRehabilitation, 15*, 57–70.

Trosset, M. W., & Kaszniak, A. W. (1996). Measures of deficit unawareness for predicted performance experiments. *Journal of the International Neuropsychological Society, 2*, 315–322.

Trudel, T. M., Tryon, W. W., & Purdum, C. M. (1998). Awareness of disability and long-term outcome after traumatic brain injury. *Rehabilitation Psychology, 43*, 267–281.

Van Weilingen, L. E., Tuokko, H. A., Cramer, K., Mateer, C. A., & Hultsch, D. F. (2004). Awareness of financial skills in dementia. *Aging and Mental Health, 8*, 374–380.

Vuilleumier, P. (2004). Anosognosia: The neurology of beliefs and uncertainties. *Cortex, 40*, 9–17.

Weinstein, E. A. (1991). Anosognosia and denial of illness. In G. P. Prigatano & D. L. Schacter (Eds.), *Awareness of deficit after brain injury: Clinical and theoretical issues* (pp. 240–257). New York: Oxford University Press.

Weinstein, E. A., Friedland, R. P., & Wagner, E. E. (1994). Denial/unawareness of impairment and symbolic behaviour in Alzheimer's disease. *Neuropsychiatry, Neuropsychology and Behavioural Neurology, 3*, 176–184.

Weinstein, E. A., & Kahn, R. L. (1955). *Denial of illness: Symbolic and physiological aspects.* Springfield, IL: Charles C Thomas.

Zaitchik, D., & Albert, M. (2004). Cognition and emotion. In R. Morris & J. Becker, (Eds.), *Cognitive neuropsychology of Alzheimer's disease* (2nd ed., pp 267–274) Oxford: Oxford University Press.

Zeman, A. (2001). Consciousness. *Brain, 124*, 1263–1289.

NEUROPSYCHOLOGICAL REHABILITATION
2006, 16 (4), 439–455

# Approaches to the assessment of awareness: Conceptual issues

Ivana S. Marková[1] and German E. Berrios[2]

[1]*Department of Psychiatry, University of Hull, Hull, UK*
[2]*Department of Psychiatry, University of Cambridge, Cambridge, UK*

Recent interest in the empirical exploration of patients' awareness in relation to their clinical states has resulted in a range of approaches taken to evaluate such awareness. These approaches vary in terms of the bases on which awareness is determined and rated, the contents of the measures used, the level of detail and complexity of judgements required, etc. The approaches use different *definitions* and *objects* of awareness and hence give rise to different (and on occasions divergent) awareness phenomena. Such differences help to explain both the contradictory nature of published results and the difficulties involved in generalising from them. In practical terms, these differences should encourage the development of management and rehabilitation strategies that are individual to specific phenomena of awareness.

## INTRODUCTION

Exploration of awareness of disease can be focused on "awareness in relation to" or "awareness of" a clinical state. The purpose of the former is to learn about the way in which a patient relates (or has insight into) his clinical condition; it is an experiential enquiry that helps to determine specific treatment or rehabilitation strategies. The purpose of the latter is to outline (with the help of the patient), in a qualitative sense, a specific clinical phenomenon, e.g., phantom limb syndrome. In other words, although the intention of both these (overlapping) perspectives is to delineate the perception of a

Correspondence should be sent to Dr. Ivana S. Marková, Department of Psychiatry, University of Hull, Hertford Building, Cottingham Road, Hull, HU6 7RX. Tel: +44 1482 464564. E-mail: ismarkova@psych.hi-net.co.uk



http://www.psypress.com/neurorehab DOI:10.1080/09602010500373396

patient, the first one seeks to evaluate his/her understanding and the second to describe the clinical phenomena he/she is suffering from. This paper will concentrate essentially only on the first perspective, namely, on the approaches taken to explore patients' awareness or insight in relation to their clinical states.

The aim of this paper is to identify some of the conceptual problems affecting the assessment of patients' awareness or insight into their clinical states. The first section will deal with definitions; the second with a review of the clinical approaches developed to explore patients' awareness; and the third with an analysis of the differences involved and with their implications for the understanding of insight, clinical practice and future research.

## TERMS AND CONCEPTS

Over the past 15 years there has been much interest in the empirical exploration of patients' awareness or insight into psychoses (Amador & David, 2004; Marková & Berrios, 1995a), brain syndromes following head injury and cerebrovascular accidents (Prigatano & Schacter, 1991), and chronic organic brain syndromes such as dementia (Marková & Berrios, 2000). This empirical work has been concerned mainly with the relationship between patients' awareness and various clinical (e.g., severity/type/duration of disorder, symptom patterns, neuropsychological performance, prognosis, brain lesions, etc.) and socio-demographic (age of onset, gender, hospitalisations, personality, etc.) variables in order to determine the extent to which impaired awareness might be related to the disease process itself and/or whether other non-disease factors are important. Results have been variable and inconsistent (Marková & Berrios, 1995a; 2000). In addition to differences in methods and measures, this variability is likely to have resulted from differences in the definitions of awareness or insight which seem to range from the more basic (i.e., direct perception or recognition of a problem such as loss of function of a limb, memory problems, etc.) to the more complex (i.e., in addition to the perception of a problem, further-judgements are demanded concerning the nature of the problem, e.g., judging the morbidity of mental symptoms, their effects on social function, etc.).

Further complications arise from the inconsistent use of terms. For example, poor awareness may be referred to as "unawareness", "lack of insight", "impaired self-awareness", "anosognosia", "denial", and "impaired self-consciousness" and any of these terms can be used in the context of schizophrenia, amnesia, hemiplegia or dementia. More seriously, the *same term* has been used to refer to different sorts of concepts (e.g., "lack of insight" could refer to both a lack or perception of a deficit as well as to a lack of an understanding of the nature and consequences of a problem) and, equally, *different terms* have been used to refer to a similar sort of concept (e.g., "unawareness", "poor insight", "anosognosia", "denial", etc., used interchangeably to refer to a particular concept of lack of recognition of problems). The interchangeable use of related terms ostensibly referring to one concept is particularly apparent in studies exploring insight in chronic organic brain syndromes (e.g., Verhey, Rozendaal, Ponds, & Jolles, 1993). And even when conceptual distinctions are made (e.g., Reed, Jagust, & Coulter, 1993; Vasterling, Seltzer, Foss, & Vanderbrook, 1995; Weinstein, Friedland, & Wagner, 1994), they are inconsistent in regards to the content of the ensuing conceptual categories (Marková et al., 2005). In this paper, the terms "awareness" and "insight" are both used to refer to the understanding the patient has about a particular clinical state. Since there is no room for discussion around possible mechanisms underlying insight, the concept of "denial" in the motivated sense (Weinstein & Kahn, 1955) will not be addressed here.

An important distinction to define at this point is that between (1) the *theoretical concept* of insight (or awareness) and (2) the *clinical phenomenon* of insight (or awareness). This distinction has been made elsewhere (Marková & Berrios, 1995a, 1995b; 2001) and here it is explained only briefly. The *concept* refers to insight as a whole, i.e., to a construct whose structure and components can be (and are) theoretically defined; and it accommodates current and past (and future) meanings and conceptualisations of insight. The *phenomenon* of insight, on the other hand, refers to the clinical manifestation (or elicitation) of what can, necessarily, be only an aspect of the concept of insight. The concept is thus wider than the phenomenon and provides the framework against which individual phenomena of insight (or awareness) can be delineated and understood. The importance of distinguishing between the concept and the phenomenon lies not only in highlighting that the clinical phenomenon may not necessarily reflect everything that is entailed by conceptualisation of insight as a whole, but allows for a more structured translation from theory to practice by identifying specific components of insight which may or may not be amenable to particular forms of clinical capture. In addition, however, separation of the clinical phenomenon from the concept enables the identification of other factors contributing to the structure of the phenomenon. Such factors, as will be seen later, include the contribution made by the clinicians and/or tests to the phenomenon obtained. This is particularly important when determining differences between different insight or awareness phenomena.

One further conceptual clarification relevant for the discussion on measures of awareness concerns the relational aspects of awareness or insight. Again, this has been presented in detail elsewhere (Marková, 2005; Marková & Berrios, 2001) but the important issue to cmphasise here is that insight (or awareness) is a *relational* concept—or an "intentional" concept in the sense of Brentano (1874/1973). It can only be understood or expressed in terms of its relation to something, be that a pathological state or a non-morbid experience. One cannot have insight (or awareness) without there being something to have insight about and this "something" has already been referred to as the "object" of insight assessment (Marková & Berrios, 2001). The "object", therefore, refers to the particular mental/physical state (e.g., mental symptoms, mental illness, neurological abnormality, neuropsychological deficit, particular behaviours, functional skills, etc.) in relation to which insight or awareness is being assessed. The "object" of insight assessment has a crucial role in determining and shaping the clinical *phenomenon* of insight. In other words, different "objects" of insight/awareness assessment (e.g., memory impairment, schizophrenia, hallucinations, personality changes, dementia) will help to determine phenomena of insight/awareness that are different, in important ways, from one another. The ways in which "objects" of insight assessment are able to shape phenomena have been described elsewhere (Marková, 2005; Marková & Berrios, 2001). In brief, however, firstly the "object" of insight is embedded within the conceptual framework guiding a particular discipline and this will naturally impose a similar structure on the phenomenon of insight elicited within that discipline (e.g., general psychiatry, neuropsychology, neurology, psychodynamic psychology, etc.). Secondly, the semantic category to which the "object" of insight assessment belongs (i.e., the sort of term the "object" refers to, Ryle, 1949/1990) will exert its particular structure on the ensuing phenomenon of insight. This is particularly apparent when considering the difference in order of meaning between "objects" referring to a wide multifactorial construct such as "mental illness" and those referring to a narrower "objectively" determined concept such as neurological or neuropsychological impairment. Thirdly, the specific nature of the "object" of insight assessment determines to some extent the sort of insight phenomenon that will be elicited. In this context, the question whether the "object" refers to a subjective mental state (e.g., depressed mood, hearing voices, feeling persecuted, etc.) or a so-called "objective" state (e.g., hemiplegia, amnesia, dysphasia, etc.), is particularly important.

## CURRENT ASSESSMENTS OF AWARENESS

Evident in the increasing numbers of studies exploring awareness/insight in patients both between and within different clinical areas and professional disciplines is the range of approaches taken to assess and measure awareness and insight. Comprehensive reviews of such approaches have been provided in relation to patients with dementia (Clare, Marková, Verhey, & Kenny, 2005), patients with general psychiatric disorders (Amador & David, 2004; Marková & Berrios, 1995a) and in patients with various neurological problems, particularly head injury (Prigatano & Schacter, 1991). A review of the current approaches to assessing awareness in relation to all such clinical areas would be beyond the scope of this paper. Given the remit of the journal, the focus here, therefore, will be on examining some of the different approaches taken to explore awareness in relation to neuropsychological impairments particularly in relation to dementia. Since the intention here is to raise and explore some of the specific conceptual problems associated with the empirical assessment of awareness, the review is limited to illustrating some of the main differences in methodologies employed. Fully comprehensive reviews of assessments of awareness can be found elsewhere (e.g., Clare et al., 2005). In broad terms, approaches to assess patients' awareness in relation to different clinical states can be divided into three main groups, namely, (1) clinician rated, (2) discrepancy methods, (3) composite methods including other specific measures. Each of these will be examined in turn.

## Clinician-rated evaluations of patients' awareness

In earlier studies, and based on loosely defined clinical judgements, clinicians categorised patients as having or not having awareness into their condition, e.g., dementia (Aminoff, Marshall, Smith, & Wyke, 1975; Gustafson & Nilsson, 1982; Neary et al., 1986). More recently, however, attempts have focused on developing more systematic methods of assessing awareness. Such approaches can be distinguished in terms of the following.

1. The basis on which ratings are made. Thus, ratings may be obtained from: structured or semi-structured interviews (Loebel, Dager, Berg, & Hyde, 1990; Seltzer, Vasterling & Buswell, 1995a; Sevush & Leve, 1993; Verhey et al., 1993; Weinstein et al., 1994), clinician-rated scales with set criteria (Cutting, 1978; Bisiach et al., 1986; Ott & Fogel, 1992; Starkstein et al., 1992), or clinician or patient-rated structured questionnaires (Feher, Larrabee, Sudilovsky, & Crook, 1994; Gil et al., 2001; Levine, Calvanio, & Rinn, 1991; Sevush, 1999).

2. The way in which ratings are made. Ratings range from simple dichotomous divisions (e.g., awareness or anosognosia are described as present or absent) (Cutting, 1978; Hier, Mondlock, & Caplan, 1983a, 1983b; Loebel et al., 1990; Lopez et al., 1994; Seltzer, Vasterling, Hale, & Khurana, 1995b) to multiple categorisations based on several point scales (e.g., in recognition of "partial" insight or "mild" denial) (Bisiach et al., 1986, Cappa, Sterzi, Vallar, & Bisiach, 1987; Sevush & Leve, 1993; Verhey et al., 1993; Weinstein et al., 1994) to continuous

scores on scales (Ott & Fogel, 1992; Gil et al., 2001). The divisions between the categories are determined by researcher-set criteria which vary from study to study. For example, Sevush and Leve (1993), on the basis of their interview of patients with Alzheimer's disease, categorise patients into having *no insight*, i.e., no acknowledgement of memory impairment; or *partial insight*, i.e., showing some awareness of the presence of memory impairment but not its full extent; or *full insight*, i.e. acknowledgement of both the presence and severity of the memory impairment. On the other hand, McDaniel et al. (1995), using the CERAD (Consortium to Establish a Registry for Alzheimer's Disease) structured interview, emphasise a different categorisation: *normal insight*, i.e., total insight into the illness and implications; or *partial awareness* of disease or implications; and *unawareness or denial* of symptoms of illness.

3. The methods employed to elicit the ratings of awareness. Some clinician judgements are based on interviews with patients only (Sevush & Leve, 1993; Weinstein et al., 1994; McDaniel et al., 1995) but others are based also on information from carers/relatives (Loebel et al., 1990; Ott & Fogel, 1992; Verhey et al., 1993). On the other hand, some researchers have determined patients' insight on the basis of information from case notes only (Auchus, Goldstein, Green, & Green, 1994; Lopez et al., 1994; Reed et al., 1993).
4. The contents of the measures themselves. Differences here can be seen in terms of both the "object" of awareness assessment (e.g., memory impairment, hemiplegia, independent living activities, dementia, etc.) and the types of judgements demanded from the patients (e.g., severity of problem, frequency of difficulties, comparison with the past, etc.). These will be discussed in more detail below as they apply to all the approaches taken to assess awareness.

## Discrepancy measures evaluating patients' awareness

Discrepancy measures have been particularly important in the exploration of patients' awareness following head injury (Allen & Ruff, 1990; Oddy, Coughlan, Tyerman, & Jenkins, 1985; Prigatano et al., 1986; Sherer et al., 1998; Sunderland, Harris, & Gleave, 1984) and in the dementias (Clare et al., 2005). Levels of awareness or insight are determined on the basis of discrepancies between the patient's assessment of abilities and either: (1) the carer's (relative's) assessment of the patient's abilities (De Bettignies, Mahurin, & Pirozzolo, 1990; Feher et al., 1991; Michon et al., 1994; Prigatano et al., 1986; Smith et al., 2000; Sunderland et al., 1984; Vasterling et al., 1995), or

(2) "objective" measures of impairment, such as a battery of neuropsychological tests (Anderson & Tranel, 1989; Dalla Barba, Parlato, Iavarone, & Boller, 1995; Kopelman, Stanhope, & Guinan, 1998; Wagner, Spangenberg, Bachman, & O'Connell, 1997), or (3) a combination of both forms of discrepancy assessments (Clare et al., 2002; Correa, Graves, & Costa, 1996; Duke, Seltzer, Seltzer & Vasterling, 2002; Green, Goldstein, Sirockman, & Green, 1993; Kapur & Pearson, 1983; McGlynn & Kaszniak, 1991a, 1991b). Discrepancy methods are based on the assumption that an "accurate" assessment of an individual's functioning (the gold standard) can be obtained either directly through the observations of another person or indirectly by means of scores on performance in certain tasks. Such assessments are then compared with the patients' own assessments of their functioning and any discrepancy found between patients' ratings and carers' ratings or test scores is attributed to the patient's lack of awareness or insight into such functioning. Consequently, the greater the discrepancy obtained, the greater the degree of unawareness or lack of insight shown by the patient. Since the questionnaires or tests involved are scored (e.g., total score on patient-rated questionnaire subtracted from total score on carer-rated questionnaire, or ratios are calculated in relation to test scores), then discrepancies have ranges of values and hence awareness or insight is quantified along a continuum of scores. Some researchers, however, while calculating such scores, subsequently set a cut-off point below which patients are said to show or not show awareness (e.g., Migliorelli et al., 1995).

As far as awareness assessments using patient–carer discrepancies are concerned, then the main differences between such measures relate to the different contents of such measures—both in terms of the "objects" of awareness concerned and also the nature of the judgements demanded of patients and carers. For example, in relation to traumatic brain injury, the Patient Competency Rating Scale (Prigatano, Fordyce, Zeiner, Roueche, Pepping, & Wood, 1986) assesses discrepancies between patients and carers in judgements relating to activities of daily living, cognitive functioning, interpersonal functioning and emotional regulation. Ratings are scored on a Likert scale ranging from 1 (cannot do) to 5 (can do with ease) and scores from carers/clinicians are subtracted from patient scores. Gasquoine and Gibbons (1994), on the other hand, explore discrepancies between patients and staff ratings in areas relating to head injury, physical impairment, communication difficulties, functional impairment and sensory/cognitive impairment. Different again is the Awareness Questionnaire developed by Sherer et al. (1998) which likewise evaluates patients' awareness on the basis of discrepancies between patients and relatives and/or clinician ratings but the judgements demanded by this questionnaire relate to comparing current and pre-injury functioning. In relation to studies exploring awareness in dementia, the differences between the "objects" of awareness assessment are particularly striking.

Thus, some questionnaires are focused on activities of daily living and patients and carers are required to rate the patients' abilities in those particular areas (De Bettignies et al., 1990; Mangone et al., 1991) while other questionnaires focus on memory and/or other cognitive problems (e.g., Feher et al., 1991; Michon et al., 1994; Seltzer et al., 1995b) and still others use questionnaires addressing both these areas (e.g., Seltzer, Vasterling, Yoder, & Thompson, 1997) and additional areas such as mood changes, behavioural problems and others (e.g., Deckel & Morrison, 1996; Kotler-Cope & Camp, 1995; Smith et al., 2000; Snow et al., 2004; Starkstein et al., 1995; Vasterling et al., 1995).

In addition, the types of judgements demanded by the measures also vary. For example, some questionnaires focusing on awareness of memory problems, ask patients (with parallel questions for carers) to rate the degree of severity of problems they perceive as having with their memory (Green et al., 1993; Duke et al., 2002) while other questionnaires ask patients to rate their memory compared with some years previously (McGlynn & Kaszniak, 1991a, 1991b; Michon et al., 1994) or even with others of a similar age (Deckel & Morrison, 1996) or to rate the frequency with which they make mistakes in various memory-related tasks (Derouesné et al., 1999; Migliorelli et al., 1995; Seltzer et al., 1995b) and some studies include various mixtures of such types of judgements (Clare et al., 2002; Feher et al., 1991). On the other hand, the memory questionnaire devised by Kopelman et al. (1998), to explore memory complaints in patients with various focal organic lesions, focuses on judgements concerning premorbid, recent and prospective memories. In other words, as is the case with discrepancy measures used in head injury, there are differences in "objects" of awareness assessment and the types of judgements demanded from patients (and carers) between the various measures.

Apart from their variety, questionnaire discrepancy measures raise issues concerning validity. One such issue relates to the extent to which a carer/relative can be expected to provide an accurate evaluation of a patient's functioning in different areas. For various reasons, carers may both overestimate or underestimate levels of impairments in patients. In general, studies exploring the "accuracy" of carers' evaluations of patients in different areas have found reasonably good correlations between carers' assessments and other measures of patients' functioning. In relation to memory assessments, for example, in contrast to patients' own evaluations, carers' evaluations of patients' difficulties have correlated significantly with neuropsychological tests of memory function in these patients (Grut et al., 1993; Koss et al., 1993; McGlone, Gupta, Humphrey, & Oppenheimer, 1990). However, some qualifications have been made by researchers. Jorm et al. (1994) found that carers' ratings were influenced by depression and anxiety in the carers and McLoughlin, Cooney, Holmes, and Levy (1996) found that the type of carer involved related directly to the accuracy of carer evaluations as compared with neuropsychology tests. They reported that spouses' evaluations were more "accurate" than first degree relatives' evaluations and that second degree relatives' evaluations of patients' memory had no significant correlations with memory tests. Likewise, in relation to exploring awareness of independent living activities, carers/relatives' evaluations of patient function have been more strongly correlated with "objective" tests of activities of daily living than patients' evaluations (Kuriansky, Gurland, & Fleiss, 1976). However, again some researchers have suggested that carers experiencing a greater burden of care were less accurate and were underestimating patients' level of functioning (De Bettignies et al., 1990). Similar findings have been reported in relation to assessment of depressive symptoms (Burke et al., 1998).

Discrepancy methods using performances on "objective" psychometric tests, rather than carers' assessments, as the gold standard against which patients' awareness is derived are complicated by other issues. For example, as Trosset and Kaszniak (1996) point out, there is poor correspondence between what is assessed by specific detailed neuropsychological tests and the assessments of memory problems in daily life that are asked of patients. Attempts have been made to reduce this particular problem by the use of prediction and/or postdiction discrepancy methods. In the former, specific neuropsychological tests (e.g., recall of word lists) are explained to patients and they are asked to predict how they would perform on such tests and the discrepancies between patient predictions and actual performance are taken as measures of patient awareness (Green et al., 1993; McGlynn & Kaszniak, 1991a, 1991b). In the latter, the patients perform the tests and afterwards are asked to rate how well they have performed and discrepancies between their judgements and performances are thus calculated (Correa et al., 1996). In acknowledgement of the problems involved in making judgements around such specialised psychometric test performance, some researchers have incorporated patients' evaluations of carers' performances on the same tests and carers' evaluations of their own performance and patients' performances (McGlynn & Kaszniak, 1991a,b; Duke et al., 2002).

## Composite and other methods

Other approaches have employed combinations of both clinician-rated assessments and discrepancy measures in an attempt to provide a more global and comprehensive picture of awareness or insight (Correa et al., 1996; Derouesné et al., 1999; Howorth & Saper, 2003; Ott et al., 1996). In addition, some studies have included novel ways of assessing awareness. For example, Giovanetti, Libon, and Hart (2002) in addition to using discrepancy measures also included a clinician-rated evaluation of patients' insight that was based on directly observable behaviours (videotaped). In this latter situation, awareness was inferred on the basis of patients' reactions to and attempts at self-corrections of mistakes occurring during the course of three set everyday tasks. Clare (2003), on the other hand, attempted to assess awareness in more depth by exploring patients' awareness in detailed interviews focusing on patients' understanding in the context of their individual and social backgrounds.

## THE PHENOMENON OF AWARENESS AS DETERMINED BY EMPIRICAL MEASURES

A number of approaches to assessing awareness in patients have been described and it is clear that there are marked differences in methods used both between the various approaches as well as within a particular type of approach. The question here, however, is what do such differences in methods for assessing awareness mean for the phenomenon of awareness that is elicited?

Earlier, the phenomenon of awareness/insight was defined as the clinical aspect of awareness or insight that was manifested or elicited as opposed to the theoretical concept of insight as a whole which, in practical terms, would be difficult to capture in its entirety. Examining the different approaches taken to assess awareness clinically, it is evident from the above that the phenomena of awareness determined by the various measures are likely to be different. There is also some empirical confirmation of this in that studies using different measures of awareness concomitantly have obtained different clinical outcomes in relation to the particular measure of awareness used (Derouesné et al., 1999; Duke et al., 2002; Green et al., 1993; Howorth & Saper, 2003; Sanz et al., 1998; Sevush, 1999). If the clinical phenomena of awareness are different in relation to the different approaches taken to evaluate awareness, questions then follow concerning the nature of such differences and the implications they carry for understanding insight, in terms of its structure, its role in disease states and in terms of its practical application in relation to communication with and management of patients with various disabilities.

Since phenomena of awareness are determined, in clinical terms, by the various measures of awareness described above, it is important to examine some of the differences between the measures. The latter vary in content, perspective, level of detail, complexity, how ratings are determined, who does the ratings, etc. In broad terms, however, these attributes can be divided into those relating to *content* and those relating to the *form* in which the evaluation takes place.

## Content and its determinations

Turning first to the contents, the question is what determines them? There are two inter-related factors that need to be considered here. First, the contents of the awareness measures must be dependent on the conceptualisation of insight held by the researchers (and the level of correspondence between this and an empirical translation) and, second, the "object" of awareness assessment itself will determine to some extent the content of the awareness measure. The problem of a lack of consistency in the conceptualisation of insight has already been raised. However, and despite the interchangeable use of related terms, there does emerge from the work reviewed in this area, a general *conceptual distinction* between insight as a concept in the *narrow* sense (i.e., solely concentrated on awareness or perception of a problem) and insight in a *wider* sense (i.e., involving other sorts of judgements in addition to the awareness of a problem) (Marková, 2005; Marková & Berrios, 1995a, 1995b). While it is apparent that the narrow and wide concepts are continuous it may be useful here to refer to them as "*awareness*" and "*insight*", respectively. The clinical phenomena of awareness/insight will, therefore, likewise reflect the narrow or wider conceptualisations held by the researchers. "Objects" of awareness assessment range from specific neurological or neuropsychological impairments (e.g., hemiplegia, amnesic syndromes, dysphasia, etc.) to diagnostic constructs (e.g., dementia, schizophrenia, brain injury) to subjective mental symptoms (depressive mood, hallucinations, delusions, irritability) to admixtures of behaviours/personality characteristics as well as to "normal" functioning. Each of these types of "objects" will determine different types of clinical phenomena of awareness or insight and the measures used to capture these reflect this. Thus, "objects" referring to specific neurological or neuropsychological deficits determine narrower phenomena of awareness than "objects", for example, referring to subjective mental states (Marková, 2005; Marková & Berrios, 2001).

In practical terms, this means that the phenomenon of awareness, as conceived in the narrow sense, and determined by an "object" likely to refer to a specific deficit or impairment, will be focused on the degree of perception of the "object" itself and the judgements constituting the phenomenon will be directed specifically at features of the particular "object" (e.g., *severity* of memory problem, *frequency* with which memory problem interferes with normal activities, *comparison* of memory difficulty with *past* function or with *contemporaries*, etc.). In contrast, the phenomenon of insight, as conceived in the wider sense, and, determined by "objects" relating more to subjective mental states, will be focused on a wider understanding the individual has concerning the particular "object". In this case awareness of the subjective state, is assumed by definition and judgements constituting the phenomenon will be directed at the sense the individual makes of the subjective experience, such as depression (e.g., the degree to which the experience is viewed as pathological, the way in which it affects feelings/activities relating to the self, etc.) (Marková & Berrios, 1995b). Measures of awareness or insight, depending on the conceptualisation of insight and the "object" of insight assessment chosen, will thus capture phenomena that are correspondingly narrow or wider and whose structures show significant differences in terms of their constitutive judgements.

## Form and its determinants

In regards to the *form* taken by awareness measures, a variety of different approaches are in use. Some approaches involve judgements made by clinicians on direct exploration of insight with patients either by means of interviews or scales; others concern indirect evaluations of patients by clinicians on the basis of questionnaires or examination of clinical notes. Yet other approaches involve comparisons of judgements with those of carers or relatives or as against specific test performance.

Differences in *form* have a direct bearing on the structure of the phenomena of awareness that are obtained. In this case, the phenomena elicited will vary in terms of the contribution made to their structure by the external individual or test. The forms of awareness measures chosen determine the type and extent of interpretation provided by the clinician/relative/test. For example, a clinician judging a patient as having or not having awareness or having "partial" awareness on the basis of loose criteria is likely to contribute more to the phenomenon of awareness elicited by means of his/her personal judgements than a clinician adding up scores on a patient-rated questionnaire. Similarly, it is likely that a greater contribution to the phenomenon of awareness is made by clinician judgements when these are based on case notes. On the other hand, in an interview situation, there will be the added contribution of the interactive process itself that helps to shape and define the awareness/insight phenomenon elicited (Marková & Berrios, 1995a, 1995b). The "object" of insight assessment also plays a part in the form of the insight measure in that "objects" refer to different kinds of "data" in relation to which awareness/insight is being determined. "Loss of function" in a leg or an obvious "speech problem" present as more directly observable "data" on which clinicians can make comparative judgements than objects such as "depressed mood" or even certain behaviours or personality attributes. In other words, the extent of interpretation by the clinician will also depend on the nature of the "object" of insight assessment and thus contribute to the phenomenon of insight elicited.

## CONCLUSION

In conclusion, approaches taken to explore patients' awareness or insight in relation to various clinical states have been determined by both the particular conceptualisation of insight held by the researchers and by the "object" of insight assessment, i.e., the clinical state or aspect of clinical state chosen in relation to which insight is examined. Differences in both these factors have contributed to the wide range of different insight measures offered. In turn, the different approaches taken to assess awareness result in different phenomena of awareness elicited. Differences between phenomena of awareness and/or insight are important because they are structural differences, referring to different types and contents of judgements constituting the phenomena and incorporating to varying extents additional external judgements.

The differences between phenomena of awareness or insight elicited by the various measures carry implications for future research on awareness and insight as well as for the management and rehabilitation of patients showing impaired awareness into their disabilities. In terms of the former, studies seeking to explore mechanisms underlying impaired awareness or poor insight in patients, whether looking at possible neurobiology or psychological and other factors, need to be clear concerning the specific phenomenon of awareness that is being examined. In this sense, it may not be valid to generalise between studies exploring different awareness phenomena. In terms of management and rehabilitation of patients with poor insight into their disabilities, then likewise, it is important to understand as clearly as possible the structure of the phenomenon under study. Communication and management strategies will depend on having an understanding of the phenomenon in terms of the types of disturbed perceptions and/or judgements held in relation to different impairments and problems.

## REFERENCES


Allen, C. C., & Ruff, R. M. (1990). Self-rating versus neuropsychological performance of moderate versus severe head-injured patients. *Brain Injury*, *4*, 7–17.

Amador, X., & David, A. (2004). *Insight and psychosis: Awareness of illness in schizophrenia and related disorders*. Oxford: Oxford University Press.

Aminoff, M. J., Marshall, J., Smith, E. M., & Wyke, M. A. (1975). Pattern of intellectual impairment in Huntington's chorea. *Psychological Medicine*, *5*, 169–172.

Anderson, S. W., & Tranel, D. (1989). Awareness of disease states following cerebral infarction, dementia and head trauma: Standardized assessment. *The Clinical Neuropsychologist*, *3*, 327–339.

Auchus, A. P., Goldstein, F. C., Green, J., & Green, R. C. (1994). Unawareness of cognitive impairments in Alzheimer's disease. *Neuropsychiatry Neuropsychology, and Behavioral Neurology*, *7*, 25–29.

Bisiach, E., Vallar, G., Perani, D., Papagno, C., & Berti, A. (1986). Unawareness of disease following lesions of the right hemisphere: Anosognosia for hemiplegia and anosognosia for hemianopia. *Neuropsychologia, 24*, 471–482.

Blonder, L. X., & Ranseen, J. D. (1994). Awareness of deficit following right hemisphere stroke. *Neuropsychiatry, Neuropsychology, and Behavioral Neurology, 7*, 260–266.

Brentano, F. (1973). *Psychology from an empirical standpoint*. Trans. Rancurello, A. C., Terrell, D. B., & McAlister, L. L. London: Routledge and Kegan Paul (1st ed., 1874).

Burke, W. J., Roccaforte, W. H., Wengel, S. P., McArthur-Miller, D., Folks, D. G., & Potter, J. F. (1998). Disagreement in the reporting of depressive symptoms between patients with dementia of the Alzheimer type and their collateral sources. *American Journal of Geriatric Psychiatry, 6*, 308–319.

Cappa, S., Sterzi, R., Vallar, G., & Bisiach, E. (1987). Remission of hemineglect and anosognosia during vestibular stimulation. *Neuropsychologia, 25*, 775–782.

Clare, L. (2003). Managing threats to self: Awareness in early stage Alzheimer's disease. *Social Science and Medicine, 57*, 1017–1029.

Clare, L., Marková, I. S., Verhey, F., & Kenny, G. (2005). Awareness in dementia: A review of assessment methods and measures. *Aging and Mental Health, 9*, 394–413.

Clare, L., Wilson, B. A., Carter, G., Roth, I., & Hodges, J. R. (2002). Assessing awareness in early-stage Alzheimer's disease: Development and piloting of the Memory Awareness Rating Scale. *Neuropsychological Rehabilitation, 12*, 341–362.

Correa, D. D., Graves, R. E., & Costa, L. (1996). Awareness of memory deficit in Alzheimer's disease patients and memory-impaired older adults. *Aging, Neuropsychology and Cognition, 3*, 215–228.

Cutting, J. (1978). Study of anosognosia. *Journal of Neurology, Neurosurgery and Psychiatry, 41*, 548–555.

Dalla Barba, G., Parlato, V., Iavarone, A., & Boller, F. (1995). Anosognosia, intrusions and "frontal" functions in Alzheimer's disease and depression. *Neuropsychologia, 33*, 247–259.

De Bettignies, B. H., Mahurin, R. K., & Pirozzolo, F. J. (1990). Insight for impairment in independent living skills in Alzheimer's disease and multi-infarct dementia. *Journal of Clinical and Experimental Neuropsychology, 12*, 355–363.

Deckel, A. W., & Morrison, D. (1996). Evidence of a neurologically based 'denial of illness' in patients with Huntington's disease. *Archives of Clinical Neuropsychology, 11*, 295–302.

Derouesné, C., Thibault, S., Lagha-Pierucci, S., Baudouin-Madec, V., Ancri, D., & Lacomblez, L. (1999). Decreased awareness of cognitive deficit in patients with mild dementia of the Alzheimer's type. *International Journal of Geriatric Psychiatry, 14*, 1019–1030.

Duke, L., Seltzer, B., Seltzer, J. E., & Vasterling, J. J. (2002). Cognitive components of deficit awareness in Alzheimer's disease. *Neuropsychology, 16*, 359–369.

Feher, E. P., Larrabee, G. J., Sudilovsky, A., & Crook, T. H. (1994). Memory self-report in Alzheimer's disease and in age-associated memory impairment. *Journal of Geriatrics, Psychiatry and Neurology, 7*, 58–65.

Feher, E. P., Mahurin, R. K., Inbody, S. B., Crook, T. H., & Pirozzolo, F. J. (1991). Anosognosia in Alzheimer's disease. *Neuropsychiatry, Neuropsychology and Behavioral Neurology, 4*, 136–146.

Gasquoine, P. G., & Gibbons, T. A. (1994). Lack of awareness of impairment in institutionalized, severely, and chronically disabled survivors of traumatic brain injury: A preliminary investigation. *Journal of Head Trauma Rehabilitation, 9*, 16–24.

Gil, R., Arroyo-Anllo, E. M., Ingrand, P., Gil, M., Neau, J. P., Ornon, C., & Bonnaud, V. (2001). Self-consciousness and Alzheimer's disease. *Acta Neurologica Scandinavica, 104*, 296–300.

Giovannetti, T., Libon, D. J., & Hart, T. (2002). Awareness of naturalistic action errors in dementia. *Journal of the International Neuropsychological Society, 8*, 633–644.

Green, J., Goldstein, F. C., Sirockman, B. E., & Green, R. C. (1993). Variable awareness of deficits in Alzheimer's disease. *Neuropsychiatry, Neuropsychology and Behavioral Neurology*, *6*, 159–165.

Grut, M., Jorm, A. F., Fratiglioni, L., Forsell, Y., Viitanen, M., & Winblad, B. (1993). Memory complaints of elderly people in a population survey: Variation according to dementia stage and depression. *Journal of the American Geriatrics Society*, *41*, 1295–1300.

Gustafson, L., & Nilsson, L. (1982). Differential diagnosis of presenile dementia on clinical grounds. *Acta Psychiatrica Scandinavica*, *65*, 194–209.

Hier, D. B., Mondlock, J., & Caplan, L. R. (1983a). Behavioral abnormalities after right hemisphere stroke. *Neurology*, *33*, 337–344.

Hier, D. B., Mondlock, J., & Caplan, L. R. (1983b). Recovery of behavioral abnormalities after right hemisphere stroke. *Neurology*, *33*, 345–350.

Howorth, P., & Saper, J. (2003). The dimensions of insight in people with dementia. *Aging and Mental Health*, *7*, 113–122.

Jorm, A. F., Christensen, H., Henderson, A. S., Korten, A. E., Mackinnon, A. J., & Scott, R. (1994). Complaints of cognitive decline in the elderly: A comparison of reports by subjects and informants in a community survey. *Psychological Medicine*, *24*, 365–374.

Kapur, N., & Pearson, D. (1983). Memory symptoms and memory performance of neurological patients. *British Journal of Psychology*, *74*, 409–415.

Kopelman, M. D., Stanhope, N., & Guinan, E. (1998). Subjective memory evaluations in patients with focal frontal, diencephalic, and temporal lobe lesion. *Cortex*, *34*, 191–207.

Koss, E., Patterson, M. B., Ownby, R., Stuckey, J. C., & Whitehouse, P. J. (1993). Memory evaluation in Alzheimer's disease, caregivers' appraisals and objective testing. *Archives of Neurology*, *50*, 92–97.

Kotler-Cope, S., & Camp, C. J. (1995). Anosognosia in Alzheimer's disease. *Alzheimer Disease and Associated Disorders*, *9*, 52–56.

Kuriansky, J. B., Gurland, B. J., & Fleiss, J. L. (1976). The assessment of self-care capacity in geriatric psychiatric patients by objective and subjective methods. *Journal of Clinical Psychology*, *32*, 95–102.

Levine, D. N., Calvanio, R., & Rinn, W. E. (1991). The pathogenesis of anosognosia for hemiplegia. *Neurology*, *41*, 1770–1781.

Loebel, J. P., Dager, S. R., Berg, G., & Hyde, T. S. (1990). Fluency of speech and self-awareness of memory deficit in Alzheimer's disease. *International Journal of Geriatric Psychiatry*, *5*, 41–45.

Lopez, O. L., Becker, J. T., Somsak, D., Dew, M. A., & DeKosky, S. T. (1994). Awareness of cognitive deficits and anosognosia in probable Alzheimer's disease. *European Neurology*, *34*, 277–282.

Mangone, C. A., Hier, D. B., Gorelick, P. B., Ganellen, R. J., Langenberg, P., Boarman, R., & Dollear, W. C. (1991). Impaired insight in Alzheimer's disease. *Journal of Geriatric Psychiatry and Neurology*, *4*, 189–193.

Marková, I. S. (2005). *Insight in psychiatry*. Cambridge: Cambridge University Press.

Marková, I. S., & Berrios, G. E. (1995a). Insight in clinical psychiatry revisited. *Comprehensive Psychiatry*, *36*, 367–376.

Marková, I. S., & Berrios, G. E. (1995b). Insight in clinical psychiatry: A new model. *Journal of Nervous and Mental Disease*, *183*, 743–751.

Marková, I. S., & Berrios, G. E. (2000). Insight into memory deficits. In G. E. Berrios & J. R. Hodges (Eds.), *Memory disorders in psychiatric practice*. Cambridge, UK: Cambridge University Press.

Marková, I. S., & Berrios, G. E. (2001). The "Object" of insight assessment: Relationship to insight "structure". *Psychopathology*, *34*, 245–252.

Marková, I. S., Clare, L., Wang, M., Romero, B., & Kenny, G. (2005). Awareness in dementia: Conceptual issues. *Aging & Mental Health, 9*, 386–393.

McDaniel, K. D., Edland, S. D., Heyman, A., & the CERAD clinical investigators (1995). Relationship between level of insight and severity of dementia in Alzheimer disease. *Alzheimer Disease and Associated Disorders, 9*, 101–104.

McGlone, J., Gupta, S., Humphrey, D., & Oppenheimer, T. (1990). Screening for early dementia using memory complaints from patients and relatives. *Archives of Neurology, 47*, 1189–1193.

McGlynn, S. M., & Kaszniak, A. W. (1991a). When metacognition fails: Impaired awareness of deficit in Alzheimer's disease. *Journal of Cognitive Neuroscience, 3*, 183–189.

McGlynn, S. M., & Kaszniak, A. W. (1991b). Unawareness of deficits in dementia and schizophrenia. In G. P. Prigatano, & D. L. Schacter (Eds.) *Awareness of deficit after brain injury*, Oxford: Oxford University Press.

McLoughlin, D. M., Cooney, C., Holmes, C., & Levy, R. (1996). Carer informants for dementia sufferers: Carer awareness of cognitive impairment in an elderly community-resident sample. *Age and Ageing, 25*, 367–371.

Michon, A., Deweer, B., Pillon, B., Agid, Y., & Dubois, B. (1994). Relation of anosognosia to frontal lobe dysfunction in Alzheimer's disease. *Journal of Neurology, Neurosurgery and Psychiatry, 57*, 805–809.

Migliorelli, R., Tesón, A., Sabe, L., Petracca, G., Petracchi, M., Leiguarda, R., & Starkstein, S. E. (1995). Anosognosia in Alzheimer's disease: A study of associated factors. *Journal of Neuropsychiatry and Clinical Sciences, 7*, 338–344.

Neary, D., Snowden, J. S., Bowen, D. M., Sims, N. R., Mann, D. M. A., Benton, J. S., Northen, B., Yates, P. O., & Davison, A. N. (1986). Neuropsychological syndromes in presenile dementia due to cerebral atrophy. *Journal of Neurology, Neurosurgery and Psychiatry, 49*, 163–174.

Oddy, M., Coughlan, T., Tyerman, A., & Jenkins, D. (1985). Social adjustment after closed head injury: A further follow-up seven years after injury. *Journal of Neurology, Neurosurgery and Psychiatry, 48*, 564–568.

Ott, B. R., & Fogel, B. S. (1992). Measurement of depression in dementia: Self vs clinician rating. *International Journal of Geriatric Psychiatry, 7*, 899–904.

Ott, B. R., Lafleche, G., Whelihan, W. M., Buongiorno, G. W., Albert, M. S., & Fogel, B. S. (1996). Impaired awareness of deficits in Alzheimer disease. *Alzheimer Disease and Associated Disorders, 10*, 67–76.

Prigatano, G. P., Fordyce, D. J., Zeiner, H. K., Roueche, J. R., Pepping, M., & Wood, B. C. (1986). *Neuropsychological rehabilitation after brain injury*. Baltimore: Johns Hopkins University Press.

Prigatano, G. P., & Schacter, D. L. (Eds.) (1991). *Awareness of deficit after brain injury*. Oxford: Oxford University Press.

Reed, B. R., Jagust, W. J., & Coulter, L. (1993). Anosognosia in Alzheimer's disease: Relationships to depression, cognitive function, and cerebral perfusion. *Journal of Clinical and Experimental Neuropsychology, 15*, 231–244.

Ryle, G. (1949/1990). *The concept of mind*. Harmondsworth: Penguin Books.

Sanz, M., Constable, G., Lopez-Ibor, I., Kemp, R., & David, A. S. (1998). A comparative study of insight scales and their relationship to psychopathological and clinical variables. *Psychological Medicine, 28*, 437–446.

Seltzer, B., Vasterling, J. J., & Buswell, A. (1995a). Awareness of deficit in Alzheimer's disease: Association with psychiatric symptoms and other disease variables. *Journal of Clinical Geropsychology, 1*, 79–87.

Seltzer, B., Vasterling, J. J., Hale, M. A., & Khurana, R. (1995b). Unawareness of memory deficit in Alzheimer's disease: Relation to mood and other disease variables. *Neuropsychiatry, Neuropsychology and Behavioral Neurology, 8*, 176–181.

Seltzer, B., Vasterling, J. J., Yoder, J., & Thompson, K. A. (1997). Awareness of deficit in Alzheimer's disease: Relation to caregiver burden. *The Gerontologist*, *37*, 20–24.

Sevush, S. (1999). Relationship between denial of memory deficit and dementia severity in Alzheimer's disease. *Neuropsychiatry, Neuropsychology & Behavioral Neurology*, *12*, 88–94.

Sevush, S., & Leve, N. (1993). Denial of memory deficit in Alzheimer's disease. *American Journal of Psychiatry*, *150*, 748–751.

Sherer, M., Bergloff, P., Boake, C., High, W., & Levin, E. (1998). The Awareness Questionnaire: Factor analysis structure and internal consistency. *Brain Injury*, *12*, 63–68.

Smith, C. A., Henderson, V. W., McCleary, C. A., Murdock, G. A., & Buckwalter, J. G. (2000). Anosognosia and Alzheimer's disease: The role of depressive symptoms in mediating impaired insight. *Journal of Clinical and Experimental Neuropsychology*, *22*, 437–444.

Snow, A. L., Norris, M. P., Doody, R., Molinari, V. A., Orengo, C. A., & Kunik, M. E. (2004). Dementia Deficits Scale. Rating self-awareness of deficits. *Alzheimer Disease and Associated Disorders*, *18*, 22–31.

Starkstein, S. E., Fedoroff, J. P., Price, T. R., Leiguarda, R., & Robinson, R. G. (1992). Anosognosia in patients with cerebrovascular lesions. A study of causative factors. *Stroke*, *23*, 1446–1453.

Starkstein, S. E., Vázquez, S., Migliorelli, R., Tesón, A., Sabe, L., & Leiguarda, R. (1995). A single-photon emission computed tomographic study of anosognosia in Alzheimer's disease. *Archives of Neurology*, *52*, 415–420.

Sunderland, A., Harris, J. E., & Gleave, J. (1984). Memory failures in everyday life following severe head injury. *Journal of Clinical Neuropsychology*, *6*, 127–142.

Trosset, M. W., & Kaszniak, A. W. (1996). Measures of deficit unawareness for predicted performance experiments. *Journal of the International Neuropsychological Society*, *2*, 315–322.

Vasterling, J. J., Seltzer, B., Foss, J. W., & Vanderbrook, V. (1995). Unawareness of deficit in Alzheimer's disease. Domain-specific differences and disease correlates. *Neuropsychiatry, Neuropsychology and Behavioral Neurology*, *8*, 26–32.

Verhey, F. R. J., Rozendaal, N., Ponds, R. W. H. M., & Jolles, J. (1993). Dementia, awareness and depression. *International Journal of Geriatric Psychiatry*, *8*, 851–856.

Wagner, M. T., Spangenberg, K. B., Bachman, D. L., & O'Connell, P. (1997). Unawareness of cognitive deficit in Alzheimer disease and related dementias. *Alzheimer Disease and Associated Disorders*, *11*, 125–131.

Weinstein, E. A., Friedland, R. P., & Wagner, E. E. (1994). Denial/unawareness of impairment and symbolic behavior in Alzheimer's disease. *Neuropsychiatry, Neuropsychology and Behavioral Neurology*, *7*, 176–184.

Weinstein, E. A., & Kahn, R. L. (1955). *Denial of illness: Symbolic and physiological aspects*. Springfield CA: Charles C. Thomas.

NEUROPSYCHOLOGICAL REHABILITATION
2006, 16 (4), 456–473

# Awareness and knowing: Implications for rehabilitation

Peter W. Halligan

*School of Psychology, Cardiff University, Cardiff, Wales*

It has been known for well over a century that brain-damaged patients are often unaware of the very deficits that impair performance in everyday life. Pathologies of awareness have been described for many neurological, psychiatric and neuropsychological deficits and the construct of "awareness" or "insight" understandably now receives attention from many researchers within the clinical and cognitive neurosciences. This paper does not attempt to explain the nature of consciousness or its impairment but rather considers four aspects of consciousness/awareness that health care professionals interested in understanding, measuring and improving deficits of awareness should consider.

## CONSCIOUSNESS AND COGNITIVE FUNCTION

Consciousness or awareness is a frustrating construct, superficially self-evident and yet, as James (1892) pointed out, difficult to characterise and define in scientific or functional terms. The situation is not helped by the often uncritical adoption and interchangeable use of different operational and functional terms ranging from direct phenomenological experience ("consciousness", "self-consciousness", "awareness"), to the more reflective monitoring capacities of ongoing experiences ("insight", "meta-cognitions"). Everyday or folk usage, however, tends to be less problematic and generally assumes that all human beings possess the qualitative and apparently effortless capacity of being aware of their own perceptions, thoughts, memories

Correspondence should be addressed to: Peter Halligan, School of Psychology, Cardiff University, PO Box 901, Cardiff CF103YG. E-mail: HalliganPW@Cardiff.ac.uk



http://www.psypress.com/neurorehab DOI:10.1080/09602010500309762

as their own, together with the ability to initiate and control actions (Chalmers, 1998).

Originally the province of philosophy, consciousness or awareness provided the obvious research platform for the early psychologists as evidenced by the work of Wilhelm Wundt, Hermann von Helmholtz, William James and Alfred Titchener. These early pioneers, however, realised that many aspects of mental processing for which awareness was claimed was in fact the product of prior levels of "unconscious" processing. Nearly a century later, in their much cited paper "Telling more than we can know: Verbal reports on mental processes", Nisbett and Wilson (1977) argued that we are only conscious of the products of our mental processes and have little or no conscious awareness of the processes themselves.

While much of the current research on consciousness is dominated by the big (or "hard") questions of where consciousness is located and how brain processes can produce it (Dennett, 1991), converging findings from cognitive neuroscience over the past 30 years have been singularly successful in confirming that most cognitive abilities are carried out by a myriad of highly efficient and largely automatic pre-conscious processes that operate outside phenomenological awareness and subjective control (Driver & Vuilleumier, 2001; Gazzaniga, 1998; Halligan & Marshall, 1997; Hassin, Uleman, & Bargh, 2004; Moscovitch & Umiltà, 1991).

The realisation that many aspects of mental life represent products of prior levels of "unconscious" processing is not surprising and indeed provides one of the reasons for the existence of a cognitive psychology in the first place. As Velmans (2000) points outs "if the complex processes which enable us to select information, attend to it, plan, organise, determine priorities, respond appropriately and so on, were available to consciousness, there would be no need for careful experiment and theoretical inference to determine their operations" (p. 68).

Despite growing evidence of an increasingly large, sophisticated and competent pre-conscious system, it has been commonly assumed that the cognitive processes involving "consciousness" have a qualitatively distinct and additional causal role in shaping and determining behaviour, particularly where these involved related notions of "self", "free will", and control of actions. In other words, consciousness was not "an epiphenomenon, inner aspect or other passive correlate of brain processes but rather an active integral part of the cerebral process itself, exerting potent causal effects in the interplay of cerebral operations" (Sperry, 1977), although the opposite view has been persuasively argued by Pockett (2004).

The distinction between conscious and preconscious processing was often implicitly incorporated into early cognitive processing models where the terms automatic (without subjective awareness) and controlled or limited capacity processes (with subjective awarencss) were typically used to justify the additional contribution of conscious awareness for behavioural output. Evidence of such a distinction was commonly claimed by appealing to the subject's first person awareness of motor control and perceptual awareness.

Consciousness as a formal topic of cognitive enquiry however remained largely neglected despite renewed emphasis in the 1960s on informational-processing accounts of memory, perception and language comprehension (Marcel & Bisiach, 1988; Shanon, 1998). Indeed it was "the norm for accounts of personal experience to be used only informally" (Shallice, 1988a) and ". . .most theories of cognition make no call at all upon consciousness" (Marcel, 1988). Neither Shallice's (1978) nor Johnson-Laird's (1983) formal cognitive models implied "a definitive causal role for consciousness" (Bisiach, 1988).

One exception was the causal role attributed to "attention". Informally, many students of visuo-spatial neglect consider the condition to be a disorder of visual awareness—where "awareness" is equated with the sub-personal psychological construct of attention (Posner, 1978). The assumed causal dependency between visual attention and visual awareness was such that intact attentional systems were considered necessary for conscious perception (Mack & Rock, 1998; Dehaene and Naccache, 2001). This assumption originated with James who, in claiming that "my experience is what I agree to attend to" (James, 1890), rendered focal or selective attention as "the experimental psychologist's code name for consciousness" (Allport, 1980). This intimate relationship is not universally accepted and recently Kentridge, Heywood, and Weiskrantz (1999, 2004) showed (in the case of blindsight) that attention could be directed by cues presented in the blind field, despite a subject's apparent unawareness, suggesting that attention's entry into conscious experience is not one and the same process.

The reality of subjective experience, however, suggests that we are not in a position to know how or from where our mental contents arise. In most cases, "objects are experienced as having colour, shape, position, size and so on and as forming scenes" and in the case of speech production "one is frequently not aware of the thought in any clear sense before the utterance occurs" (Shallice, 1988a). Consciousness gives no clue as to where the answer comes from, since the processes that produce it are unconscious. "It is the *result* of thinking, not the process of thinking that appears in consciousness" (Miller, 1962).

The nature of conscious awareness therefore does not depend upon whether it can be reported or acted upon but rather on whether it gives rise to "an experience" (Nagel, 1979). Phenomenological consciousness simply occurs too late to affect the outcomes of the cognitive processes to which it is apparently linked (Blackmore, 2001, 2003; Halligan & Oakley, 2000; Pockett, 2004). Hence, following acquired brain injury, the failure or impairment of normal experience and behaviours clinically observed (e.g., anosognosia) results from damage to those early cognitive processes that mediate and provide for conscious awareness (Prigatano & Schacter, 1991). Consequently, it may be best to accept, as Chalmers (1997) suggests, that phenomenal consciousness, while central to much of our mental lives, does not of itself involve any distinctive functional property or cognitive function.

## PHENOMENAL VERSUS ACCESS CONSCIOUSNESS

In an effort to resolve some of the confusion arising from this "ill-defined concept", the neuropsychologist, Edoardo Bisiach (1988) and philosopher Ned Block (1995) suggested a conceptual distinction between different types of consciousness: *phenomenal consciousness* (C1or P-consciousness) and *access consciousness* (C2 or A-consciousness). For Bisiach and Block, the phenomenal properties of consciousness are immediate, non-reflective, experiential properties inaccessible to an external observer. P-consciousness includes all the experiential properties, including sensations, feelings, perceptions, thoughts, wants and emotions. Non-reflective consciousness is considered self-evident, irreducible, private and not in need of further justification. At the phenomenal level, the established operating rules (e.g., objectivity, testability, reliability) of the third person scientific perspective do not apply.

From a first person perspective, P-consciousness appears to be involved in most forms of complex or novel processing (Velmans, 2000) but providing an adequate cognitive explanation for why this type of awareness does not involve previous stages of automatic preconscious systems proves difficult. Regression into more primitive unconscious stages is avoided by employing a functional, third sub-personal perspective, despite the fact that most of the relevant evidence (thoughts, ideas, memories, beliefs, feelings) used to construct this understanding of conscious awareness remains within first person experience. Without direct access to P-consciousness (C1), the search for neurobiological or cognitive correlates to predict and control behaviour remains problematic, and cognitive psychology and neuropsychology research turned from introspection to an approach where the experimenter (not the participant) became the observer, and the target of those observations became the participant's behaviour and reflexive reflective accounts. Although Bisiach and Block both recognise that P-consciousness and A-consciousness co-occur, they distinguish phenomenal experience from the ability to subsequently evaluate experiences and report on them. This reflective capacity (what Block terms *access consciousness*) is considered a more elaborate activity involving the ability to self-monitor and engage cognitive functions such as reasoning and actions, including verbal reports of mental states. In operational terms, one has access consciousness (or Bisiach's C2) of something when a verbal or non-verbal description can be provided regarding a particular object or experience or when a voluntary response can be made. In this respect, much of "our knowledge of perception, for example, is almost entirely based on what Weiskrantz (1977) called commentary procedures" (Shallice, 1988a). This ability to monitor and report is considered a more reliable indicator of consciousness, since it is accessible to the external observer and can be the subject of externally administered tests.

Although many clinical conditions are assumed to involve impairment of the patient's subjective experience (P-consciousness), disorders of awareness tend to be defined in terms of disorders of A-consciousness namely, as a "condition in which there is failure to acknowledge acquired impairments of cognitive or motor function in response to explicit questioning" (Anderson & Tranel, 1989). The operational method of choice relies on the patient's *subjective report* about a current or recent experience (Berti, Ladavas, & Della Corte, 1996).Consequently, most current assessments involve questionnaires that contain both *global and domain-specific items*, (Berti et al., 1996; Bisiach et al., 1986; Cutting, 1978; Levine, Calvanio, & Rinn, 1991; Starkstein et al., 1992), comparisons between patients' self-ratings and objective test performance (Allen & Ruff, 1990; Anderson & Tranel, 1989; Trudel, Tyron, & Purdum, 1998), patients' self-ratings and competencies as adjudged by informants, (Newman, Garmoe, Betty, & Ziccardi, 2000), patients'-relatives (Godfrey, Partridge, Knight, & Bishara 1993; Prigatano & Klonoff, 1998), and professionals (Ranseen, Bohaska, & Schmitt, 1990). The capacity to comment on the outputs of self-monitoring thus provides the main operational focus for much of the current clinical assessments of anosognosia and disorders of awareness.

## BEING AWARE BUT NOT AWARE

Much of what is known about neuropsychology is largely inferred from research carried out to explain the functional level of the patient's performance. Cognitive neuropsychology has achieved an understanding of the functional architecture of cognitive systems by charting dissociations between cognitive tasks that occur in patients with selective brain damage (Shallice, 1988b). Pathology based fractionations or dissociations have provided valuable insights into the intact and damaged mechanisms in language (Margolin, 1991), amnesia (Cermak, 1982), dyslexia, (Coslett & Saffran, 1994), prosopagnosia (Young, 1994), and neglect (Halligan & Marshall, 1994).

Although adequate cognitive accounts of awareness still remain to be developed (Dehaene & Naccache, 2001; Farah & Feinberg, 1997), productive contributions towards the emerging cognitive neuroscience of consciousness have relied on pathologies of awareness and the tasks used to reveal them

(Babinski, 1914; Bisiach & Berti, 1987; Forstl, Owen, & David, 1993; Prigatano & Schacter, 1991). Indeed, the study of clinical cases is probably one of oldest and most valuable avenues of research into the nature of consciousness. In a letter addressed to his friend Lucilius *(Liber V, Epistula* IX), the philosopher Seneca (4BC–65AD) related the following anecdote:

> *You know that Harpastes, my wife's fatuous companion, has remained in my home as an inherited burden ... This foolish woman has suddenly lost her sight. Incredible as it might appear, what I am going to tell you is true; she does not know she is blind. Therefore, again and again she asks her guardian to take her elsewhere. She claims that my home is dark.* (from Bisiach & Geminiani, 1991).

Some of the most striking dissociations in neuropsychology appear to result from disconnections between conscious (explicit awareness, e.g., what the subject reports) and non-conscious (or implicit processing, e.g., how the subject performs). Traditionally, the method employed to demonstrate such dissociation involved comparing the patient's subjective report with their behavioural or physiological performance. In the case of prosopagnosia, patients demonstrate differential electrical skin conductance or evoked potentials to familiar faces despite an explicit inability to identify them (Bauer, 1984; Tranel & Damasio, 1985). In the case of memory, amnesic patients show significant improvements in overall accuracy when a test is repeated, despite denying conscious recollection of the test or its content items. In aphasia, patients who fail on explicit tests of comprehension show normal semantic priming and semantic context effects on lexical decision tasks (Milberg, Blumstein, & Dworetsky, 1987); in dyslexia, patients who cannot read when tested explicitly can nevertheless guess correctly what the words denote using drawings (Shallice & Saffran, 1986). One of the better known illustrations of access consciousness without phenomenal consciousness is "blindsight" (Stoerig, 1996; Weiskrantz, 1986), where patients unaware of the stimuli in their blind field can nevertheless indicate (at levels significantly above chance) the location of stimuli when requested to guess. In cases of visual neglect, there is considerable evidence that when tested indirectly, many patients show some degree of information processing for the stimulus on the affected side (Berti & Rizzolatti, 1992; Marshall & Halligan, 1988; McGlinchey-Berroth et al., 1993; McIntosh et al., 2004).

While theoretical studies are concerned with showing what a patient can do without explicit awareness of their clinical condition using experimental task performance (Berti & Rizzolatti, 1992; Bisiach & Rusconi, 1990; Marshall & Halligan, 1988), many clinical studies are concerned with diagnostic issues (Cutting, 1978; Ellis & Small, 1994; Levine et al., 1991; Nathanson, Bergman, & Gordon, 1952), in particular characterising the anatomical and functional consequences of the reported and behavioural unawareness (Pia, Neppi-Modona, Ricci, & Berti, 2004; Samuelsson et al., 1997; Stone, Halligan, & Greenwood, 1993).

However, a patient does not need to be *explicitly unaware of their cognitive or neurological deficit*—at the level of reporting (A–consciousness)—to continue to demonstrate significant pathologies of awareness on formal testing. Indeed several patients with intractable chronic neglect show what appears to be considerable conceptual and experiential insight (A–consciousness) into their deficit and its consequences while continuing to demonstrate attentional deficits (e.g., neglect) on selective tasks (see Cantagallo & Della Sala, 1998). Moreover, stroke patients with anosognosia may verbally admit to being hemiplegic yet appear to ignore the consequences of such statements when planning and programming their functional motor activities (House & Hodges, 1988; Marcel, Tegner, & Nimmo-Smith, 2004).

An illustration of a patient who reliably showed explicit awareness *of her neuropsychological deficit*, while at the same time showing severe deficits of awareness on formal testing, was PP—a 60-year-old woman previously described by Halligan and Marshall (1998). PP's main cognitive deficit after her stroke in 1987 was a persisting florid visual neglect. On a variety of standard visuo-spatial neglect tests, PP reliably showed marked inattention. Examples of her performance are shown in Figures 1–3.

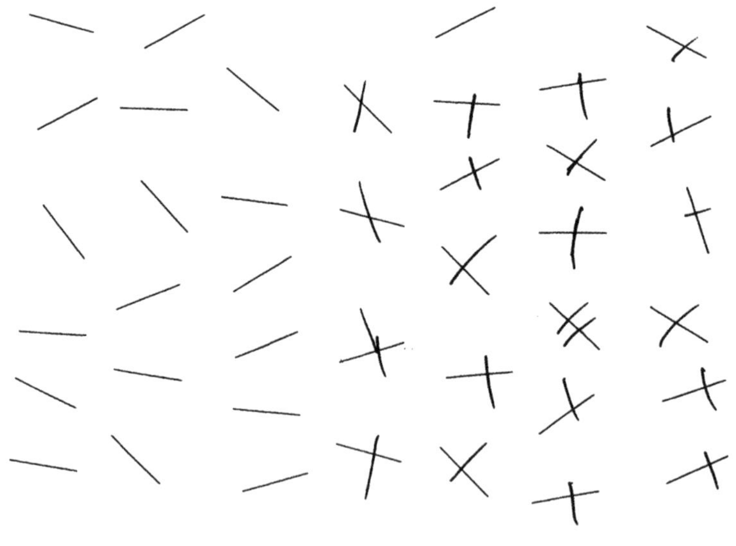

**Figure 1.** Characteristic left sided neglect on PP's line cancellation test.

**Figure 2.** Evidence of selective face and body neglect on PP's drawing performance.

PP's line cancellation performance shows characteristic omission of items located on the left side of the A4 display. When drawing from memory, PP (who knew perfectly well that people had two eyes, two arms and two legs) nevertheless reliably drew in free vision only one eye, one arm or one leg to the right of the vertical axis of a front-on configuration (Figure 2). Despite impressive insight into her condition, PP almost always omitted the left side in most of her drawing sketches.

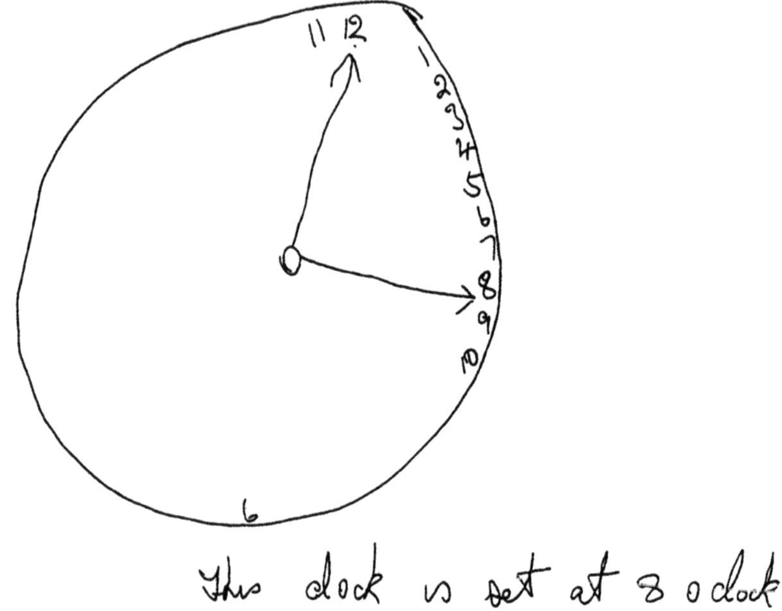


**Figure 3.** PP's clock drawing showing left neglect and right sided crowding of all 12 numbers on right side of clock face.

When drawing a clock face (Figure 3), despite clearly stating how many numbers there were on a standard clock, PP nonetheless located all the numbers on the right side of the clockface. Furthermore, on direct questioning with the incomplete production in front of her, she claimed that her drawing was finished.

Apart from visual neglect, PP was well oriented, articulate and displayed considerable awareness of the functional consequences and indeed interest in the conceptual and diagnostic basis of her visual neglect. Nonetheless, she continued to produce neglect performances (as shown in Figures 1–3). Requested to describe her experience of neglect in a short letter 12 months after her stroke, PP's performance clearly showed neglect dysgraphia despite articulating many of the symptoms of neglect in her written performance. Asked to reflect further upon her condition several months later (Halligan, 1988), she again provided a detailed functional account detailing (on video tape) her awareness of the disruptive consequences of her deficit, while showing florid neglect on most behavioural tests.

"I kept turning to the right. I was going round each little building and coming to another little building. I got myself lost several times and it began to frighten me. . . .. I kept on walking round and round in circles to the right because each little building was on its own. I still actually leave a certain amount of food on the left hand side of my plate because I don't see it there. I don't have quite so much of a problem with dressing now. . . .. If there is a long telephone number I can't see the left hand side of the numbers. I miss the first few figures. I get many more wrong numbers than I ever got. Very often I miss the first few figures and then I can't get the number I'm trying to dial. I think the kitchen is one of the worse places, because when you're cooking and doing things in the kitchen it takes a long time to find things in the kitchen. It takes a long time to find things if they are on the left hand side. Combing and brushing my hair I tend to do one side and not the other." (Halligan & Marshall, 1998)

Finally, asked to provide an explanation for her "visual neglect", she takes issue with the clinical term "neglect" suggesting that it is an unfortunate and inaccurate description of her experience. As far as PP was concerned, left space and its contents did not appear to exist and hence there was nothing to neglect!

"I heard the word 'neglect' mentioned but I couldn't understand what it meant. I thought they were saying I was actually neglecting to look to the left. I couldn't move my eyes to the left. It was quite fixed. It was scary. I used to bump into things because I couldn't move my eyes to the left. Because I never used to look to the left at all. I knew the word 'neglect' was a sort of medical term for whatever was wrong but the word bothered me because you only neglect something that is actually there don't you? If it's not there how can you neglect it? It doesn't seem right to me that the word neglect should be used to describe it. I think they thought I was definitely, deliberately not looking to the left. I wasn't really. It was painful looking to the left. . . . People think you are not looking . . .you are neglecting to look but it's not there. If it's not there you are not neglecting it. I think concentrating is a better word than neglect. It's definitely concentration. If I am walking anywhere and there's something in my way, if I'm concentrating on what I'm doing I will see it and avoid it. The slightest distraction and I won't see it. (Halligan & Marshall, 1998)

Most of the above phenomena are clinically well-known to staff working in rehabilitation and can be seen in many (but not all) patients diagnosed with left visual spatial neglect and other conditions.

The selective lack of awareness during neglect task behaviours is hard to reconcile with the patients' explicit and often detailed insights regarding their condition. In these cases, where the performance is reliably *impaired* on behavioural tests (despite reflective awareness for both the condition and test performance), there is some merit in considering neglect performance as a partial disconnection of the normal binding that integrates phenomenological and access consciousness (Halligan & Marshall, 1998). In the case of PP, there was no general alteration of her consciousness; rather specific aspects of phenomenal awareness were lost together with a deficit in self-monitoring and ability to report the selective absence of information during a relevant task.

## UNAWARENESS: COMPETING EXPLANATIONS

Since one can never be in a position to verify or refute a patient's subjective report regarding their phenomenological experience (Frith, Perry, & Lumer, 1999), most clinicians and neuropsychologists understandably assume that "when a patient disclaims awareness, there is no awareness" (Milner, 1995). However, unawareness of deficits is an equivocal symptom observed across a large range of conditions (Vuilleumier, 2000) and explanations, for the "absence of reportable awareness" can be considered in terms of at least four basic (and probably interacting) accounts; neurogenic, psychosocial, psychogenic and non-medical. Although none of these accounts are mutually exclusive, it is meaningful conceptually to distinguish them for the purposes of discussing their relative characteristics.

### Neurogenic factors

Central to the neurogenic account is the assumption that lack of awareness results from malfunctions in previously intact neurologically-mediated monitoring systems (Heilman, Barrett, & Adair, 1998; Levine et al., 1991; Ramachandran, 1996; Stuss, Picton, & Alexander, 2001). Although neuropsychological models currently dominate most explanations of awareness deficits (Prigatano & Schacter, 1991), it seems unlikely that selective neurological damage within and/or between modalities alone can adequately explain why all patients appear unaware of their condition(s) or its consequences (see Ownsworth, McFarland, & Young, 2002).

### Psychosocial factors

Biomedical models have been rightly criticised for failing to take account of the complex constitutional beliefs, coping strategies and experiences that individuals in their social context bring to any physical or psychological dysfunction (Wade & Halligan, 2004). In response to the perceived and growing need to consider more complex, interactional and contextual paradigms, "biopsychosocial models" applied to health sciences emerged in the late 1970s (Engel, 1977). Biopsychosocial models are still emerging for symptom complexes and syndromes including somatisation, fibromyalgia, conversion hysteria, irritable bowel syndrome and factitious disorders (White, 2005). One influential version developed by Waddell (2004) based on chronic back pain serves as a useful example of why such models are clearly relevant when explaining disorders of awareness. According to Waddell (2004) acute or chronic symptoms that originate from benign or mild forms of physical or mental impairment are re-experienced as amplified perceptions with accompanying distress which, when filtered through the presenting patient's attitudes, beliefs, coping skills and occupational or cultural social context, alter a patient's perceptions of their impairment and associated disability. In the case of acquired brain damage, it is likely that a patient's response to his or her illness is determined to a significant extent by the psychosocial environment in which behaviours are elicited and understood (Clare, 2004; Prigatano &Weinstein, 1996).

## Psychogenic factors

The explanation of impaired awareness arising from a non-conscious "defensive adaptation" against stress was strongly argued by Weinstein and Kahn (1955). These authors suggested that "the effect of the brain damage is to provide the milieu of altered function in which the patient may deny anything that he feels is wrong with him. The "motivation" to deny illness and incapacity was considered to exist in everyone and the level of brain function determines the particular perceptual-symbolic organisation, or language in which it is expressed. Although individuals may employ a range of psychological defence mechanisms, the term "denial" is the term most commonly used in the brain injury literature as the main non-conscious method of psychological reaction that contributes to awareness deficits (Weinstein, 1991). Denial is typically conceptualised within a more general psychodynamic account of human behaviour and is considered to be largely beyond the patient's conscious volitional choice. From an assessment point of view, the critical problem remains how to reliably and conceptually distinguish "between defensive and non-defensive forms of unawareness and to delineate the underlying bases for them" (Prigatano & Schacter, 1991). Short of the patient's own admission, there is no formal clinical procedure that can claim to reliably distinguish "defensive" from "non-defensive" coping and hence infer the degree of any consciously mediated intention and motivations. Moreover, the likelihood of a complex interplay involving more than one type of conscious and non-conscious coping strategies makes this distinction impractical and unrealistic in clinical practice.

## Non-medical factors

Sensitivity to issues surrounding the nature of illness deception continue to be a major feature of modern occupational medicine and while it is understandable that most disorders of awareness are framed in medical, psychosocial or psychiatric parameters, there is a growing clinical literature on dissimulation after brain injury (Reynolds, 1998) which focuses on the subject's intention to fabricate or exaggerate physical or psychological symptoms (Halligan, Bass, & Oakley, 2003; Rogers, 1997). A study by Mittenberg, Patton, Canyock, & Condir (2002) of 131 practising clinical neuropsychologists in the US provided estimates of the prevalence of 'bad' malingering and symptom exaggeration for a variety of clinical conditions. They reported base rates of 39% in the case of mild head injury, 35% in the case of fibromyalgia-chronic fatigue, 31% in the case of chronic pain, 15% for depressive disorders, and 11% in the case of dissociative disorders. In a separate review of 1,363 compensation-seeking cases after mild head injury, Larrabee (2003) found similar figures for mild head injury (40%).

Less well known forms of dissimulation include "defensiveness" or "faking good" described by Rogers (1984) as the "conscious denial or gross minimization of physical non psychological symptoms". In such cases, the motivation is neither compensation nor financial gain but avoiding the potential consequences of illness and the sick role including prescribed medication, long-term involuntary hospitalisation, concern for occupational prospects and/or potential suitability for childcare custody.

One example of a patient who showed what appeared to be explicit awareness of motor weakness was MH, a 53-year-old women who had suffered a sub-arachnoid haemorrhage involving ischaemic damage to frontal lobes. Although fully oriented in time and place, she refused rehabilitation, denying or minimising her symptomatology (right side hemiparesis), severe mobility and dressing problems (2/20 Barthel). Her denial, however, was selective for medical staff only. Family members and junior rehabilitation staff claimed no such denial with regard to diagnosis or symptomatology. Following several unproductive months at the rehabilitation centre, MH finally confided to a psychiatrist that she had explicitly denied her illness (to medical staff) out of a fear of losing her job as a nurse.

# CONCLUSION

Pathologies of awareness and its functional consequences are associated with poor recovery and sub-optimal benefit from rehabilitation (Prigatano, 2005). Inprovements in awareness are associated with better functional outcomes (Sherer et al., 1998). This is hardly surprising as awareness of the consequences of neurological and psychological deficits seem an intuitive and logical starting point for both therapist and patient to begin when perusing rehabilitation. Consequently, it is important that the growing emergence of interest in the neurobiological and psychosocial underpinnings of consciousness/awareness should feed into those accounts used for understanding and treating patients with deficits of awareness. There is certainly a wealth of information on awareness that still awaits analysis and explanation.

Deficits of awareness (as clinically indexed in terms of subjective report and behavioural performance) do not constitute a unitary coherent disorder traceable to the disruption of a single unitary neural process but is best conceived as involving the interaction of several conceptually different factors. The traditional neurological accounts need to embrace the contribution of strategic and psychosocial determinants given that a patient's attitudes, beliefs, coping skills, and cultural social context can also significantly affect perceptions of their impairment and its associated disability (Waddell, 1998). The question remains, whether intelligible sub-syndromes of awareness deficits can be derived which both inform and constrain therapeutic interventions and realistic goal setting. To ensure the optimal targeting of rehabilitation, comprehensive, functionally orientated and evidence-based assessment tools are both needed.

## REFERENCES

Allen, C. C., & Ruff, R. M. (1990). Self-rating versus neuropsychological performance on moderate versus severe head-injured patients. *Brain Injury*, *4*, 7–17.

Allport, D. A. (1980). Patterns and actions: Cognitive mechanisms are content specific. In G. Claxton (Ed.), *Cognitive psychology: New directions*. London: Routledge, Kegan Paul.

Anderson, S. W., & Tranel, D. (1989). Awareness of disease states following cerebral infarction, dementia, and head trauma. *Clinical Neuropsychology*, *3*, 327–339.

Babinski, M. J. (1914). Contribution to the study of mental disturbance in organic cerebral hemiplagia (anosognosia) [in French], *Revue Neurologique*, *12*, 845–848.

Bauer, R. M. (1984). Autonomic recognition of names and faces in prosopagnosia: A neuropsychological application of the guilty knowledge test. *Neuropsychologia*, *22*, 457–469.

Berti, A., Ladavas, E., & Della Corte, M. (1996). Anosognosia for hemiplegia, neglect dyslexia, and drawing neglect: Clinical findings and theoretical considerations. *Journal of the International Neuropsychological Society*, *2*, 426–440.

Berti A., & Rizzolatti, G. (1992). Visual processing without awareness: Evidence from unilateral neglect. *Journal of Cognitive Neuroscience*, *4*, 345–351.

Bisiach, E. (1988). The haunted brain and consciousness. In A. E. Marcel & E. Bisiach (Eds.), *Consciousness in contemporary science* (p. 115). Cambridge: Cambridge University Press.

Bisiach, E., & Berti, A. (1987). Dyschiria. An attempt at its systemic explanation. In M. Jeannerod (Ed.), *Neurophysiological and neuropsychological aspects of spatial neglect* (pp. 183–201). Amsterdam: Elsevier Science Publishers.

Bisiach, E., & Geminiani, G. (1991). Anosognosia related to hemiplegia and hemianopia. In G. P. Prigatano & D. L. Schacter (Eds), *Awareness of deficit after brain injury: Clinical and theoretical issues*. New York: Oxford University Press.

Bisiach, E., & Rusconi, M. L. (1990). Breakdown of perceptual awareness in unilateral neglect. *Cortex, 26*, 643–649.

Bisiach, E., Vallar, G., Perani, D., Papagno, C., & Berti, A. (1986). Unawareness of disease following lesions of the right hemisphere: Anosognosia for hemiplegia and anosognosia for hemianopia. Neuropsychologia. *24*(4), 471–482.

Blackmore, S. J. (1999). *The meme machine*, Oxford: Oxford University Press.

Blackmore, S. J. (2001). Consciousness. *The Psychologist, 14*, 522–525.

Blackmore, S. (2003). *Consciousness: An introduction.* London: Hodder and Stoughton.

Block, N. (1995). On a confusion about the function of consciousness. *Behavioral and Brain Sciences, 18*, 227–247.

Cantagallo, A., & Della Sala, S. (1998). Preserved insight in an artist with extrapersonal spatial neglect. *Cortex, 34*(2), 163–189.

Cermak, L. S. (1982). *Human memory and amnesia.* Hillsdale, N J: Lawrence Erlbaum Associates.

Chalmers, D. (1997). Availability: The cognitive basis of experience? *Behavioral and Brain Sciences, 20*, 148–149.

Chalmers, D. (1998). The problems of consciousness. In H. Jasper, L. Descarries, V. Castellucci, & S. Rossignol (Eds.), *Consciousness: At the frontiers of neuroscience* (*Advances in Neurology*, Vol. 77). New York: Lippincott-Raven Press.

Clare, L. (2004). Awareness in early-stage Alzheimer's disease: A review of methods and evidence. *British Journal of Clinical Psychology, 43*(Pt 2), 177–196.

Coslett, H. B., & Saffran, E. M. (1994). Mechanisms of implicit reading in pure alexia. In M. J. Farah & G. Ratcliff (Eds.), *The neuropsychology of high-level vision.* Hillsdale, NJ: Lawrence Erlbaum Associates.

Cutting, J. (1978). Study of anosognosia. *Journal of Neurology, Neurosurgery and Psychiatry, 41*, 548–555.

Dehaene, S., & Naccache, L. (2001). Towards a cognitive neuroscience of consciousness: Basic evidence and a workspace framework. *Cognition*, 79, 1–37.

Dennett, D. (1991). *Consciousness explained.* Boston, MA: Little, Brown and Company.

Driver, J., & Vuilleumier, P. (2001). Perceptual awareness and its loss in unilateral neglect and extinction. *Cognition, 79*(1–2), 39–88.

Ellis, S. J., & Small, M. (1994). Denial of eye closure in acute stroke. *Stroke, 25*(10), 1958–1962.

Engel, G. L. (1977). The need of a new medical model: A challenge for biomedicine. *Science, 196*, 129–136.

Farah, M. J., & Feinberg, T. E. (1997). Consciousness of perception after brain damage. *Seminars in Neurology, 17*(2), 145–152.

Forstl, H., Owen, A. M., & David, A. (1993). Gabriel Anton and "Anton's symptom": "On focal diseases of the brain which are not perceived by the patient" (1898). *Neuropsychiatry, Neuropsychology and Behavioral Neurology, 6*, 1–6.

Frith, C., Perry, R., & Lumer, E. (1999). The neural correlates of conscious experience: An experimental framework. *Trends in Cognitive Sciences, 3*, 105–114.

Gazzaniga, M. S. (1998). *The minds past.* Berkeley, CA: University of California Press.

Godfrey, H. P., Partridge, F. M., Knight, R. G., & Bishara, S. (1993). Course of insight disorder and emotional dysfunction following closed head injury: A controlled cross-sectional follow-up study. *Journal of Clinical Experimental Neuropsychology, 15*, 503–515.

Halligan, P. W. (1988). *The experience of visual neglect* [Video]. Produced by Oxford Medical Illustration/distributed by LEA.

Halligan, P. W., Bass, C., & Oakley, D. A. (Eds.). (2003). *Malingering and illness deception.* Oxford: Oxford University Press.

Halligan, P. W., & Marshall, J. C. (1994). Toward a principled explanation of unilateral neglect. *Cognitive Neuropsychology, 11*, 167–206.

Halligan, P. W., & Marshall, J. C. (1997). Cognitive neuropsychology: The good the bad and the bizarre. In R. Fuller, P. Walsh, & P. McGinley (Eds.), *A century of psychology: Progress, paradigms and prospects for the new millennium*. London: Routledge.

Halligan, P. W., & Marshall, J. C. (1998). Neglect of awareness. *Consciousness and Cognition, 7*(3), 356–380.

Halligan, P. W., & Oakley, D. (2000). Greatest myth of all. *New Scientist, 168*(2265), 35–39.

Hassin, R. R., Uleman, J. S., & Bargh, J. A. (Eds.) (2004). *The new unconscious*. New York: Oxford University Press.

Heilman, K. M., Barrett, A., & Adair, J. (1998). Possible mechanisms of anosognosia: A defect in self-awareness. *Philosophical Transactions: Biological Sciences* (The Royal Society), 353.

House, A., & Hodges, J. (1988). Persistent denial of handicap after infarction of the right basal ganglia: A case study. *Journal of Neurology, Neurosurgery and Psychiatry, 51*(1), 112–115.

Johnson-Laird, P. N. (1983). *Mental models: Towards a cognitive science of language, inference, and consciousness*. Cambridge, MA: Harvard University Press.

James, W. (1890). *The principles of psychology* (pp. i; 402). New York: Henry Holt & Co.

James, W. (1892). The stream of consciousness. In *Psychology* (chapter XI). Cleveland & New York: World.

Kentridge, R. W., Heywood, C. A., & Weiskrantz, L. (1999). Attention without awareness in blindsight. *Proceedings of the Royal Society of London, Series B, 266*, 1805–1811.

Kentridge, R. W., Heywood, C. A., & Weiskrantz, L. (2004). Spatial attention speeds discrimination without awareness in blindsight. *Neuropsychologia, 42*(6), 831–835.

Larrabee, G. J. (2003). Detection of malingering using atypical performance patterns on standard neuropsychological tests. *Clinical Neuropsychology, 17*(3), 410–425.

Levine, D. N., Calvanio, R., & Rinn, W. E. (1991). The pathogenesis of anosognosia for hemiplegia. *Neurology, 41*, 1770–1781.

Mack, A., & Rock, I. (1998). *Inattentional blindness*. Cambridge, MA: MIT Press.

Marcel, A. (1988). Phenomenal experience and functionalism. In A. J. Marcel, & E. Bisiach (Eds.), *Consciousness in contemporary science* (pp. 121–158). Oxford: Clarendon Press.

Marcel, A. E., & Bisiach, E. (Eds.) (1988). *Consciousness in contemporary science*. Oxford: Clarendon Press.

Marcel, A. J., Tegner, R., & Nimmo-Smith, I. (2004). Anosognosia for plegia: Specificity, extension, partiality and disunity of bodily unawareness. *Cortex, 40*(1), 19–40.

Margolin, D. I. (1991). Cognitive neuropsychology. Resolving enigmas about Wernicke's aphasia and other higher cortical disorders. *Archives of Neurology 48*(7), 751–765.

Marshall, J. C., & Halligan, P. W. (1988). Blindsight and insight in visuo-spatial neglect. *Nature, 336*, 766–767.

McGlinchey-Berroth, R., Milberg, W. P., Verfaellie, M., Alexander, M., &, Kilduff, P. T. (1993). Semantic processing in the neglected visual field: Evidence from a lexical decision task. *Cognitive Neuropsychology, 10*, 79–108.

McIntosh, R. D., McClements, K. I., Schindler, I., Cassidy, T. P., Birchall, D., & Milner, A. D. (2004). Avoidance of obstacles in the absence of visual awareness. *Proceedings of the Royal Society of London B, 271*, 15–20.

Milberg, W., Blumstein, S., & Dworetsky, B. (1987). Processing of lexical ambiguities in aphasia. *Brain and Language, 31*, 138–150.

Miller, G. A. (1962). *Psychology: The science of mental life* (p. 71). New York: Penguin Books.

Milner, A. D. (1995). Cerebral correlates of visual awareness. *Neuropsychologia, 33*, 1117–1130.

Moscovitch, M., & Umiltà, C. (1991). Conscious and nonconscious aspects of memory: A neuropsychological framework of modules and central systems. In R. Lister, & H. Weigartner, (Eds.), *Perspectives on cognitive neuroscience*. Oxford: Oxford University Press.

Mittenberg, W., Patton, C., Canyock, E. M., & Condit, D. (2002). Base rates of malingering and symptom exaggeration. *Journal of Clinical and Experimental Neuropsychology, 24*, 1094–1102.

Nagel, T. (1979). Panpsychism. In T. Nagel (Ed.), *Mortal questions*. Cambridge: Cambridge University Press.

Nathanson, M., Bergman, P., & Gordon, G. (1952). Denial of illness. Its occurrence in one hundred consecutive cases of hemiplegia. *Archives of Neurology and Psychiatry, 68*, 380–387.

Newman, A. C., Garmoe, W., Beatty, P., & Ziccardi, M. (2000). Self-awareness of traumatically brain injured patients in the acute inpatient rehabilitation setting. *Brain Injury, 14*(4), 333–344.

Nisbett, R. E., & Wilson, T. D. (1977). Telling more than we can know: Verbal reports on mental processes. *Psychological Reports, 84*(3), 231–259.

Ownsworth, T., McFarland, K., & Young, R. (2002). The investigation of factors underlying deficits in self-awareness and self-regulation. *Brain Injury, 16*, 291–309.

Pia, L., Neppi-Modona, M., Ricci, R., & Berti, A. (2004). The anatomy of anosognosia for hemiplegia: A meta-analysis. *Cortex, 40*, 367–377.

Pockett, S. (2004). Does consciousness cause behaviour? *Journal of Consciousness Studies, 11*, 23–40.

Posner, M. I. (1978). *Chronometric explorations of mind*. Hillsdale, NJ: Erlbaum.

Prigatano, G. P. (2005). Impaired self-awareness after moderately severe to severe traumatic brain injury. *Acta Neurochir Suppl. 93*, 39–42.

Prigatano, G. P., & Klonoff, P. S. (1998). A clinician's rating scale for evaluating impaired self-awareness and denial of disability after brain injury. *The Clinical Neuropsychologist, 12*, 56–67.

Prigatano, G. P., & Schachter, D. L. (Eds.). (1991). *Awareness of deficit after brain injury: Clinical and theoretical issues*. Oxford: Oxford University Press.

Prigatano, G. P., & Weinstein, E. A. (1996). Edwin A. Weinstein's contributions to neuropsychological rehabilitation. *Neuropsychological Rehabilitation, 6*, 305–326.

Ramachandran, V. S. (1996). Synaesthesia in phantom limbs induced with mirrors. *Proceedings of the Royal Society London, 263*, 377–386.

Ranseen, J. D., Bohaska, L. A., & Schmitt, F. A. (1990). An investigation of anosognosia following traumatic brain injury. *International Journal of Clinical Neuropsychology, 7*, 29–36.

Reynolds, C. (1998). 'Common sense, clinicians, and actuarialism.' In C. R. Reynolds (Eds.), *Detection of malingering during head injury litigation*. New York: Plenum Press.

Rogers, R. (1997). Introduction. In R. Rogers (Ed.), *Clinical assessment of malingering and deception* (2nd ed., pp. 1–19). New York: Guilford Press.

Rogers, R. (1984). *Rogers Criminal Responsibility Assessment Scales (R-CRAS) and Test Manual*. Odessa, FL: Psychological Assessment Resources.

Samuelson, H., Jensen, C., Ekholm, S., Naver, H., & Blomstrand, C. (1997). Anatomical and neurological correlates of acute and chronic visuospatial neglect following right hemisphere stroke. *Cortex, 33*, 271–285.

Shallice, T. (1978), The Dominant Action System: An Information-processing approach to consciousness. In K. S. Pope & J. L. Singer (Eds.), *The stream of consciousness: Scientific investigations into the flow of experience*. New York: Plenum.

Shallice, T. (1988a). Information-processing models of consciousness: Possibilities and problems. In A. E. Marcel & E. Bisiach (Eds.), *Consciousness in contemporary science*. Oxford: Clarendon Press.

Shallice, T. (1988b). *From neuropsychology to mental structure*. Cambridge: Cambridge University Press.

Shallice, T., & Saffran, E. (1986). Lexical processing in the absence of explicit word identification: Evidence from a letter-by-letter reader. *Cognitive Neuropsychology, 3*, 429–458.

Shanon, B. (1998). What is the function of consciousness? *Journal of Consciousness Studies, 5*(3), 295–308.

Sherer, M., Bergloff, P., Levin, E., High, W.M. Jr., Oden, K.E., & Nick, T.G. (1998). Impaired awareness and employment outcome after traumatic brain injury. *Journal of Head Trauma Rehabilitation, 13*(5), 52–61.

Sperry, R. W. (1977). Forebrain commissurotomy and conscious awareness. *Journal of Medicine and Philosophy, 2*(2), 101.

Starkstein, S. E., Federoff, J. P., Price, T. R., Leiguarda, R., Robinson, R. G. (1992). Anosognosia in patients with cerebrovascular lesions: A study of causative factors, *Stroke, 23*, 1446–1453.

Stoerig, P. (1996). Varieties of vision: From blind responses to conscious recognition. *Trends Neuroscience, 19*, 401–405.

Stone, S. P., Halligan, P. W., & Greenwood, R. J. (1993). The incidence of neglect phenomena and related disorders in patients with an acute right or left hemisphere stroke. *Age & Ageing, 22*, 46–52.

Stuss, D. T., Picton, T. W., & Alexander, M. P. (2001). Consciousness, self-awareness and the frontal lobes. In S. P. Salloway, P. F. Malloy, & J. D. Duffy (Eds.), *The frontal lobes and neuropsychiatric illness* (pp. 101–109). Washington, DC: American Psychiatric Publishing.

Tranel D., & Damasio, A. R. (1985). Knowledge without awareness: An autonomic index of facial recognition by prosopagnosics. *Science, 228*, 1453–1454.

Trudel, T. M., Tyron, W. W., & Purdum, C. M. (1998). Awareness of disability and long-term outcome after traumatic brain injury. *Rehabilitation Psychology, 43*(4), 267–281.

Velmans, M. (2000). *Understanding consciousness*. London: Routledge.

Vuilleumier, P. (2000). Anosognosia. In J. Bogousslavsky & J. L. Cummings (Eds.), *Behaviour and mood disorders in focal brain lesions* (pp. 465–519). Cambridge: Cambridge University Press.

Wade, D. T., & Halligan, P. W. (2004). Do biomedical models of illness make for good healthcare systems? *British Medical Journal, 329*, 1398–1401.

Waddell, G. (2004). *The back pain revolution* (2nd ed.). Edinburgh: Churchill Livingstone.

Weinstein, E. A. (1991). Anosognosia and denial of illness. In G. P. Prigatano & D. L. Schacter (Eds.), *Awareness of deficit after brain injury: Clinical and theoretical issues* (pp. 240–257). New York: Oxford University Press.

Weinstein, E. A., & Kahn, R. L. (1955). *Denial of illness: Symbolic and physiological aspects*. Springfield, IL: Charles C. Thomas Publishing.

Weiskrantz, L. (1977). Trying to bridge some neuropsychological gaps between monkey and man. *British Journal of Psychology, 68*, 431–445.

Weiskrantz, L. (1986). *Blindsight*. Oxford: Oxford University Press.

White, P. (2005). *Biopsychosocial medicine: An integrated approach to understanding illness*. Oxford: Oxford University Press.

Young, A. W. (1994). Covert recognition. In M. J. Farah & G. Ratcliff (Eds.), *The neuropsychology of higher level vision* (pp. 331–358). Hillsdale, NJ: Erlbaum.

NEUROPSYCHOLOGICAL REHABILITATION
2006, 16 (4), 474–500

# A review of awareness interventions in brain injury rehabilitation

J. M. Fleming[1,2] and T. Ownsworth[1]

[1]*Division of Occupational Therapy, School of Health and Rehabilitation Sciences, The University of Queensland, Australia*
[2]*Occupational Therapy Department, Princess Alexandra Hospital, Bristane, Australia*

Unawareness related to brain injury has implications for participation in rehabilitation, functional outcomes, and the emotional well-being of clients. Addressing disorders of awareness is an integral component of many rehabilitation programmes, and a review of the literature identified a range of awareness interventions that include holistic milieu-oriented neuropsychological programmes, psychotherapy, compensatory and facilitatory approaches, structured experiences, direct feedback, videotaped feedback, confrontational techniques, cognitive therapy, group therapy, game formats and behavioural intervention. These approaches are examined in terms of their theoretical bases and research evidence. A distinction is made between intervention approaches for unawareness due to neurocognitive factors and approaches for unawareness due to psychological factors. The socio-cultural context of unawareness is a third factor presented in a biopsychosocial framework to guide clinical decisions about awareness interventions. The ethical and methodological concerns associated with research on awareness interventions are discussed. The main considerations relate to the embedded nature of awareness interventions within rehabilitation programmes, the need for individually tailored interventions, differing responses according to the nature of unawareness, and the risk of eliciting emotional distress in some clients.

Over the past 15–20 years there has been increasing recognition of disorders of awareness as a critical and over-riding issue in all forms of

Correspondence should be sent to Dr J. Fleming, Division of Occupational Therapy, School of Health and Rehabilitation Sciences, The University of Queensland, Brisbane, 4072, Australia. Tel: +61 7 3365 2808, Fax: +61 7 3365 1622. E-mail: j.fleming@uq.edu.au


http://www.psypress.com/neurorehab DOI:10.1080/09602010500505518

neuropsychological rehabilitation. During this time considerable research has amassed focusing on various methods of assessment, and describing the clinical presentation of unawareness and its correlates at different stages of recovery from brain injury. It has emerged that unawareness is not a unitary or an "all or nothing" construct (Hart, Giovannetti, Montgomery, & Schwartz, 1998; Schacter & Prigatano, 1991), and that awareness is a complex construct incorporating neural and cognitive processes, as well as psychological factors (McGlynn & Schacter, 1989). Additionally, authors suggest that to some extent the social environment may influence individuals' presentations of unawareness (Prigatano & Weinstein, 1996). Research suggests that level of awareness is related to rehabilitation outcomes (Fleming, Strong, & Ashton, 1998; Prigatano & Wong, 1999; Sherer et al., 1998a), indicating that awareness is an important issue to address in brain injury rehabilitation.

Awareness, or self-awareness as it is often termed, is defined as "the capacity to perceive the 'self' in relatively 'objective' terms while maintaining a sense of subjectivity" (Prigatano & Schacter, 1991, p. 13). A disorder of self-awareness refers to a person's "inability to recognise deficits or problem circumstances caused by neurological injury" (Barco et al., 1991, p. 129). There has been some description of intervention approaches to manage disorders of awareness in clients with brain injury, but limited formal evaluation of these approaches. In many cases, interventions have been developed in response to a perceived clinical need, and have limited theoretical bases. It is generally assumed that interventions to facilitate awareness are necessary and beneficial to clients, yet there has been a lack of critical debate about the value and implications of intervening to improve awareness. This paper aims to review awareness interventions that have been described for adults with acquired brain injury, and to present the related empirical evidence and underlying theoretical approaches.

Several authors have presented reviews of existing interventions for clients with brain injury who lack awareness (Deaton, 1986; Lucas & Fleming, 2005; Sherer et al., 1998b). This paper extends upon these reviews, presenting a new framework for intervention, and identifying future challenges and directions. A review of the literature identified a variety of awareness interventions including holistic milieu-oriented neuropsychological programmes, psychotherapy, compensatory and facilitatory approaches, structured experiences, direct feedback, videotaped feedback, confrontational techniques, cognitive therapy, group therapy, game formats, and behavioural intervention. Many of these interventions use a combination of approaches, and will be described commencing with the earliest approaches. Samples of the interventions and research evidence are presented in Table 1 in the order consistent with the following discussion.

TABLE 1
Research evidence for awareness interventions

| *Author* | *Intervention* | *Participants* | *Design* | *Outcomes* |
|---|---|---|---|---|
| Prigatano et al. (1984, 1986) | Holistic milieu-oriented Neuropsychological programme involving a combination of cognitive retraining and psychotherapy | 18 TBI clients receiving intervention and untreated comparison group of 17 clients | Comparative study with concurrent controls, allocation not randomised | Intervention group showed trend towards better emotional adjustment and higher incidence of employment (50%) compared to untreated group (36%) |
| Ben-Yishay et al. (1987) | Holistic neuropsychological day rehabilitation programme involving cognitive remediation, small group procedures, and guided occupational trials | 94 clients with brain injury | Case series reporting post-intervention outcomes | 84% classified as able to engage in productive activity with 63% at a competitive level |
| Klonoff et al. (1989) | Daily cognitive retraining hour as part of a larger neuropsychological rehabilitation programme | 2 clients with traumatic brain injury drawn from a larger unspecified client group | Case study descriptions | Subsequent work trial and placement was successful for one client and unsuccessful for the other |
| Fordyce & Roueche (1986) | Neuropsychological rehabilitation programme using small group intensive treatments (6 hours/day, 4 days/week for 6 months) | 28 clients with brain injury in 3 subgroups: Group 1 ($n = 11$) initial high awareness, Group 2 ($n = 9$) initial low awareness but improved by discharge, Group 3 ($n = 8$) initial low awareness which did not improve | Retrospective case series with pre–post intervention comparisons | At discharge: Group 1 – reduced emotional distress; Group 3 – increased emotional distress<br>No group differences on vocational outcome, but trend towards group 2 having better outcome than group 3 |

| | | | | |
|---|---|---|---|---|
| Malec & Moessner (2000) | Comprehensive day treatment programme modelled on the programmes of Prigatano and Ben-Yishay | 62 consecutive programme graduates with brain injury | Cohort study with pre-post intervention comparisons | Impaired awareness and distress diminished after programme. Better awareness and less distress predicted positive behavioural outcomes but not vocational outcomes |
| Sherer et al. (1998b) | The Challenge Program of community re-integration using multi-faceted awareness interventions | Brief case examples only | Nil presented | |
| Ownsworth (2005) | Individual psychotherapy approach with generalisation of skills in a group setting | 1 client with TBI and persisting denial due to a highly defensive personality style | Single case study with pre–post intervention comparisons | Significant reduction in social anxiety, depression, defensiveness and functional impairment. Significant improvement in cognitive performance. |
| Crosson et al. (1989)<br>Barco et al. (1991) | Facilitation of and compensation for impaired awareness based on the pyramid model of awareness | 1 client with TBI (Barco et al.)<br>2 brief descriptions of clients with TBI (Crosson et al.) | Case study descriptions | Clients demonstrated some gains in awareness during the course of rehabilitation |
| DeHope & Finegan (1999) | Three-stage community-based intervention incorporating psychotherapy | 3 clients with severe brain injury and maladaptive behaviours | Case study descriptions | Clients demonstrated improved social functioning, independence in activities of daily living or work |

*(Table continued)*

Table 1 (Continued)

| *Author* | *Intervention* | *Participants* | *Design* | *Outcomes* |
|---|---|---|---|---|
| Ownsworth et al. (2005) | A metacognitive contextual intervention to improve error awareness and self-correction of errors during real-life functional tasks | 1 client with TBI displaying severe awareness deficits relating to neuro-cognitive deficits, non-defensive coping and social environmental factors | A multiple baseline single case study design | The client displayed a significant reduction in errors and greater self-correction of errors, although this did not spontaneously generalise across settings and his global self-awareness was unchanged |
| Toglia (1998) | Metacognitive training techniques within a multicontextual treatment approach | 2 clients with stroke | Case descriptions | Outcomes not stated |
| Landa-Gonzales (2001) | Multicontextual community re-entry occupational therapy programme | 1 client 8 years post-TBI | Single case study design with pre-post intervention comparisons and follow-up | Improvements in occupational function, client satisfaction with performance, and self-awareness at post-intervention. Maintained 8 weeks later |
| Fleming et al. (2006) | 10 week occupation-based programme incorporating elements of the multicontextual approach | 4 clients with acquired brain injury | Single case design with baseline/follow-up assessments | Clients showed modest gains in awareness. One client withdrawn |
| Rebmann & Hannon (1995) Schacter et al. (1990) Schlund (1999) | All studies used self-prediction of performance on memory tasks followed by feedback on actual performance | In total, 5 clients with brain injury | All used a single case design | All clients showed improvements in awareness of memory performance |

| | | | | |
|---|---|---|---|---|
| Alexy et al. (1983) | Audiovisual feedback of interpersonal and communication skills | Groups of clients 2–6 months post-brain injury | Qualitative description | Improved interpersonal behaviour on functional tasks |
| Youngjohn & Altman (1989) | Feedback on self-predicted vs actual performance of verbal recall and arithmetic tasks in a single group session | 6 clients with brain injury | Pre–post intervention comparisons | Prediction on both tasks improved significantly after group session with gains maintained 1 week later for arithmetic task only |
| Ranseen et al. (1990) | Group therapy approach providing feedback on interpersonal skills (twice weekly for approx. 1 month) | 32 rehabilitation inpatients | Pre–post intervention comparisons | No significant improvements in awareness |
| Liu et al. (2002) | Self-regulatory skills training using audiovisual feedback of daily tasks | 3 elderly clients with acute stroke | Case study descriptions | Clients showed improved independence on functional tasks |
| Zhou et al. (1996) | Educational board game focused on general knowledge of residual impairments following brain injury (3 × week) | 3 male residents of a neuro-rehabilitation programme | Multiple baseline case study design | Clients showed improved general knowledge of brain injury impairments but not accuracy of self-ratings |
| Chittum et al. (1996) | Extension of board game format to focus on specific cognitive and behavioural sequelae relevant to the individual plus instructor-facilitated discussion before game | 3 male residents of a neuro-rehabilitation programme | Multiple baseline case study design | Participants' knowledge of personal impairments improved and was maintained 1–2 months later |

(*Table continued*)

Table 1 (Continued)

| *Author* | *Intervention* | *Participants* | *Design* | *Outcomes* |
| --- | --- | --- | --- | --- |
| Ownsworth et al. (2000) | 16 week group support and psychoeducation programme based on cognitive-behavioural therapy, cognitive rehabilitation and social skills training and the pyramid model | 21 clients with long-term acquired brain injury | Pre–post intervention comparisons with a 6-month follow-up | Participants showed significant improvement in emergent and anticipatory awareness and strategy use, as well improved psychosocial function. Gains maintained 6 months later |
| Ylvisaker et al. (1998) | Continuum of low to high confrontation options for children | Brief case examples of children with brain injury | Nil presented | |
| Beardmore et al. (1999) | Single 30 minute individual educational feedback session | 21 children with TBI aged 9–16 years | Randomised controlled with attention-placebo group | No significant between-group differences in awareness or knowledge at 1 month follow-up |
| Bieman-Copland & Dywan (2000) | Behavioural intervention focusing on reducing target behaviours | 1 client with inappropriate behaviour and anosognosia | Single case study design | Clients showed decreased target behaviours over 2–3 months of intervention. Gains maintained 2 months later |

TBI = traumatic brain injury

## OVERVIEW OF AWARENESS INTERVENTIONS

### Neuropsychological rehabilitation programmes

Prigatano et al. (1984, 1986; Prigatano, 1999a) and Ben-Yishay et al. (1985; Ben-Yishay & Prigatano, 1990; Ben-Yishay, Silver, Piasetsky, & Rattock, 1987) pioneered the incorporation of management of unawareness into brain injury rehabilitation programmes. Prigatano et al. (1984, 1986) described a holistic milieu-oriented programme which involves a combination of cognitive retraining and psychotherapeutic intervention and addresses affective issues as an integral component of the programme. This programme recognises and targets the problem of disturbances of self-awareness as a "substantial barrier to successful rehabilitation outcome" (Prigatano, 1999b, p. 146). Prigatano (1991) also demonstrated that patients who successfully completed the programme rated their level of self-awareness as similar to staff ratings, whereas those who "failed" in the programme universally overestimated their level of self-awareness compared to staff ratings. These findings not only illustrate the role played by self-awareness in rehabilitation outcome, but also suggest that some people with disorders of self-awareness may not respond to this treatment approach.

Another early approach incorporated the use of a daily cognitive retraining hour to facilitate awareness into a larger neuropsychological rehabilitation programme (Klonoff et al., 1989). The cognitive retraining hour involved clients working alongside each other on cognitive retraining activities, receiving well-timed therapist feedback and being involved in keeping records, timing tasks, graphing their own performance, and writing strength and weakness lists. The supportive group context and strong working alliance with the therapist were seen as important in addressing emotional responses as they arose.

In a retrospective study of clients in an intensive neuropsychological rehabilitation programme, Fordyce and Roueche (1986) identified a group of clients who originally underestimated their impairments as compared with staff and relatives' reports. One subgroup of these clients displayed improved awareness in their self-reports over the course of the programme, whereas the self-reports of another subgroup showed increased discrepancy from staff and relative's ratings and an increase in emotional distress over the programme. There was a nonsignificant trend for the improved self-awareness subgroup to experience more favourable vocational outcomes than the subgroup with unchanged low self-awareness. The results reinforced previous findings that not all individuals benefit from interventions to enhance awareness and that increased awareness can be associated with emotional distress (Prigatano et al., 1986).

Sherer et al. (1998b) described a comprehensive community re-integration rehabilitation programme based on the assumption that increasing self-awareness facilitates the achievement of better community re-integration in clients with brain injury. They drew upon a number of techniques for increasing awareness including establishing a therapeutic alliance, family interventions, peer feedback, education, roleplays, videotaped feedback, real world experiences, therapeutic milieu and psychotherapy. A systematic evaluation of changes using pre- and post-intervention measures of awareness was not presented.

Most of the above programmes are based on a theoretical approach that recognises the contribution of both neuropsychological and psychological elements to disorders of awareness. Prigatano and Klonoff (1998) distinguished between unawareness that has neuropsychological origin, which was termed "impaired self-awareness," and unawareness with psychological origin, named "denial of disability", but it was later suggested that this model be reconceptualised as four syndromes of unawareness determined by lesion site (Prigatano, 1999a, b). Prigatano proposed that these syndromes will be "complete" in clients with bilateral brain impairment, who are likely to be unmotivated, passive but non-resistant participants in rehabilitation. In contrast, following unilateral brain impairment, these syndromes may be "partial" and clients are likely to demonstrate different methods of coping, including non-defensive and defensive methods, and hence respond better to different types of intervention. Prigatano (1999a) proposed that clients with non-defensive reactions are using premorbid ways of coping that may no longer be effective, and with rehabilitation will realise that their impairments are preventing them from performing activities successfully. Clients with defensive coping styles may employ denial and projection, show resistance to therapy, and accuse therapists of obstructing them from achieving their goals. Prigatano (1999a) predicted that the group with non-defensive coping would respond best to the milieu-oriented neuropsychological rehabilitation programmes, while those with defensive coping methods might benefit more from individual psychotherapy approaches. Preliminary support for these predictions concerning the efficacy of different interventions for clients with defensive and non-defensive coping styles was provided by Ownsworth (2005) and Ownsworth, Fleming, and Desbois (2005).

## Psychotherapeutic treatment

The emphasis of psychotherapy after brain injury is to assist clients to explore the meaning of their losses and impairments (Langer & Padrone, 1992) and to re-establish a sense of meaning in their lives and form realistic goals (Prigatano, 1986). As previously mentioned, this is an integral component of many rehabilitation programmes and various authors have advocated for the use of psychotherapy with people with brain injury (Andersson,

Gundersen, & Finset, 1999; Butler & Satz, 1988; Cicerone, 1989; Langer & Padrone, 1992; Mateer, 1999; Prigatano, 1986; Sherer et al., 1998b). Langer and Padrone (1992) proposed a tripartite model of awareness which integrates psychological (motivational) factors with the neuropsychological/cognitive factors underlying self-awareness. The model conceptualises the three sources of individuals "not knowing" about their injury-related deficits. The first source of limitation is not having the information due to a lack of access to or inability to understand the problem, which manifests as unawareness in the individual client. This can be addressed in rehabilitation by providing information and feedback about deficits to the client. The second source of "not knowing" is a neuropsychological problem with gleaning the implications of the information, and thus, the problem is minimised. In this case, the clinician needs to work with the client to build structures to help support the processing of information and use repetition to facilitate learning. The third source has an emotional origin, in which the client denies or minimises information that is too painful for him or her to deal with at a conscious level. At this level, awareness interventions need to be preceded or accompanied by efforts to strengthen the client's ego functions to support the knowledge.

Langer and Padrone recommended that such awareness issues be dealt with early in the acute phase of rehabilitation, using group and individual psychotherapy. This may involve the performance of meaningful and concrete activities, review of the client's past work and progress with him or her, and use of symbols and language that are relevant to the client. They stressed the need to continually monitor the client's neuropsychological and emotional readiness to face losses without experiencing too much distress. Ownsworth (2005) employed a psychotherapeutic approach, guided by Langer and Padrone's (1992) recommendations, with a client to reduce persisting denial of traumatic brain injury-related disability due to a highly defensive personality style. However, further research evidence is required to support psychotherapeutic interventions based on the tripartite model of awareness for people with acquired brain injury.

## Interventions based on the pyramid model of awareness

The pyramid model (Barco et al., 1991; Crosson et al., 1989) conceptualises awareness on three levels. *Intellectual* awareness (a basic knowledge of one's brain injury deficits and their implications) is at the base of the pyramid and is believed to provide a foundation for the higher levels of *emergent* awareness (the person's ability to recognise a problem while it is happening) and *anticipatory* awareness (the ability to predict that a problem may occur). Barco et al. (1991) used the pyramid model as a basis for a range of awareness interventions. To facilitate intellectual awareness, the authors recommended client and family education about brain injury deficits, providing consistent feedback during therapy, videotaped feedback, strength-and-weakness lists, and "planned failure" in task performance accompanied by emotional support and discussion. Emergent awareness can also be facilitated by providing feedback during and after task performance, including videotaped feedback, with a focus on identifying observable signs of the problem, and comparison of self-ratings and therapist's ratings of performance. To facilitate anticipatory awareness, Barco et al. suggested assisting the client to plan and anticipate problems prior to task performance in a variety of situations.

The client may also be taught a compensation technique appropriate to his or her level of awareness (Crosson et al., 1989). For example, at the highest level, clients with intact anticipatory awareness can employ anticipatory compensation (i.e., plan ahead to employ a compensatory strategy in situations where a problem is anticipated). At the lowest level, clients who lack intellectual awareness require external compensation (cueing or environmental modification) initiated by another person in the client's support system for safety reasons and to maximise independence (Crosson et al., 1989). Although this approach seems to be structured around disorders of awareness with a neuropsychological basis, Barco et al. (1991) also acknowledged the coexistence of denial (either conscious or unconscious) based upon psychological factors, and recognised the role of psychotherapy in treating denial. Despite its intuitive sense and widespread adoption, the pyramid model has limited empirical support, and in fact Abreu et al. (2001) found no evidence for the hierarchy of levels of awareness in the pyramid model.

DeHope and Finegan (1999) reported on a self-determination approach to enhance self-awareness and social functioning in adults with severe traumatic brain injury, based upon the pyramid model of awareness overlapped with a leisure education model (Dattilo, 1994) and Willer and Corrigan's (1994) "Whatever it Takes" model of community integration. The intervention involved three steps (i.e., education, practice in safe and structured settings, and real-life consequences) and was accompanied by individual psychotherapy and family involvement. The self-determination approach was successful in improving social functioning and independence for three individuals with very severe maladaptive social behaviours in community-based rehabilitation programmes spanning several years. Gains were attributed to improved self-awareness and self-monitoring, although this did not appear to be measured in a systematic way, and the repetitive practice of strategies. However none of the individuals progressed to achieve full anticipatory awareness. This study illustrated the intensive and lengthy nature of interventions required to address severe awareness deficits in people with traumatic brain injury, and to translate gains in awareness into functional gains.

## Structured experiences

Toglia and Kirk (2000) expanded upon the pyramid model to develop the Comprehensive Dynamic Interactional Model of awareness which highlights the dynamic, rather than hierarchical nature of self-awareness, by drawing upon parallel themes from cognitive psychology, social psychology and neuropsychology. This model describes a dynamic relationship between clients' knowledge of the task, self-knowledge and beliefs prior to task performance (termed metacognitive knowledge), and their situational awareness activated during task performance (termed on-line awareness). Other influences on clients' awareness and responses to feedback include cognitive and perceptual impairment, emotional state, motivation, meaningfulness and characteristics of tasks, value, culture, and context.

Intervention strategies recommended by Toglia and Kirk (2000) include the use of "guided mastery", as originally proposed by Bandura (1997), which involves engaging the client in structured experiences that allow for self-monitoring and self-evaluation. As the individual exercises some control and gains mastery over the task, his or her self-efficacy or metacognitive knowledge is restructured and strengthened. This is most likely to occur with familiar tasks pitched at the level of "just right challenge". Tasks can be accompanied by structured methods of self-questioning and self-evaluation, or be videotaped to provide later opportunity for self-evaluation (Toglia & Kirk, 2000). Ownsworth et al. (2005) provided some preliminary support for using structured experiences or a "metacognitive contextual intervention" for improving self-monitoring and self-correction of errors during real-life tasks (i.e., cooking and volunteer work) in a client with severe awareness deficits. However, the development of metacognitive skills using context specific training was not found to generalise across settings and the client's global deficits in awareness were relatively unchanged.

Toglia (1998) has also described a number of metacognitive training techniques that can be used within a multicontext treatment approach based upon a more general dynamic interactional model of cognition. Like the comprehensive model of awareness (Toglia & Kirk, 2000), the dynamic interactional model of cognition recognises the interaction between the individual, task and environment in determining cognitive function. In the multicontext treatment approach, tasks and environments are gradually changed, but strategies and techniques remain constant. Training strategies suggested for use prior to structured experiences include *anticipation* of obstacles and outcomes and the need for strategies, and *self-prediction* of the level of difficulty and speed and accuracy of performance, which can be compared to self-evaluations after actual performance. At intervals during task performance, strategies such as *time-monitoring, self-checking* and *self-evaluation* can be used, and *self-questioning* can be facilitated by key questions on a cue card.

Another technique is *role reversal* in which the therapist performs the task with errors and the client gives feedback. Toglia (1998) presented a case study to illustrate the use of some of these techniques, but did not systematically evaluate the efficacy of the approach.

Using a single case study design, Landa-Gonzalez (2001) demonstrated the effectiveness of Toglia's (1998) multicontext treatment approach and awareness training techniques combined with those recommended by Barco et al. (1991). During the six-month programme, the participant, who was 8 years post-brain injury, received one hour of occupational therapy and eight hours of "coach-supervised life skills practice" per week in his home and community. Metacognitive training using structured experiences incorporated strategy training, task gradation and practice in multiple environmental contexts.

Another occupation-based approach to facilitating self-awareness incorporated elements of the multicontext approach in a 10-week programme (Fleming, Lucas, & Lightbody, 2006). Four participants with brain injury showed modest gains in self-awareness over this time, but these gains were accompanied by an increase in emotional distress. One client withdrew from treatment after six weeks, and it was considered that this approach was less suitable for this particular client due to his complex presentation of defensive denial and neuropsychologically-based unawareness (see Katz et al., 2002). Similar occupation-based approaches, which also considered the relative contribution of neuropsychological unawareness and denial of disability, were reported as successful for two other clients with stroke and schizophrenia (Katz et al., 2002).

## Direct feedback

The use of direct feedback from the therapist regarding task performance is a fundamental component of many awareness interventions, with emphasis placed on the specific, timely, consistent and respectful nature of the feedback (Barco et al., 1991; Cicerone, 1989; DeHope & Finegan, 1999; Klonoff et al., 1989; Langer & Padrone, 1992; Mateer, 1999). Therapist feedback can be compared with client's self-ratings of performance to enhance self-awareness. Giacino and Cicerone (1998) recommended that direct feedback methods work best with clients who have unawareness secondary to impairment of cognitive subsystems, as opposed to those displaying unawareness due to psychological denial who tend to demonstrate resistance and heightened emotional arousal in response to feedback, and those with neurologically-based unawareness who show a passive response and indifference.

The use of this method with individual clients has been evaluated with positive results in three studies of self-awareness of memory impairment as described in Table 1 (Rebmann & Hannon, 1995; Schacter, Glisky, & McGlynn, 1990; Schlund, 1999). Two studies have investigated the effect of giving direct feedback in a group situation with contrasting results (Ranseen, Bohaska, & Schmidt, 1990; Youngjohn & Altman, 1989). Youngjohn and Altman (1989) reported that gains in awareness were maintained for an arithmetic task, where as Ranseen et al. (1990) reported no significant change in awareness for interpersonal skills, suggesting that awareness deficits for certain areas of function may be easier to remediate than others using a feedback approach.

Videotaped feedback has been recommended as an effective method of direct feedback, particularly for improving awareness of behavioural and communication problems in group therapy situations (Alexy, Foster, & Baker, 1983; Barco et al., 1991; Mateer, 1999; Sherer et al., 1998b). Alexy et al. (1983) used audiovisual feedback within group sessions to improve awareness of interpersonal and communication skills of clients with brain injury. However, despite general clinical observations of participants' improvement in awareness, this intervention was not systematically evaluated. Lui et al. (2002) also used videotaped feedback to improve performance of activities of daily living in three people with stroke. Individuals were initially shown a video of a non-injured person performing a self-selected functional task (e.g., laundry) and then, after performing the task, watched their own performance on video to identify problems and solutions, and then practised the task over a one-week period. Although all three participants showed functional gains, these changes could not be reliably separated from functional gains arising from neurological recovery and the specific impact of the intervention upon metacognitive skills could not be determined.

## Game formats

Two studies have used an educational board-game format to improve knowledge and awareness in clients with acquired brain injury (Chittum et al., 1996; Zhou et al., 1996). The authors proposed that games provide a non-threatening opportunity for clients to use exploration, imitation and repetition to learn about brain injury. However, while clients' knowledge of brain injury might be improved by the game format, not all individuals appear to benefit in terms of increased accuracy of self-appraisal (Zhou et al., 1996).

## Group support programme

Ownsworth, McFarland, and Young (2000) described a 16-week group support and psychoeducation programme for participants with long-term acquired brain injury. A pre- and post-intervention assessment demonstrated significant gains in self-awareness and psychosocial functioning. While this study lacked a control group, the authors noted that the clients were a chronic group, who had not responded well to previous interventions, and actually endorsed more emotional and behavioural problems after the programme as a function of improved awareness. Thus, it appeared that clients' self-reported improvement in psychosocial functioning at post-intervention and follow-up was not simply due to non-specific therapeutic effects.

In an evaluation of 28 participants completing the 16-week programme, Ownsworth and McFarland (2004) found that individuals with impaired executive functioning benefited from the group programme and improved their self-regulation skills, whereas individuals displaying a defensive personality style did not appear to benefit from the programme. However, the latter group appeared to have developed a sound level of self-regulation skills prior to the programme. Individuals who minimised their symptoms as a coping method also made few gains in the programme and appeared to under-report their psychosocial difficulties. Interestingly, improvement in strategy behaviour was not associated with improvement in awareness or psychosocial functioning, but there was some support for an association between increased awareness and improved psychosocial functioning.

## Awareness interventions with children

Ylvisaker, Szekeres, and Feeney (1998) presented intervention options for children and adolescents with disorders of awareness within a cognitive rehabilitation approach for executive deficits. However, they also considered the contribution made to awareness by psychologically based denial, the stage of developmental maturation of the child, and the role of the social environment. For example, high levels of support usually provided by family and professionals to ensure that the child experiences success at all times might prevent opportunities for the child to develop awareness. Treatment options were presented on a continuum from relatively low-confrontation to relatively high-confrontation interventions.

Low-confrontation tasks included: daily conversational interaction to help the child to understand which tasks are easy and which are hard for him/her; a self-monitoring system or log of school activities incorporating self-prediction and self-evaluation; peer teaching in which students tutor younger students thereby identifying strengths and weaknesses in others; and students training and orientating teachers to their own needs (e.g., creating a self-advocacy video). High-confrontation methods included: verbal recitation of deficits, presentation of low test results, peer confrontation, and self-observation of videotaped performances on difficult tasks. Decisions about type of intervention are made based on the child's age, emotional fragility, consequences of unawareness (e.g., risk-taking behaviours in adolescents), and the resources available to the family. Ylvisaker et al. cautioned against premature use of confrontational methods, suggesting that serious confrontation before two years post-injury may result in increased anger and denial. A case study of a child developing a self-advocacy video was provided to illustrate gains in self-awareness from this method (Ylvisaker et al., 1998). Further research evidence and consideration of how this approach could be adapted for use with adults is required.

Beardmore, Tate, and Liddle (1999) used a randomised controlled design to evaluate a 30-minute individual educational session for improving knowledge and awareness in children with TBI. Overall, they found no evidence to support the efficacy of this approach, which questions the long-term effectiveness of the type of information typically provided in "feedback" sessions in rehabilitation. Beardmore et al. also found that higher self-awareness was associated with lower self-esteem, and advocated the need to be careful about facilitating awareness in children by focusing on the child's deficits. The authors of this study identified five possible origins of unawareness in children with brain injury; namely neurologically based unawareness, emotionally motivated denial, insufficient information, developmental issues, and other cognitive or memory sequelae. It could be argued that the use of an information session might have some potential for addressing unawareness based on insufficient information, and that the lack of treatment effect might have been due to the other origins of unawareness.

## Behavioural intervention

Bieman-Copland and Dywan (2000) argued that confrontational strategies, such as education and providing direct and experiential feedback, may actually cause agitation and entrench confabulatory beliefs, and they recommended a behavioural approach as an alternative. This approach involves therapists working collaboratively with clients, with a focus on reducing clients' targeted behaviours. A descriptive case study supported the use of a behavioural intervention for reducing a client's inappropriate behaviours, and raised the issue of whether or not self-awareness is relevant for rehabilitative gains in certain clients. However, this intervention was based upon an assumption that the client's unawareness was neuropsychologically based and, consequently, the possible role of psychological factors such as pre-morbid personality and coping methods were not explored.

Sohlberg et al. (1998) in a nine-month longitudinal study of three individuals with acquired brain injury found that behavioural indicators of awareness did not co-vary with caregivers' and individuals' perceptions, suggesting that behaviour may improve without a change in awareness. The findings also suggested that some individuals might learn to use compensatory strategies with training, despite not understanding the need to use them, by relying on implicit learning and habit formation. It is also possible, however, that any improvement in awareness relating to the specific behaviours targeted by Sohlberg et al. was not reflected in global measures of awareness that were employed.

## Summary

A fairly broad range of interventions has been described in the literature for improving awareness in people with acquired brain injury or for achieving functional gains despite impaired awareness. This review also suggests that the best intervention for any particular individual may depend upon the factors which contribute to the disorder of awareness. Various possible contributing factors were identified including neuropsychological factors, psychological factors and social-environmental factors. Neuropsychological or neuro-cognitive factors include higher order cognitive impairment which results from damage to frontal systems and is related to more generalised disorders of awareness. In contrast, selective unawareness of physical, sensory or cognitive changes is thought to be related to more focal lesions (McGlynn & Schacter, 1989; Prigatano & Weinstein, 1996). These neurocognitive impairments interfere with the process of self-monitoring one's internal status to recalibrate self-knowledge based upon experience with deficits (Vuilleumier, 2004). Psychological factors contributing to impaired awareness include pre-morbid personality and coping styles, non-disclosure of information and defensive reactions such as denial and resistance (Gainotti, 1993; Ownsworth & McFarland, 2004). Some intervention approaches also recognise that, to a certain extent, socio-cultural and environmental factors may influence individuals' presentations of awareness. Socio-cultural and environmental factors relate to the specific context in which disorders of awareness are observed and may include the degree of opportunity afforded by the social, physical and cultural environment for feedback and experience of limitations by the individual (Beardmore et al., 1999; Ylvisaker et al., 1998). In particular, cross-cultural research has demonstrated that cultural background plays a role in determining level of awareness (Prigatano & Leathem, 1993; Prigatano, Ogano, & Amakusa, 1997).

Despite a number of authors emphasising the need to examine the factors contributing to unawareness, there have been few systematic or evidence-based guidelines documented for tailoring interventions accordingly for an individual client. Of the studies reviewed, the type of unawareness observed in participants was not typically described (see Katz et al., 2002, Ownsworth, 2005; Ownsworth et al., 2005; Ownsworth & McFarland, 2004 for exceptions) and this appears to be an important next step in progressing effective interventions for this problem. The following section provides some suggestions based upon recommendations in the literature, a preliminary evidence-base and the authors' own experiences in designing individual awareness interventions.

## A BIOPSYCHOSOCIAL APPROACH TO AWARENESS INTERVENTIONS

A theme emerging from the models for awareness intervention described is that neuropsychologically based disorders of awareness require different intervention approaches to psychologically based unawareness (e.g., Katz et al., 2002; Langer & Padrone, 1992; Ownsworth, 2005; Ownsworth & McFarland, 2004; Prigatano & Klonoff, 1998), and that such approaches need to consider the social and environmental factors that potentially contribute to impaired awareness (Beardmore et al., 1999; Toglia & Kirk, 2000; Ylvisaker et al., 1998). Overall, this highlights that a "biopsychosocial" approach is necessary to understand awareness deficits in people with brain injury. Elsewhere in this issue, Ownsworth, Clare and Morris identify that, to some degree, unawareness may be shaped by the environment in which behaviours are interpreted. They presented "an integrated biopsychosocial approach to understanding awareness disorders" which distinguishes between the three factors, namely, neurocognitive, psychological and socio-environmental influences, which contribute to disorders of awareness in people with acquired brain injury.

A biopsychosocial approach can be used to guide the selection of appropriate interventions according to the nature of factors contributing to the individual's unawareness (see Table 2). In reality, all of these factors may be present in one individual, and establishing the main cause of unawareness may be a major undertaking for the clinician. According to the literature, the relative contribution of the different factors may be gleaned from information on lesion location, neuropsychological assessment results, the client's reaction to feedback or difficulties with rehabilitation tasks, collateral information from significant others (e.g., concerning premorbid personality), specific measures of coping style and personality, and analysis of the client's social and cultural environment (McGlynn & Schacter, 1989; Ownsworth & McFarland, 2004; Ownsworth et al., 2005; Toglia & Kirk, 2000; Ylvisaker et al., 1998).

As shown in Table 2, interventions recommended for individuals with unawareness related to neuro-cognitive factors include the following: (1) selecting key tasks and environments (e.g., Fleming et al., 2006; Katz et al., 2002; Landa-Gonzales, 2001; Toglia, 1998); (2) providing clear feedback and structured learning opportunities (e.g., Klonoff et al., 1989; Ownsworth et al., 2005; Rebmann & Hannon, 1995); (3) promoting habit formation through procedural learning (e.g., Barco et al., 1991); (4) specifically training for application outside the learning environment (e.g., Ben-Yishay et al., 1987; DeHope & Finegan, 1999); (5) involving clients in group therapy (e.g., Chittum et al., 1996; Ownsworth et al., 2000); and (6) educating family and enhancing social environment supports (e.g., Barco et al., 1991;

TABLE 2

A summary of awareness intervention approaches based upon an integrated biopsychosocial approach

| *Bases for unawareness* | *Specific factor contributing to awareness deficits* | *Corresponding treatment guidelines and intervention components* |
|---|---|---|
| Neurocognitive factors | Damage to the right hemisphere or parietal regions (domain-specific awareness deficits), frontal systems or diffuse brain injury (global awareness deficits and difficulty self-monitoring and assimilating experiences into self-knowledge)<br>Impaired executive functioning or significant cognitive impairment contributing to the onset or maintenance of awareness deficits | Select key tasks and environments in which awareness behaviours are most important within everyday activities and roles<br>Provide clear feedback and structured opportunities to help people to evaluate their performance, discover errors and compensate for deficits<br>Focus on habit formation through repetition and procedural or implicit learning Specifically train for application outside the learning environment. Be realistic: some people might be taught to recognise a mismatch but not retain this experience or generalise learning<br>Group therapy, family education and environmental supports to provide external compensation |
| Psychological factors | Information about self is partially or fully recognised but may not be disclosed due to pre-morbid personality characteristics or coping methods | Building the therapeutic alliance to initially get a "foot in the door" with an individual and validate any frustration or distress<br>Commence with non-confrontational approaches such as teaching individuals a range of adaptive coping strategies (e.g., relaxation techniques) before attempting to change any maladaptive strategies that may be protecting them from emotional distress<br>Enhance perceived control over the therapy process by presenting a lot of choices and allowing the individual to direct sessions |

| | | |
|---|---|---|
| | | Psychotherapy and adjustment counselling techniques can help to re-establish sense of self and self-mastery by exploring the subjective meaning of loss and to acknowledge grief. Techniques for working through grief include reading books or watching videos, writing a personal story or a poem, artwork, compiling a photo album or scrap book, keeping a journal on thoughts and feelings and joining a support group<br>Promote and reinforce acceptance of change and gradually develop modified goals for the future |
| Socio-environmental context | Information about self is not disclosed due to concerns about how such information will be used in the referral context; or<br>Individuals have not had relevant information or meaningful opportunities to observe post-injury changes<br>Cultural values impact upon individual's understanding of the assessment or rehabilitation process | Clarify the rationale for the assessment or rehabilitation programme and help the person to identify any concerns (e.g., discuss the "pros and cons" of the individual being involved in an assessment or rehabilitation programme)<br>Consider the timing of the intervention and need for safe and supportive opportunities to observe post-injury changes. Educate significant others to provide appropriate feedback and support. Link people to support or educational groups to provide a positive social context and normalise people's experiences<br>Seek advice from a cultural liaison officer and speak to the family and friends of the individual to develop a shared understanding |

Ownsworth et al., 2005; Sherer et al., 1998b). Individuals who present with psychologically based unawareness are more likely to respond to interventions that place emphasis on the following: (1) building the therapeutic alliance (Ownsworth, 2005; Sherer et al., 1998b); (2) commencing with non-confrontational approaches (Ownsworth, 2005; Ylvisaker et al., 1998); (3) teaching a range of adaptive coping strategies before attempting to change any maladaptive strategies that may be protecting the individual from emotional distress (Langer & Padrone, 1992); and (4) using psychotherapy and adjustment counselling techniques to explore the meaning of loss and promote acceptance (Ownsworth, 2005; Prigatano, 1986; Prigatano & Klonoff, 1998).

Interventions that consider social environmental influences recognise how these factors might either hinder the development of awareness, or influence the degree to which individuals acknowledge their post-injury impairments in a social context (Allen & Ruff, 1990; Beardmore et al., 1999; Ylvisaker et al., 1998). For example, some individuals might perceive that disclosing their problems in a specific referral context would be more disadvantageous than beneficial for them personally. It is proposed that social environmental considerations for interventions include: (1) clarifying the rationale for assessment or treatment and eliciting personal concerns (Ownsworth, 2005), (2) providing relevant information and creating meaningful and concrete opportunities to learn about post-injury changes (Ylvisaker et al., 1998); (3) educating significant others and linking individuals to support/educational groups or peer-mentoring programmes (Ownsworth et al., 2000, 2005); and (4) seeking advice and involvement from a cultural liaison officer.

In summary, Table 2 provides a range of suggestions for developing interventions for clients with brain injury who display awareness deficits. However, the systematic application of these intervention guidelines needs to be based upon careful examination of the extent to which different factors are impacting upon a given individual's presentation of unawareness. Further guidelines for determining this have been provided by Ownsworth et al. in this issue. Other considerations when conducting awareness interventions arising from the literature review will now be discussed.

## CONSIDERATIONS FOR AWARENESS INTERVENTIONS

Another theme linking many of the treatment approaches previously described is that they do not solely focus on facilitating awareness, but occur in the context of interventions to improve other aspects of functioning such as emotional well-being, strategy use, social functioning, independence and vocational outcome. It would appear pointless or even harmful for an intervention to mainly focus upon increasing awareness of post-injury impairments (as indicated, for example, by a person verbally reciting their deficits) unless this development was accompanied by gains in other relevant areas of skill and well-being. Therefore, rather than representing the main desired outcome of treatment, it might be more apt to view increasing awareness as an important goal in the process of treatment (see also Ezrachi et al., 1991) that promotes change in other areas (e.g., acceptance, readiness to change, realistic goal setting, use of compensatory strategies) which, in combination, contribute to functional gains.

A number of studies have demonstrated a link between increased self-awareness and emotional distress (Fleming et al., 1998; Godfrey, Partridge, Knight, & Bishara, 1993; Wallace & Bogner, 2000) which has important implications for any intervention aiming to facilitate awareness in this population, which is at risk of developing secondary psychological disorders (Ownsworth & Oei, 1998). As mentioned above, interventions should not have the sole aim of improving self-awareness without also improving function, and therefore awareness interventions are best provided within the context of a holistic rehabilitation, allowing necessary follow-up support and to facilitate translation of enhanced awareness into functional gains. From a methodological point of view, this makes it difficult for researchers to isolate the effects of specific awareness interventions from the rehabilitation contexts in which they are embedded.

Furthermore, the outcome measures available to assess level of self-awareness in intervention studies tend to be general in nature, and may not be sensitive to changes in awareness relating to a particular aspect of functioning which is the target of the intervention (Sohlberg et al., 1998). Therefore, a diverse range of clinical indicators of improvements in awareness may need to be considered which include explicit verbal reports of difficulties by the client, more accurate predictions of performance, reduced discrepancy between self-ratings and others' ratings, emotional changes, increased strategy use, fewer errors in task performance, and increased compliance with therapy (Sohlberg et al., 1998). Toglia and Kirk (2000) identified a range of responses to feedback including agreement, perplexity, surprise, confusion, indifference, resistance, hostility, and anger. Awareness assessments that take into account this broad range of responses and awareness indicators would be useful in documenting clinical changes in response to awareness interventions.

Many of these outcomes are difficult to operationalise for formal evaluation in intervention studies, and a review of Table 1 indicates that very little empirical research, beyond case study and group outcome descriptions, has been reported. Another explanation for the lack of research may lie in the diverse nature of disorders of awareness requiring differing approaches with each individual according to the underlying factors contributing to his or her unawareness. This, coupled with the fact that an inappropriate approach may exacerbate emotional distress in some clients, makes it ethically and methodologically difficult to apply a standard randomised controlled design to the study of awareness interventions. This highlights the need for innovative research approaches in this area, which seems to point towards the use of single case experimental designs and qualitative studies. For an example of a qualitative evaluation of change in clients' goals and self-perceptions throughout rehabilitation, see Kristensen (2004). Alternatively, group treatment studies that employ a clear set of inclusion criteria to reflect specific factors underlying unawareness could be evaluated using a matched comparison group that does not receive treatment.

Increased awareness has been associated with better functional outcomes in a number of studies (e.g., Fordyce & Roueche, 1986; Sherer et al., 1998a). However, further research is needed to examine the mechanism of these functional gains (Fischer, Gauggel, & Trexler, 2004), whether it is as a result of improved motivation, compliance with therapy, more realistic goal setting, or some other means. Dirette (2002) recommended investigation into the process of development of awareness, including qualitative evaluation of methods from the client's perspective. Dirette also drew attention to the issue of timing of awareness intervention, which is a consideration included in the guidelines presented in Table 2, but one that requires further investigation. Furthermore, for some clients it appears that functional gains can be made without awareness, raising the question of the relevance of awareness interventions (Sohlberg et al., 1998) and the need for guidelines to indicate when behavioural interventions may be more suitable.

## SUMMARY

This review of the literature pertaining to awareness interventions for people with acquired brain injury has identified a broad theoretical basis from which interventions are derived, spanning neuropsychology, psychotherapy, social psychology, cognitive psychology, occupational therapy, and education. The more sophisticated theoretical models of awareness integrate a number of these approaches and draw on multiple techniques to provide awareness interventions tailored to a given individual's type of awareness disorder. Here we have proposed that a biopsychosocial approach for understanding awareness disorders be used to guide therapists in the choice of intervention approaches for individual clients. In light of the limited empirical research base, the ethical and methodological dilemmas associated with conducting intervention studies in this area were identified. The challenge for the future is to develop innovative research methods to evaluate critically the effectiveness of theoretically driven approaches to awareness interventions.

# REFERENCES

Abreu, B. C., Seale, G., Scheibel, R. S., Huddleston, N., Zhang, L., & Ottenbacher, K. J. (2001). Levels of self-awareness after acute brain injury: How patients' and rehabilitation specialists' perceptions compare. *Archives of Physical and Medical Rehabilitation*, *82*, 49–56.

Alexy, W. D., Foster, M., & Baker, A. (1983). Audiovisual feedback: An exercise in self-awareness for the head injured patient. *Cognitive Rehabilitation*, *1*, 8–10.

Allen, C. C., & Ruff, R. M. (1990). Self-rating versus neuropsychological performance of moderate versus severe head-injured patients. *Brain Injury*, *4*, 7–17.

Andersson, S., Gundersen, P. M., & Finset, A. (1999). Emotional activation during therapeutic interaction in traumatic brain injury: Effect of apathy, self-awareness and implications for rehabilitation. *Brain Injury*, *13*, 393–404.

Bandura, A. (1997). *Self-efficacy: The exercise of control.* New York: W.H. Freeman and Company.

Barco, P. P., Crosson, B., Bolesta, M. M., Werts, D., & Stout, R. (1991). Training awareness and compensation in postacute head injury rehabilitation. In J. S. Kreutzer & P. H. Wehman (Eds.), *Cognitive rehabilitation for person's with traumatic brain injury: A functional approach* (pp. 129–146). Baltimore: Paul H. Brookes.

Beardmore, S., Tate, R., & Liddle, B. (1999). Does information and feedback improve children's knowledge and awareness of deficits after traumatic brain injury? *Neuropsychological Rehabilitation*, *9*, 45–62.

Ben-Yishay, Y., & Prigatano, G. (1990). Cognitive remediation. In M. Rosenthal, E. R. Griffith, M. R. Bond, & J. D. Miller (Eds.), *Rehabilitation of the adult and child with traumatic brain injury* (pp. 393–409). Philadelphia: F.A. Davis Company.

Ben-Yishay, Y., Rattok, J., Lakin, P., Piasetsky, E. D., Ross, B., Silver, S., Zide, E., & Ezrachi, O. (1985). Neuropsychologic rehabilitation: Quest for a holistic approach. *Seminars in Neurology*, *5*, 252–259.

Ben-Yishay, Y., Silver, S. M., Piasetsky, E., & Rattok, J. (1987). Relationship between employability and vocational outcome after intensive holistic cognitive rehabilitation. *Journal of Head Trauma Rehabilitation*, *2*(1), 35–48.

Bieman-Copland, S., & Dywan, J. (2000). Achieving rehabilitative gains in anosognosia after TBI. *Brain and Cognition*, *1*, 1–18.

Butler, R. W., & Satz, P. (1988). Individual psychotherapy with head-injured adults: Clinical notes for the practitioner. *Professional Psychology: Research and Practice*, *19*, 536–541.

Cicerone, K. D. (1989). Psychotherapeutic interventions with traumatically brain-injured patients. *Rehabilitation Psychology*, *34*, 105–114.

Chittum, W. R., Johnson, K., Chittum, J. M., Guercio, J. M., & McMorrow, M. J. (1996). Road to awareness: An individualised training package for increasing knowledge and comprehension of personal deficits in persons with acquired brain injury. *Brain Injury*, *10*, 763–776.

Crosson, B., Barco, P. P., Velezo, C. A., Bolesta, M. M., Cooper, P. V., Werts, D., & Brobeck, T. C. (1989). Awareness of compensation in postacute head injury rehabilitation. *Journal of Head Trauma Rehabilitation*, *4*, 46–54.

Dattilo, J. (1994). *Inclusive leisure services.* State College, PA: Venture Publishing.

Deaton, A. V. (1986). Denial in the aftermath of traumatic head injury: Its manifestations, measurement and treatment. *Rehabilitation Psychology*, *31*, 231–240.

DeHope, E., & Finegan, J. (1999). The self determination model: An approach to develop awareness for survivors of traumatic brain injury. *NeuroRehabilitation*, *13*, 3–12.

Dirette, D. (2002). The development of awareness and the use of compensatory strategies for cognitive deficits. *Brain Injury*, *16*, 861–871

Ezrachi, O., Ben-Yishay, Y., Kay, T., Diller, L., & Rattock, J. (1991). Predicting employment in traumatic brain injury following neuropsychological rehabilitation. *Journal of Head Trauma Rehabilitation*, *6*, 71–84.

Fisher, S., Gauggel, S., & Trexler, L. E. (2004). Awareness of activity limitations, goal setting and rehabilitation outcome in patients with brain injuries. *Brain Injury, 18*, 547–562.

Fleming, J. M., Lucas, S. E., & Lightbody (2006). Using occupation to facilitate self-awareness in people who have acquired brain injury. *Canadian Journal of Occupational Therapy, 73*, 44–55.

Fleming, J. M., Strong, J., & Ashton, R. (1998). Cluster analysis of self-awareness levels in adults with traumatic brain injury and relationship to outcome. *Journal of Head Trauma Rehabilitation, 13*(5), 39–51.

Fordyce, D. J., & Roueche, J. R. (1986). Changes in perspectives of disability among patients, staff, and relatives during rehabilitation of brain injury. *Rehabilitation Psychology, 31*, 217–229.

Gainotti, G. (1993). Emotional and psychosocial problems after brain injury. *Neuropsychological Rehabilitation, 3*, 259–277.

Giacino, J. T., & Cicerone, K. D. (1998). Varieties of deficit unawareness after brain injury. *Journal of Head Trauma Rehabilitation, 13*(5), 1–15.

Godfrey, H. P. D., Partridge, F. M., Knight, R. G., & Bishara, S. (1993). Course of insight disorder and emotional dysfunction following closed head injury: A controlled cross-sectional follow-up study. *Journal of Clinical and Experimental Neuropsychology, 15*, 503–515.

Hart, T., Giovannetti, T., Montgomery, M. W., & Schwartz, M. F. (1998). Awareness of errors in naturalistic action after traumatic brain injury. *Journal of Head Trauma Rehabilitation, 13*(5), 16–28.

Katz, N., Fleming, J., Hartman-Maeir, A., Keren, N., & Lightbody, S. (2002). Unawareness and/or denial of disability: Implications for occupational therapy intervention. *Canadian Journal of Occupational Therapy, 69*, 281–292.

Klonoff, P. S., O'Brien, K. P., Prigatano, G. P., Chiapello, D. A., & Cunningham, M. (1989). Cognitive retraining after traumatic brain injury and its role in facilitating awareness. *Journal of Head Trauma Rehabilitation, 4*, 37–45.

Kristensen, O. F. (2004). Changing goals and intentions among participants in a neuropsychological rehabilitation: An exploratory case study evaluation. *Brain Injury, 10*, 1049–1062.

Landa-Gonzalez, B. (2001). Multicontextual occupational therapy intervention: A case study of traumatic brain injury. *Occupational Therapy International, 8*, 49–62.

Langer, K. G., & Padrone, F. J. (1992). Psychotherapeutic treatment of awareness in acute rehabilitation of traumatic brain injury. *Neuropsychological Rehabilitation, 2*, 59–70.

Liu, K. P. Y., Chan, C. C. H., Lee, T. M. C., Li, L. S. W., & Hui-Chan, C. W. Y. (2002). Self-regulatory learning and generalization for people with brain injury. *Brain Injury, 16*, 817–824.

Lucas, S., & Fleming, J. M. (2005). Interventions for improving self-awareness following acquired brain injury. *Australian Occupational Therapy Journal, 52*, 160–170.

Malec, J. F., & Moessner, A. M. (2000). Self-awwareness, distress, and postacute rehabilitation outcome. *Rehabilitation Psychology, 45*, 227–241.

Mateer, C. A. (1999). The rehabilitation of executive disorders. In D. T. Stuss, G. Winocur, & I. H. Robertson (Eds.), *Cognitive neurorehabilitation* (pp. 314–332). London: Cambridge University Press.

McGlynn, S. M., & Schacter, D. L. (1989). Unawareness of deficits in neuropsychological syndromes. *Journal of Clinical and Experimental Neuropsychology, 11*, 143–205.

Ownsworth, T. (2005). The impact of defensive denial upon adjustment following traumatic brain injury. *Neuropsychoanalysis, 7*, 83–94.

Ownsworth, T., Fleming, J., & Desbois, J. (2005). A metacognitive intervention for enhancing error awareness and functional performance in naturalistic settings: A single case experimental design. *Paper presented at the joint International Neuropsychological Society and British Psychological Society meeting*, Dublin, July 6–9.

Ownsworth, T., & McFarland, K. (2004). Investigation of psychological and neuropsychological factors associated with clinical outcome following a group rehabilitation programme. *Neuropsychological Rehabilitation, 14*, 535–562.

Ownsworth, T. L., McFarland, K., & Young, R. M. (2000). Self-awareness and psychosocial functioning following acquired brain injury: An evaluation of a group support programme. *Neuropsychological Rehabilitation, 10*, 465–484.

Ownsworth, T. L., & Oei, T. P. S. (1998). Depression after traumatic brain injury: Conceptualisation and treatment considerations. *Brain Injury, 12*, 735–751.

Prigatano, G. P. (1986). Psychotherapy after brain injury. In G. P. Prigatano, D. J. Fordyce, H. K. Zeiner, J. R. Roueche, M. Pepping, & B. C. Wood (Eds.), *Neuropsychological rehabilitation after brain injury* (pp. 67–95). Baltimore, MD: Johns Hopkins University Press.

Prigatano, G. P. (1991). Disturbances of self-awareness of deficit after traumatic brain injury. In G. P. Prigatano & D. L. Schacter (Eds.), *Awareness of Deficit after Brain Injury: Clinical and Theoretical Issues* (pp. 111–126). New York: Oxford University Press.

Prigatano, G. P. (1999a). *Principles of neuropsychological rehabilitation.* New York: Oxford University Press.

Prigatano, G. P. (1999b). Diller lecture: Impaired awareness, finger tapping, and rehabilitation outcome after brain injury. *Rehabilitation Psychology, 44*, 145–159.

Prigatano, G. P., Fordyce, D., Zeiner, H. K., Roueche, J. F., Pepping, M., & Wood, B. (1984). Neuropsychological rehabilitation after closed head injury in young adults. *Journal of Neurology, Neurosurgery, and Psychiatry, 47*, 505–513.

Prigatano, G. P., Fordyce, D., Zeiner, H., Roueche, J., Pepping, M., & Wood, B. (1986). *Neuropsychological rehabilitation after brain injury*. Baltimore, MD: Johns Hopkins University Press.

Prigatano, G. P., & Klonoff, P. S. (1998). A clinician's rating scale for evaluating impaired self-awareness and denial of disability after brain injury. *Clinical Neuropsychologist, 12*, 56–67.

Prigatano, G. P., & Leathem, J. M. (1993). Awareness of behavioural limitations after traumatic brain injury: A cross-cultural study of New Zealand Maoris and Non-Maoris. *Clinical Neuropsychologist, 7*, 123–135.

Prigatano, G. P., Ogano, M., & Amakusa, B. (1997). A cross-cultural study on impaired self-awareness in Japanese patients with brain dysfunction. *Neuropsychiatry, Neuropsychology, and Behavioural Neurology, 10*, 135–143.

Prigatano, G. P., & Schacter, D. L. (1991). Introduction. In G. P. Prigatano & D. L. Schacter (Eds.), *Awareness of deficit after brain injury: Clinical and theoretical issues* (pp. 3–15). New York: Oxford University Press.

Prigatano, G. P., & Weinstein, E. A. (1996). Edwin A. Weinstein's contributions to neuropsychological rehabilitation. *Neuropsychological Rehabilitation, 6*, 306–326.

Prigatano, G. P., & Wong, J. L. (1999). Cognitive and affective improvement in brain dysfunctional patients who achieve inpatient rehabilitation goals. *Archives of Physical Medicine and Rehabilitation, 80*, 77–84.

Ranseen, J. D., Bohaska, L. A., & Schmitt, F. A. (1990). An investigation of anosognosia following traumatic head injury. *Clinical Neuropsychology, 12*, 29–36.

Rebmann, M. J., & Hannon, R. (1995). Treatment of unawareness of memory deficits in adults with acquired brain injury: Three case studies. *Rehabilitation Psychology, 40*, 279–287.

Schacter, D. L., Glisky, E. L., & McGlynn, S. M. (1990). Impact of memory disorder on everyday life: Awareness of deficits and return to work. In D. E. Tupper & K. D. Cicerone (Eds.), *The neuropsychology of everyday life: Assessment and basic competencies* (pp. 231–257). Boston, MA: Kluwer Academic.

Schacter, D. L., & Prigatano, G. P. (1991). Forms of unawareness. In G. P. Prigatano & D. L. Schacter (Eds.), *Awareness of deficit after brain injury: clinical and theoretical issues* (pp. 258–262). New York: Oxford University Press.

Schlund, M. W. (1999). Case Study—Self-awareness: Effects of feedback and review on verbal self reports and remembering following brain injury. *Brain Injury, 13*, 375–380.

Sherer, M., Bergloff, P., Levin, E., High, W. M., Oden, K. E., & Nick, T. G. (1998a). Impaired awareness and employment outcome after traumatic brain injury. *Journal of Head Trauma Rehabilitation, 13*, 52–61.

Sherer, M., Oden, K., Bergloff, P., Levin, E., & High Jr, W. M. (1998b). Assessment and treatment of impaired awareness after brain injury: Implications for community re-integration. *NeuroRehabilitation, 10*, 25–37.

Sohlberg, M. M., Mateer, C. A., Penkman, L., Gland, A., & Todis, B. (1998). Awareness intervention: Who needs it? *Journal of Head Trauma Rehabilitation, 13*, 62–78.

Toglia, J. P. (1998). A dynamic interactional model to cognitive rehabilitation. In N. Katz (Ed.), *Cognition and occupation in rehabilitation: Models for intervention in occupational therapy* (pp. 5–50). Bethesda, MD: American Occupational Therapy Association.

Toglia, J., & Kirk, U. (2000). Understanding awareness deficits following brain injury. *Neurorehabilitation, 15*, 57–70.

Vuilleumier, P. (2004). Anosognosia: The neurology of beliefs and uncertainties. *Cortex, 41*, 67–75.

Wallace, C. A., & Bogner, J. (2000). Awareness of deficits: Emotional implications for persons with brain injury and their significant others. *Brain Injury, 14*, 549–562.

Willer, B., & Corrigan, J. (1994). Whatever it takes: A model for community-based services. *Brain Injury, 8*, 647–659.

Ylvisaker, M., Szekeres, S., & Feeney, T. (1998). Cognitive rehabilitation: Executive functions. In M. Ylvisaker (Ed.), *Traumatic brain injury rehabilitation: Children and adolescents* (pp. 221–269). Boston: Butterworth-Heinemann.

Youngjohn, J. R., & Altman, I. M. (1989). A performance-based group approach to the treatment of anosognosia and denial. *Rehabilitation Psychology, 34*, 217–222.

Zhou, J., Chittum, R., Johnson, K., Poppen, R., Guercio, J., & McMorrow, M. J. (1996). The utilization of a game format to increase knowledge of residuals among people with acquired brain injury. *Journal of Head Trauma Rehabilitation, 11*, 51–61.

NEUROPSYCHOLOGICAL REHABILITATION
2006, 16 (4), 501–504

# Subject Index

www.ingramcontent.com/pod-product-compliance
Ingram Content Group UK Ltd.
Pitfield, Milton Keynes, MK11 3LW, UK
UKHW020349010325
455677UK00021B/359